"*The Writer's Journey* is a lucid and readable application of Joseph Campbell's theories about mythical structure in film and is of real value to filmmakers in learning to more effectively appeal to audiences."
—Gary A. Berg
Directors Guild of America

"An evocative vision of the creative process that will stimulate directors, teachers, writers and actors for years to come."
—David McKenna
Graduate Film Department
Columbia University

"...a must read book for anyone who wants to write and tell a good story"
—D. B. Gilles
Tisch School of the Arts
New York University

"This book should come with a warning: You're going to learn about more than just writing movies—you're going to learn about life! *The Writer's Journey* is the perfect manual for developing, pitching and writing stories with universal human themes that will forever captivate a global audience. It's the secret weapon I hope every writer finds out about."
—Jeff Arch
Screenwriter
SLEEPLESS IN SEATTLE

"My writing partner and I struggled with the climax of our story until we read *The Writer's Journey* and found the solution in Vogler's lucid explanation of the "Supreme Ordeal." I can't recommend this book highly enough.

The Writer's Journey may just be the best book on the market today for practical advice and quick help for the script in trouble. Every novice writer and seasoned pro alike should get a copy."
—Meera Lester, *Director*
Writers Connection &
Selling to Hollywood

"This is a book I constantly refer to in my day-to-day business. It offers basic solutions to the most complex story problems. A seminal work for anyone entering the field."
—Charlie Fink
Former VP of Production
Walt Disney Pictures

THE WRITER'S JOURNEY

Mythic Structure for Storytellers and Screenwriters

by

Christopher Vogler

Published by Michael Wiese Productions, 11288 Ventura Boulevard, Suite #821, Studio City, CA 91604, (818) 379-8799.

Cover design, photograph and illustrations by Charles Field
Interior design and layout by Gina Mansfield

Printed by Braun-Brumfield, Inc., Ann Arbor, Michigan.
Manufactured in the United States of America

The publisher plants two trees for every tree used in the manufacturing of this book. Printed on recycled stock.

ISBN 0-941188-13-2

Library of Congress Cataloging - in - Publication Data

Vogler, Christopher, 1949-
    The Writer's Journey: Mythic Structures for Storytellers and Screenwriters / by Christopher Vogler.
    p.   cm.
    Includes bibliographical references and index.
    ISBN 0-941188-13-2
    1. Motion picture authorship. 2. Narration (rhetoric)
    3. Myth in literature. I. Title
    PN1996.V64 1992   92-37885
    806 . 2' 3 – DC20   CIP

For Mom and Dad

TABLE OF CONTENTS

PREFACE

The purpose of this book is to explore the Writer's Journey — the fascinating maze of myth, dreams, psychology, screenwriting, storytelling, and life in general. I hope it will give writers, students, filmmakers, and lovers of story some hint of what a powerful source of inspiration myths can be.

What is a myth? For our purposes a myth is not the untruth or fanciful exaggeration of popular expression. A myth, as Joseph Campbell was fond of saying, is a metaphor for a mystery beyond human comprehension. It is a comparison that helps us understand, by analogy, some aspect of our mysterious selves. A myth, in this way of thinking, is not an untruth but a way of reaching profound truth.

Then what is a story? A story is also a metaphor, a model of some aspect of human behavior. It is a thought machine, by which we test out our ideas and feelings about some human quality and try to learn more about it.

A myth is a special kind of story that deals with the gods or the forces of creation, and the relationship of those forces to human beings. Not all modern stories are myths, nor do they all have mythic dimensions, but the stories we tell today have much in common with the ancient energy of myths. The structural patterns and archetypal characters of myths provide the basis of all modern storytelling, and all writers should be familiar with these elements. My intention is to map out some of the patterns of mythology and relate them to modern storytelling and screenwriting.

A journey such as this is not possible without many mentors, guides, allies, and friends. First, I am eternally grateful to the pioneering work of Joseph Campbell and all those who travel in his generous spirit. To my fellow wayfarer David McKenna I owe thanks for a lifetime of enthusiastically roadtesting the theory and never failing to believe. The quest has been brightened by the comradeship of Tom Schlesinger, another trailblazer in the country of heroes.

Thanks to Keith Cunningham, Richard Beban, and Phil Cousineau for their wise insight on matters of myth, story, and survival. Many thanks to my friend Chris Fabiaschi for intelligently critiquing the manuscript. I am grateful to Dr. Alex Vilumsons for being a virtual reincarnation of Merlin and for helping me understand the roles of mentors and shamans in a hero's quest. Many thanks to my friend Ron Deutsch for putting the wires together to make this book happen. I am also indebted to Bettina Moss for setting me straight about *The Odyssey*.

Thanks to my mother for continuing to remind me, as late as last week, that I'd better hurry up and write this. Thanks to my father, God bless him, for being so proud of his son. I am grateful to two professors at the USC film school, Ken Evans and Drew Casper, for helping to set me on the path. Linda Venis and all the wonderful people at the UCLA Extension Writers' Program have provided an unparalleled proving ground for the Hero's Journey model, and I thank them. I must also acknowledge that legion of guinea pigs, my students who challenged and tested the concepts. I am grateful for the interest of Disney executives Jeffrey Katzenberg, Ricardo Mestres, David Hoberman, Charlie Fink, Tom Schumacher, and all those who gave me a chance to try out these ideas in the real world.

Thanks to Michael Wiese for seeing the possibilities and to Ken Lee for incredible patience and guidance during the development of the book. Finally, I am most deeply grateful for the assistance of Alice Plato who cared enough to edit the manuscript with heroic fervor. Thank you, Alice, for sharing my dreams and opening your heart to mine.

C. E. Vogler
Fall 1992

INTRODUCTION:

Preparing for the Journey

INTRODUCTION: PREPARING FOR THE JOURNEY

"This is the tale I pray the divine Muse to unfold to us. Begin it, goddess, at whatever point you will."

The Odyssey of Homer

I invite you to join me on a Writer's Journey, a mission of discovery to explore and map the elusive borderlands between myth and modern storytelling. We will be guided by a simple idea: **All stories consist of a few common structural elements found universally in myths, fairy tales, dreams, and movies.** They are known collectively as **The Hero's Journey**. Understanding these elements and their use in modern writing is the object of our quest. Used wisely, these ancient tools of the storyteller's craft still have tremendous power to heal our people and make the world a better place.

My own Writer's Journey begins with the peculiar power storytelling has always had over me. I got hooked on the fairy tales and Little Golden Books read out loud by my mother and grandmother. I devoured the cartoons and movies pouring out of TV in the 1950s, the thrilling adventures on the drive-in screens, the lurid comic books and mind-stretching science fiction of the day. When I was laid up with a sprained ankle, my father went to the local library and brought back wonder stories of Norse and Celtic mythology that made me forget the pain.

A trail of stories eventually led me to reading for a living as a story analyst for Hollywood studios. Though I evaluated thousands of novels and screenplays, I never got tired of exploring the labyrinth of story with its stunningly repeated patterns, bewildering variants, and puzzling questions. Where do stories come from? How do they work? What do they tell us about ourselves? What do they mean? Why do we need them? How can we use them to improve the world?

3

Above all, how do storytellers manage to make the story mean something? Good stories make you feel you've been through a satisfying, complete experience. You've cried or laughed or both. You finish the story feeling you've learned something about life or about yourself. Perhaps you've picked up a new awareness, a new character or attitude to model your life on. How do storytellers manage to pull that off? What are the secrets of this ancient trade? What are its rules and design principles?

Over the years I began to notice some common elements in adventure stories and myths, certain intriguingly familiar characters, props, locations, and situations. I became vaguely aware there was a pattern or a template of some sort guiding the design of stories. I had some pieces of the puzzle but the overall plan eluded me.

Then at the U.S.C. film school I was fortunate enough to cross paths with the work of the mythologist Joseph Campbell. The encounter with Campbell was, for me and many other people, a life-changing experience. A few days of exploring the labyrinth of his book *The Hero With a Thousand Faces* produced an electrifying reorganization of my life and thinking. Here, fully explored, was the pattern I had been sensing. Campbell had broken the secret code of story. His work was like a flare suddenly illuminating a deeply shadowed landscape.

I worked with Campbell's idea of the Hero's Journey to understand the phenomenal repeat business of movies such as *Star Wars* and *Close Encounters*. People were going back to see these films as if seeking some kind of religious experience. It seemed to me these films drew people in this special way because they reflected the universally satisfying patterns Campbell found in myths. They had something people needed.

The Hero With a Thousand Faces was a lifesaver when I began to work as a story analyst for major movie studios. In my first jobs I was deeply grateful for Campbell's work which became a reliable set of tools for diagnosing story problems and prescribing solutions. Without the guidance of Campbell and mythology, I would have been lost.

4

It seemed to me the Hero's Journey was exciting, useful story technology which could help filmmakers and executives eliminate some of the guesswork and expense of developing stories for film. Over the years, I ran into quite a few people who had been affected by encounters with Joe Campbell. We were like a secret society of true believers, commonly putting our faith in "the power of myth".

Shortly after going to work as a story analyst for the Walt Disney Company, I wrote a seven-page memo called "A Practical Guide to *The Hero With a Thousand Faces*" in which I described the idea of the Hero's Journey, with examples from classic and current movies. I gave the memo to friends, colleagues, and several Disney executives to test and refine the ideas through their feedback. Gradually I expanded the "Practical Guide" into a longer essay and began teaching the material through a story analysis class at the UCLA Extension Writers' Program.

At writers' conferences around the country I tested the ideas in seminars with screenwriters, romance novelists, children's writers, and all kinds of storytellers. I found many others were exploring the intertwined pathways of myth, story, and psychology.

The Hero's Journey, I discovered, is more than just a description of the hidden patterns of mythology. It is a useful guide to life, especially the writer's life. In the perilous adventure of my own writing, I found the stages of the Hero's Journey showing up just as reliably and usefully as they did in books, myths, and movies. In my personal life, I was thankful to have this map to guide my quest and help me anticipate what was around the next bend.

The usefulness of the Hero's Journey as a guide to life was brought home forcefully when I first prepared to speak publicly about it in a large seminar at UCLA. A couple of weeks before the seminar two articles appeared in the Los Angeles *Herald-Examiner*, in which a film critic attacked filmmaker George Lucas and his movie *Willow*. Somehow the critic had got hold of the "Practical Guide" and claimed it had deeply influenced and corrupted Hollywood storytellers. The critic blamed the "Practical Guide" for every flop from *Ishtar* to *Howard the Duck*, as well as for the hit *Back to the Future*. According to him, lazy, illiterate studio executives, eager to find a quick-bucks formula, had seized upon the "Practical Guide" as a cureall and were busily stuffing it down the throats of writers, stifling their creativity with a technology the executives hadn't bothered to understand.

While flattered that someone thought I had such a sweeping influence on the collective mind of Hollywood, I was also devastated. Here, on the threshold of a new phase of working with these ideas, I was shot down before I even started. Or so it seemed.

Friends who were more seasoned veterans in this war of ideas pointed out that in being challenged I was merely encountering an **archetype**, one of the familiar characters who people the landscape of the Hero's Journey, namely a **Threshold Guardian**.

That information instantly gave me my bearings and showed me how to handle the situation. Campbell had described how heroes often encounter these "unfamiliar yet strangely intimate forces, some of which severely threaten" them. The Guardians seem to pop up at the various **thresholds** of the journey, the narrow and dangerous passages from one stage of life to the next. Campbell showed the many ways in which heroes can deal with Threshold Guardians. Instead of attacking these seemingly hostile powers head on, journeyers learn to outwit them or join forces with them, absorbing their energy rather than being destroyed by it.

I realized that this Threshold Guardian's apparent attack was potentially a blessing, not a curse. I had thought of challenging the critic to a duel (laptops at twenty paces) but now reconsidered. With a slight change in attitude I could turn his hostility to my benefit. I contacted the critic and invited him to talk over our differences of opinion at the seminar. He accepted and joined a panel discussion which turned into a lively and entertaining debate, illuminating corners of the story world that I had never glimpsed before. The

6

seminar was better and my ideas were stronger for being challenged. Instead of fighting my Threshold Guardian, I had absorbed him into my adventure. What had seemed like a lethal blow had turned into something useful and healthy. The mythological approach had proven its worth in life as well as story.

Around this time I realized "The Practical Guide" and Campbell's ideas *did* have an influence on Hollywood. I began to get requests from studio story departments for copies of "The Practical Guide". I heard that executives at other studios were giving the pamphlet to writers, directors, and producers as guides to universal, commercial story patterns. Apparently Hollywood was finding the Hero's Journey useful.

Meanwhile Joseph Campbell's ideas exploded into a wider sphere of awareness with the Bill Moyers interview show on PBS, "The Power of Myth". The show was a hit, cutting across lines of age, politics, and religion to speak directly to people's spirits. The book version, a transcript of the interviews, was on the *New York Times* bestseller list for over a year. *The Hero With a Thousand Faces*, Campbell's venerable warhorse of a textbook, suddenly became a hot bestseller after forty years of slow but steady backlist sales.

The PBS show brought Campbell's ideas to millions and illuminated the impact of his work on filmmakers such as George Lucas, John Boorman, Steven Spielberg, and George Miller. Suddenly I found a sharp increase in awareness and acceptance of Campbell's ideas in Hollywood. More executives and writers were versed in these concepts and interested in learning how to apply them to moviemaking and screenwriting.

The Hero's Journey model continued to serve me well. It got me through reading and evaluating over six thousand screenplays for half a dozen studios. It was my atlas, a book of maps for my own writing journeys. It guided me to a new role in the Disney company, as a story consultant for the Feature Animation division at the time *The Little Mermaid* and *Beauty and the Beast* were being conceived.

Campbell's ideas were of tremendous value as I researched and developed stories based on fairy tales, mythology, science fiction, comic books, and historical adventure.

Joseph Campbell died in 1987. I met him briefly a couple of times at seminars. He was still a striking man in his eighties, tall, vigorous, eloquent, funny, full of energy and enthusiasm, and utterly charming. Just before his passing, he told me "Stick with this stuff. It'll take you a long way."

I recently discovered that for some time "The Practical Guide" has been required reading for Disney development executives. Daily requests for it, as well as countless letters and calls from novelists, screenwriters, producers, writers, and actors, indicate that the Hero's Journey ideas are being used and developed more than ever.

And so I come to the writing of this book, the descendant of the "Practical Guide". The book is designed somewhat on the model of the *I Ching*, with an introductory overview followed by commentaries that expand on the typical stages of the Hero's Journey. Book One, **Mapping the Journey**, is a quick survey of the territory. Chapter One is a revision of "The Practical Guide" and a concentrated presentation of the twelve-stage Hero's Journey. You might think of this as the map of a journey we are about to take together through the special world of story. Chapter Two is an introduction to the archetypes, the *dramatis personae* of myth and story. It describes seven common character types or psychological functions found in all stories.

Book Two, **Stages of the Journey**, is a more detailed examination of the twelve elements of the Hero's Journey. Each chapter is followed by suggestions for your further exploration, **Questioning the Journey**. An Epilogue, **Looking Back on the Journey**, deals with the special adventure of the Writer's Journey and some pitfalls to avoid on the road. It includes a Hero's Journey analysis of the films *The Last of the Mohicans* and *Death Becomes Her*.

Throughout the book I make reference to movies, both classic and current. You might want to view some of these films to see how the Hero's Journey works in practice. A representative list of films appears in Appendix 1.

You might also select a single movie or story of your choice and keep it in mind as you take the Writer's Journey. Get to know the story of your choice by reading or viewing it several times, taking brief notes on what happens in each scene and how it functions in the drama. Running a movie on a VCR is ideal, because you can stop to write down the content of each scene while you grasp its meaning and relation to the rest of the story.

I suggest you go through this process with a story or movie and use it to test out the ideas in this book. See if your story reflects the stages and archetypes of the Hero's Journey. (A sample worksheet for the Hero's Journey can be found in Appendix 3.) Observe how the stages are adapted to meet the needs of the story or the particular culture for whom the story was written. Challenge these ideas, test them in practice, adapt them to your needs, and make them yours. Use these concepts to challenge and inspire your own stories.

The Hero's Journey has served storytellers and their listeners since the very first stories were told, and it shows no signs of wearing out. Let's begin the Writer's Journey together to explore these ideas. I hope you find them useful as magic keys to the world of story and the labyrinth of life.

BOOK ONE:

MAPPING
THE JOURNEY

A PRACTICAL GUIDE

"There are only two or three human stories, and they go on repeating themselves as fiercely as if they had never happened before."

Willa Cather, in *O Pioneers*

In the long run, one of the most influential books of the 20th century may turn out to be Joseph Campbell's *The Hero with a Thousand Faces*.

The ideas expressed in Campbell's book are having a major impact on storytelling. Writers are becoming more aware of the ageless patterns which Campbell identifies, and are enriching their work with them.

Inevitably Hollywood has caught on to the usefulness of Campbell's work. Filmmakers like George Lucas and George Miller acknowledge their debt to Campbell and his influence can be seen in the films of Steven Spielberg, John Boorman, Francis Coppola, and others.

It's little wonder that Hollywood is beginning to embrace the ideas Campbell presents in his books. For the writer, producer, director, or designer his concepts are a welcome tool kit, stocked with sturdy instruments ideal for the craft of storytelling. With these tools you can construct a story to meet almost any situation, a story that will be dramatic, entertaining, and psychologically true. With this equipment you can diagnose the problems of almost any ailing plotline, and make the corrections to bring it to its peak of performance.

These tools have stood the test of time. They are older than the Pyramids, older than Stonehenge, older than the earliest cave paintings.

Joseph Campbell's contribution to the tool kit was to gather the ideas together, recognize them, articulate them, name them, organize them. He exposed for the first time the pattern that lies behind every story ever told.

The Hero with a Thousand Faces is his statement of the most persistent theme in oral tradition and recorded literature: the myth of the hero. In his study of world hero myths Campbell discovered that they are all basically the same story, retold endlessly in infinite variation.

He found that all storytelling, consciously or not, follows the ancient patterns of myth and that all stories, from the crudest jokes to the highest flights of literature, can be understood in terms of the Hero's Journey: the "monomyth" whose principles he lays out in the book.

The pattern of the Hero's Journey is universal, occurring in every culture, in every time. It is as infinitely varied as the human race itself and yet its basic form remains constant. The Hero's Journey is an incredibly tenacious set of elements that springs endlessly from the deepest reaches of the mind of man; different in its details for every culture, but fundamentally the same.

Campbell's thinking runs parallel to that of the Swiss psychologist, Carl G. Jung, who wrote about the **archetypes**: constantly repeating characters or energies which occur in the dreams of all people and the myths of all cultures. Jung suggested that these archetypes reflect different aspects of the human mind — that our personalities divide themselves into these characters to play out the drama of our lives. He noticed a strong correspondence between his patients' dream figures and the common archetypes of mythology. He suggested that both were coming from a deeper source, in the **collective unconscious** of the human race.

The repeating characters of world myth such as the young hero, the wise old man or woman, the shapeshifter, and the shadowy antagonist are the same as the figures who appear repeatedly in our dreams and fantasies. That's why myths and most stories constructed

14

on the mythological model have the ring of psychological truth.

Such stories are accurate models of the workings of the human mind, true maps of the psyche. They are psychologically valid and emotionally realistic even when they portray fantastic, impossible, or unreal events.

This accounts for the universal power of such stories. Stories built on the model of the Hero's Journey have an appeal that can be felt by everyone, because they well up from a universal source in the shared unconscious and reflect universal concerns.

They deal with the child-like universal questions: Who am I? Where did I come from? Where will I go when I die? What is good and what is evil? What must I do about it? What will tomorrow be like? Where did yesterday go? Is there anybody else out there?

The ideas embedded in mythology and identified by Campbell in *The Hero with a Thousand Faces* can be applied to understanding almost any human problem. They are a great key to life as well as a major instrument for dealing more effectively with a mass audience.

If you want to understand the ideas behind the Hero's Journey, there's no substitute for actually reading Campbell's work. It's an experience that has a way of changing people.

It's also a good idea to read a lot of myths, but it amounts to the same thing since Campbell is a master storyteller who delights in illustrating his points with examples from the rich storehouse of mythology.

Campbell gives an outline of the Hero's Journey in Chapter IV, "The Keys", of *The Hero with a Thousand Faces*. I've taken the liberty of amending the outline slightly, trying to reflect some of the common themes in movies with illustrations drawn from contemporary films and a few classics. You can compare the two outlines and terminology by examining Table One.

TABLE ONE

Writer's Journey	The Hero With A Thousand Faces
Act One	**Departure, Separation**
Ordinary World	World Of Common Day
Call To Adventure	Call To Adventure
Refusal Of The Call	Refusal Of The Call
Meeting With The Mentor	Supernatural Aid
Crossing The 1st Threshold	Crossing The 1st Threshold
	Belly Of The Whale
Act Two	**Descent, Initiation, Penetration**
Tests, Allies, Enemies	Road Of Trials
Approach To The Inmost Cave	
Supreme Ordeal	Meeting With The Goddess
	Woman As Temptress
	Atonement With The Father
	Apothesis
Reward	The Ultimate Boon
Act Three	**Return**
The Road Back	Refusal Of The Return
	The Magic Flight
	Rescue From Within
	Crossing The Threshold
	Return
Resurrection	Master Of The Two Worlds
Return With Elixir	Freedom To Live

I'm retelling the hero myth in my own way, and you should feel free to do the same. Every storyteller bends the mythic pattern to his own purpose or the needs of her culture.

That's why the hero has a thousand faces.

THE HERO'S JOURNEY

At heart, despite its infinite variety, the hero's story is always a journey. A hero leaves her comfortable, ordinary surroundings to venture into a challenging, unfamiliar world. It may be an outward journey to an actual place: a labyrinth, forest or cave, a strange city or country, a new locale that becomes the arena for her conflict with antagonistic, challenging forces.

But there are as many stories that take the hero on an inward journey, one of the mind, the heart, the spirit. In any good story the hero grows and changes, making a journey from one way of being to the next: from despair to hope, weakness to strength, folly to wisdom, love to hate, and back again. It's these emotional journeys that hook an audience and make a story worth watching.

The stages of the Hero's Journey can be traced in all kinds of stories, not just those that feature "heroic" physical action and adventure. The protagonist of every story is the hero of a journey, even if the path leads only into his own mind or into the realm of relationships.

The way stations of the Hero's Journey emerge naturally even when the writer is unaware of them, but some knowledge of this most ancient guide to storytelling is useful in identifying problems and telling better stories. Consider these twelve stages as a map of the Hero's Journey, one of many ways to get from here to there, but one of the most flexible, durable and dependable.

A note about the term "hero": As used here, the word, like "doctor" or "poet", may refer to a woman or a man.

17

THE STAGES OF THE HERO'S JOURNEY

1.) Ordinary World
2.) Call To Adventure
3.) Refusal Of The Call
4.) Meeting With The Mentor
5.) Crossing The 1st Threshold
6.) Tests, Allies, Enemies

7.) Approach
8.) Supreme Ordeal
9.) Reward
10.) The Road Back
11.) Resurrection
12.) Return With Elixir

The Hero's Journey Model

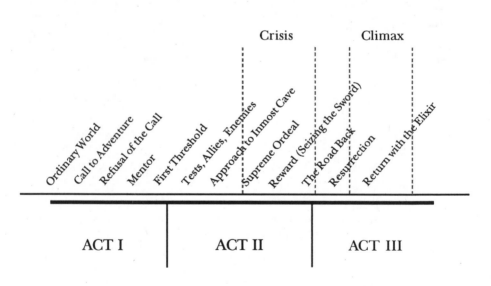

1.) THE ORDINARY WORLD

Most stories take the hero out of the ordinary, mundane world and into a Special World, new and alien. This is the familiar "fish out of water" idea which has spawned countless films and TV shows ("The Fugitive", "The Beverly Hillbillies", *Mr. Smith Goes to Washington, A Connecticut Yankee in King Arthur's Court, The Wizard of Oz, Witness, 48 Hours, Trading Places, Beverly Hills Cop,* etc.)

If you're going to show a fish out of his customary element, you first have to show him in that **Ordinary World** to create a vivid contrast with the strange new world he is about to enter.

In *Witness* you see both the city policeman and the Amish mother and son in their normal worlds before they are thrust into totally alien environments: the Amish being overwhelmed by the city, and the city cop encountering the 19th century world of the Amish. You first see Luke Skywalker, hero of *Star Wars*, being bored to death as a farmboy before he sets out to tackle the universe.

Likewise in *The Wizard of Oz*, considerable time is spent to establish Dorothy's drab normal life in Kansas before she is blown to the wonderworld of Oz. Here the contrast is heightened by shooting the Kansas scenes in stern black and white while the Oz scenes are shot in vibrant Technicolor.

An Officer and a Gentleman sketches a vivid contrast between the Ordinary World of the hero — that of a tough Navy brat with a drunken, whore-chasing father — and the Special World of the spit-and-polish Navy flight school which the hero enters.

2.) THE CALL TO ADVENTURE

The hero is presented with a problem, challenge, or adventure to undertake. Once presented with a **Call to Adventure**, she can no longer remain indefinitely in the comfort of the Ordinary World.

19

Perhaps the land is dying, as in the King Arthur stories of the search for the Grail, the only treasure that can heal the wounded land. In *Star Wars*, the Call to Adventure is Princess Leia's desperate holographic message to wise old Obi Wan Kenobi who asks Luke to join in the quest. Leia has been snatched by evil Darth Vader, like the Greek springtime goddess Persephone who was kidnapped to the underworld by Pluto, lord of the dead. Her rescue is vital to restoring the normal balance of the universe.

In many detective stories, the Call to Adventure is the private eye being asked to take on a new case and solve a crime which has upset the order of things. A good detective should right wrongs as well as solve crimes.

In revenge plots, the Call to Adventure is often a wrong which must be set right, an offense against the natural order of things. In *The Count of Monte Cristo*, Edmond Dantes is unjustly imprisoned and is driven to escape by his desire for revenge. The plot of *Beverly Hills Cop* is set in motion by the murder of the hero's best friend. In *First Blood* Rambo is motivated by his unfair treatment at the hands of an intolerant sheriff.

In romantic comedies, the Call to Adventure might be the first encounter with the special but annoying someone the hero or heroine will be pursuing and sparring with.

The Call to Adventure establishes the stakes of the game, and makes clear the hero's goal: to win the treasure or the lover, to get revenge or right a wrong, to achieve a dream, confront a challenge, or change a life.

What's at stake can often be expressed as a question posed by the call. Will E. T. or Dorothy in *The Wizard of Oz* get home again? Will Luke rescue Princess Leia and defeat Darth Vader? In *An Officer and a Gentleman,* will the hero be driven out of Navy flight school by his own selfishness and the needling of a fierce Marine drill instructor, or will he earn the right to be called an officer and a gentleman? Boy meets girl, but does boy get girl?

3. REFUSAL OF THE CALL (THE RELUCTANT HERO)

This one is about fear. Often at this point the hero balks at the threshold of adventure, **Refusing the Call** or expressing reluctance. After all, she is facing the greatest of all fears, terror of the unknown. The hero has not yet fully committed to the journey and may still be thinking of turning back. Some other influence — a change in circumstances, a further offense against the natural order of things, or the encouragement of a Mentor — is required to get her past this turning point of fear.

In romantic comedies, the hero may express reluctance to get involved (maybe because of the pain of a previous relationship). In a detective story, the private eye may at first turn down the case, only to take it on later against his better judgment.

At this point in *Star Wars*, Luke refuses Obi Wan's Call to Adventure and returns to his aunt and uncle's farmhouse, only to find they have been barbecued by the Emperor's stormtroopers. Suddenly Luke is no longer reluctant and is eager to undertake the quest. The evil of the Empire has become personal to him. He is motivated.

4. MENTOR (THE WISE OLD MAN OR WOMAN)

By this time many stories will have introduced a Merlin-like character who is the hero's **Mentor**. The relationship between hero and Mentor is one of the most common themes in mythology, and one of the richest in its symbolic value. It stands for the bond between parent and child, teacher and student, doctor and patient, god and man.

The Mentor may appear as a wise old wizard (*Star Wars*), a tough drill sergeant (*Officer and a Gentleman*), or a grizzled old boxing coach (*Rocky*). In the mythology of "The Mary Tyler Moore Show", it was Lou Grant. In *Jaws* it's the crusty Robert Shaw character who knows all about sharks.

The function of Mentors is to prepare the hero to face the unknown. They may give advice, guidance or magical equipment. Obi Wan in *Star Wars* gives Luke his father's light saber which he will need in his battles with the dark side of The Force. In *The Wizard of Oz*, Glenda the Good Witch gives Dorothy guidance and the ruby slippers that will eventually get her home again.

However the Mentor can only go so far with the hero. Eventually the hero must face the unknown alone. Sometimes the Mentor is required to give the hero a swift kick in the pants to get the adventure going.

5.) CROSSING THE FIRST THRESHOLD

Now the hero finally commits to the adventure and fully enters the Special World of the story for the first time by **Crossing the First Threshold**. He agrees to face the consequences of dealing with the problem or challenge posed in the Call to Adventure. This is the moment when the story takes off and the adventure really gets going. The balloon goes up, the ship sails, the romance begins, the plane or the spaceship soars off, the wagon train gets rolling.

Movies are often built in three acts, which can be regarded as representing 1) the hero's decision to act, 2) the action itself, and 3) the consequences of the action. The First Threshold marks the turning point between Acts One and Two. The hero, having overcome fear, has decided to confront the problem and take action. She is now committed to the journey and there's no turning back.

This is the moment when Dorothy sets out on the Yellow Brick Road. The hero of *Beverly Hills Cop*, Axel Foley, decides to defy his boss's order, leaving his Ordinary World of the Detroit streets to investigate his friend's murder in the Special World of Beverly Hills.

6.) TESTS, ALLIES AND ENEMIES

Once across the First Threshold, the hero naturally encounters new challenges and **Tests**, makes **Allies and Enemies**, and begins to learn the rules of the Special World.

Saloons and seedy bars seem to be good places for these transactions. Countless Westerns take the hero to a saloon where his manhood and determination are tested, and where friends and villains are introduced. Bars are also useful to the hero for obtaining information, for learning the new rules that apply to the Special World.

In *Casablanca*, Rick's Cafe is the den of intrigue in which alliances and enmities are forged, and in which the hero's moral character is constantly tested. In *Star Wars*, the cantina is the setting for the creation of a major alliance with Han Solo, and the making of an important enmity with Jabba the Hutt which pays off two movies later in *Return of the Jedi*. Here, in the giddy, surreal, violent atmosphere of the cantina swarming with bizarre aliens, Luke also gets a taste of the exciting and dangerous Special World he has just entered.

Scenes like these allow for character development as we watch the hero and his companions react under stress. In the Star Wars cantina, Luke gets to see Han Solo's way of handling a tight situation, and learns that Obi Wan is a warrior wizard of great power.

There are similar sequences in *An Officer and a Gentleman* at about this point, in which the hero makes allies and enemies and meets his "love interest". Several aspects of the hero's character — aggressiveness and hostility, knowledge of street fighting, attitudes about women — are revealed under pressure in these scenes, and sure enough, one of them takes place in a bar.

Of course not all Tests, Alliances, and Enmities are confronted in bars. In many stories, such as *The Wizard of Oz*, these are simply encounters on the road. At this stage on the Yellow Brick Road,

Dorothy acquires her companions the Scarecrow, Tin Woodman and Cowardly Lion, and makes enemies such as a orchard full of grumpy talking trees. She passes a number of Tests such as getting Scarecrow off the nail, oiling the Tin Woodman, and helping the Cowardly Lion deal with his fear.

In *Star Wars* the Tests continue after the cantina scene. Obi Wan teaches Luke about the Force by making him fight blindfolded. The early laser battles with the Imperial fighters are another Test which Luke successfully passes.

7.) APPROACH TO THE INMOST CAVE

The hero comes at last to the edge of a dangerous place, sometimes deep underground, where the object of the quest is hidden. Often it's the headquarters of the hero's greatest enemy, the most dangerous spot in the Special World, the **Inmost Cave**. When the hero enters that fearful place he will cross the second major threshold. Heroes often pause at the gate to prepare, plan, and outwit the villain's guards. This is the phase of **Approach**.

In mythology the Inmost Cave may represent the land of the dead. The hero may have to descend into hell to rescue a loved one (Orpheus), into a cave to fight a dragon and win a treasure (Sigurd in Norse myth), or into a labyrinth to confront a monster (Theseus and the Minotaur).

In the Arthurian stories the Inmost Cave is the Chapel Perilous, the dangerous chamber where the seeker may find the Grail.

In the modern mythology of *Star Wars* the Approach to the Inmost Cave is Luke Skywalker and company being sucked into the Death Star where they will face Darth Vader and rescue Princess Leia. In *The Wizard of Oz* it's Dorothy being kidnapped to the Wicked Witch's baleful castle, and her companions slipping in to save her. The title of *Indiana Jones and the Temple of Doom* reveals the Inmost Cave of that film.

Approach covers all the preparations for entering the Inmost Cave and confronting death or supreme danger.

8.) THE SUPREME ORDEAL

Here the fortunes of the hero hit bottom in a direct confrontation with his greatest fear. He faces the possibility of death and is brought to the brink in a battle with a hostile force. **The Supreme Ordeal** is a "black moment" for the audience, as we are held in suspense and tension, not knowing if he will live or die. The hero, like Jonah, is "in the belly of the beast."

In *Star Wars* it's the harrowing moment in the bowels of the Death Star when Luke, Leia, and company are trapped in the giant trashmasher. Luke is pulled under by the tentacled monster that lives in the sewage and is held down so long that the audience begins to wonder if he's dead. In *E.T.*, the lovable alien momentarily appears to die on the operating table. In *The Wizard of Oz* Dorothy and her friends are trapped by the Wicked Witch, and it looks like there's no way out. At this point in *Beverly Hills Cop* Axel Foley is in the clutches of the villain's men with a gun to his head.

In *An Officer and a Gentleman*, Zack Mayo endures a Supreme Ordeal when his Marine drill instructor launches an all-out drive to torment and humiliate him into quitting the program. It's a psychological life-or-death moment, for if he gives in, his chances of becoming an officer and a gentleman will be dead. He survives the Ordeal by refusing to quit, and the Ordeal changes him. The drill sergeant, a foxy Wise Old Man, has forced him to admit his dependency on others, and from this moment on he is more cooperative and less selfish.

In romantic comedies the death faced by the hero may simply be the temporary death of the relationship, as in the second movement of the old standard plot, "Boy meets girl, boy loses girl, boy gets girl." The hero's chances of connecting with the object of affection look their bleakest.

25

This is a critical moment in any story, an Ordeal in which the hero must die or appear to die so that she can be born again. It's a major source of the magic of the heroic myth. The experiences of the preceding stages have led us, the audience, to identify with the hero and her fate. What happens to the hero happens to us. We are encouraged to experience the brink-of-death moment with her. Our emotions are temporarily depressed so that they can be revived by the hero's return from death. The result of this revival is a feeling of elation and exhilaration.

The designers of amusement park thrill rides know how to use this principle. Roller coasters make their passengers feel as if they're going to die, and there's a great thrill that comes from brushing up against death and surviving it. You're never more alive than when you're looking death in the face.

This is also the key element in rites of passage or rituals of initiation into fraternities and secret societies. The initiate is forced to taste death in some terrible experience, and then is allowed to experience resurrection as he is reborn as a new member of the group. The hero of every story is an initiate being introduced to the mysteries of life and death.

Every story needs such a life-or-death moment in which the hero or his goals are in mortal jeopardy.

9.) REWARD (SEIZING THE SWORD)

Having survived death, beaten the dragon, or slain the Minotaur, hero and audience have cause to celebrate. The hero now takes possession of the treasure she has come seeking, her **Reward**. It might be a special weapon like a magic sword, or a token like the Grail or some elixir which can heal the wounded land.

Sometimes the "sword" is knowledge and experience that leads to greater understanding and a reconciliation with hostile forces.

In *Star Wars*, Luke rescues Princess Leia and captures the plans of the Death Star, keys to defeating Darth Vader.

Dorothy escapes from the Wicked Witch's castle with the Witch's broomstick and the ruby slippers, keys to getting back home.

At this point the hero may also settle a conflict with a parent. In *Return of the Jedi*, Luke is reconciled with Darth Vader, who turns out to be his father and not such a bad guy after all.

The hero may also be reconciled with the opposite sex, as in romantic comedies. In many stories the loved one is the treasure the hero has come to win or rescue, and there is often a love scene at this point to celebrate the victory.

From the hero's point of view, members of the opposite sex may appear to be **Shapeshifters**, an archetype of change. They seem to shift constantly in form or age, reflecting the confusing and constantly changing aspects of the opposite sex. Tales of vampires, werewolves and other shapechangers are symbolic echoes of this shifting quality which men and women see in each other.

The hero's Supreme Ordeal may grant a better understanding of the opposite sex, an ability to see beyond the shifting outer appearance, leading to a reconciliation.

The hero may also become more attractive as a result of having survived the Supreme Ordeal. He has earned the title of "hero" by having taken the supreme risk on behalf of the community.

10). THE ROAD BACK

The hero's not out of the woods yet. We're crossing into Act Three now as the hero begins to deal with the consequences of confronting the dark forces of the Supreme Ordeal. If she has not yet managed to reconcile with the parent, the gods, or the hostile forces, they may come raging after her. Some of the best chase scenes spring up at this

27

point, as the hero is pursued on **The Road Back** by the vengeful forces she has disturbed by Seizing the sword, the elixir or the treasure.

Thus Luke and Leia are furiously pursued by Darth Vader as they escape the Death Star. The Road Back in *E. T.* is the moonlight bicycle flight of Elliott and E. T. as they escape from "Keys" (Peter Coyote) who represents repressive governmental authority.

This stage marks the decision to return to the Ordinary World. The hero realizes that the Special World must eventually be left behind, and there are still dangers, temptations, and tests ahead.

11.) RESURRECTION

In ancient times, hunters and warriors had to be purified before they returned to their communities, because they had blood on their hands. The hero who has been to the realm of the dead must be reborn and cleansed in one last Ordeal of death and **Resurrection** before returning to the Ordinary World of the living.

This is often a second life-and-death moment, almost a replay of the death and rebirth of The Supreme Ordeal. Death and darkness get in one last, desperate shot before being finally defeated. It's a kind of final exam for the hero, who must be tested once more to see if he has really learned the lessons of the Supreme Ordeal.

The hero is transformed by these moments of death-and-rebirth, and is able to return to ordinary life reborn as a new being with new insights.

The Star Wars films play with this element constantly. All three of the films to date feature a final battle scene in which Luke is almost killed, appears to be dead for a moment, and then miraculously survives. Each ordeal wins him new knowledge and command over the Force. He is transformed into a new being by his experience.

Axel Foley in the climactic sequence of *Beverly Hills Cop* once again faces death at the hands of the villain, but is rescued by the intervention of the Beverly Hills police force. He emerges from the experience with a greater respect for cooperation, and is a more complete human being.

An Officer and a Gentleman offers a more complex series of final ordeals, as the hero faces death in a number of ways. Zack's selfishness dies as he gives up the chance for a personal athletic trophy in favor of helping another cadet over an obstacle. His relationship with his girlfriend seems to be dead, and he must survive the crushing blow of his best friend's suicide. As if that weren't enough, he also endures a final hand-to-hand, life-or-death battle with his drill instructor, but survives it all and is transformed into the gallant "officer and gentleman" of the title.

12.) RETURN WITH THE ELIXIR

The hero Returns to the Ordinary World, but the journey is meaningless unless she brings back some **Elixir**, treasure, or lesson from the Special World. The Elixir is a magic potion with the power to heal. It may be a great treasure like the Grail that magically heals the wounded land, or it simply might be knowledge or experience that could be useful to the community someday.

Dorothy returns to Kansas with the knowledge that she is loved, and that "There's no place like home." E. T. returns home with the experience of friendship with humans. Luke Skywalker defeats Darth Vader (for the time being) and restores peace and order to the galaxy.

Zack Mayo wins his commission and leaves the Special World of the training base with a new perspective. In the sparkling new uniform of an officer (with a new attitude to match) he literally sweeps his girlfriend off her feet and carries her away.

Sometimes the Elixir is treasure won on the quest, but it may be love, freedom, wisdom, or the knowledge that the Special World exists and can be survived. Sometimes it's just coming home with a good story to tell.

29

Unless something is brought back from the ordeal in the Inmost Cave, the hero is doomed to repeat the adventure. Many comedies use this ending, as a foolish character refuses to learn his lesson and embarks on the same folly that got him in trouble in the first place.

To recap the Hero's Journey:

1.) Heroes are introduced in the ORDINARY WORLD, where
2.) they receive the CALL TO ADVENTURE.
3.) They are RELUCTANT at first or REFUSE THE CALL, but
4.) are encouraged by a MENTOR to
5.) CROSS THE FIRST THRESHOLD and enter the Special World, where
6.) they encounter TESTS, ALLIES AND ENEMIES.
7.) They APPROACH THE INMOST CAVE, crossing a second threshold
8.) where they endure the SUPREME ORDEAL.
9.) They take possession of their REWARD and
10.) are pursued on THE ROAD BACK to the Ordinary World.
11.) They cross the third threshold, experience a RESURRECTION, and are transformed by the experience.
12.) They RETURN WITH THE ELIXIR, a boon or treasure to benefit the Ordinary World.

⤛⟹ ⟸⤜

The Hero's Journey is a skeletal framework that should be fleshed out with the details and surprises of the individual story. The structure should not call attention to itself, nor should it be followed too precisely. The order of the stages given here is only one of many possible variations. The stages can be deleted, added to, and drastically shuffled without losing any of their power.

The values of the Hero's Journey are what's important. The images of the basic version — young heroes seeking magic swords from old wizards, maidens risking death to save loved ones, knights riding off to fight evil dragons in deep caves, and so on — are just symbols of universal life experiences. The symbols can be changed infinitely to suit the story at hand and the needs of the society.

The Hero's Journey is easily translated to contemporary dramas, comedies, romances, or action-adventures by substituting modern equivalents for the symbolic figures and props of the hero's story. The wise old man or woman may be a real shaman or wizard, but may also be any kind of Mentor or teacher, doctor or therapist, "crusty but benign" boss, tough but fair top sergeant, parent, grandparent, or guiding, helping figure.

Modern heroes may not be going into caves and labyrinths to fight mythical beasts, but they do enter a Special World and an Inmost Cave by venturing into space, to the bottom of the sea, into the depths of a modern city, or into their own hearts.

The patterns of myth can be used to tell the simplest comic book story or the most sophisticated drama. The Hero's Journey grows and matures as new experiments are tried within its framework. Changing the traditional sex and relative ages of the archetypes only makes it more interesting, and allows ever more complex webs of understanding to be spun among them. The basic figures can be combined, or each can be divided into several characters to show different aspects of the same idea.

The Hero's Journey is infinitely flexible, capable of endless variation without sacrificing any of its magic, and it will outlive us all.

Now that we've looked over the map, let's meet the characters who populate the landscape of storytelling: the **Archetypes**.

31

THE ARCHETYPES

THE ARCHETYPES

"Summoned or not, the god will come."

Motto over the door of Carl Jung's house.

As soon as you enter the world of fairy tales and myths, you become aware of recurring character types and relationships: questing heroes, heralds who call them to adventure, wise old men and women who give them magical gifts, threshold guardians who seem to block their way, shapeshifting fellow travelers who confuse and dazzle them, shadowy villains who try to destroy them, tricksters who upset the status quo and provide comic relief. In describing these common character types, symbols, and relationships the Swiss psychologist Carl G. Jung employed the term **archetypes**, meaning ancient patterns of personality that are the shared heritage of the human race.

Jung suggested there may be a **collective unconscious**, similar to the personal unconscious. Fairy tales and myths are like the dreams of an entire culture, springing from the collective unconscious. The same character types seem to occur on both the personal and the collective scale. The archetypes are amazingly constant throughout all times and cultures, in the dreams and personalities of individuals as well as in the mythic imagination of the entire world. An understanding of these forces is one of the most powerful elements in the modern storyteller's bag of tricks.

The concept of archetypes is an indispensable tool for understanding the purpose or **function** of characters in a story. If you grasp the function of the archetype which a particular character is expressing, it can help you determine if the character is pulling her full weight in the story. The archetypes are part of the universal language of storytelling, and a command of their energy is as essential to the writer as breathing.

33

Joseph Campbell spoke of the archetypes as biological; as expressions of the organs of the body, built into the wiring of every human being. The universality of these patterns makes possible the shared experience of storytelling. Storytellers instinctively choose characters and relationships that resonate to the energy of the archetypes, to create dramatic experiences that are recognizable to everyone. Becoming aware of the archetypes can only expand your command of your craft.

ARCHETYPES AS FUNCTIONS

When I first began working with these ideas I thought of an archetype as a fixed role which a character would play exclusively throughout a story. Once I identified a character as a mentor, I expected her to remain a mentor and only a mentor. However as I worked with fairy tale motifs as a story consultant for Disney Animation, I encountered another way of looking at the archetypes — not as rigid character roles but as functions performed temporarily by characters to achieve certain effects in a story. This observation comes from the work of the Russian fairy tale expert Vladimir Propp, whose book, *Morphology of the Folktale*, analyzes motifs and recurrent patterns in hundreds of Russian tales.

Looking at the archetypes in this way, as flexible character functions rather than as rigid character types, can liberate your storytelling. It explains how a character in a story can manifest the qualities of more than one archetype. The archetypes can be thought of as **masks**, worn by the characters temporarily as they are needed to advance the story. A character might enter the story performing the function of a herald, then switch masks to function as a trickster, a mentor, and a shadow.

FACETS OF THE HERO'S PERSONALITY

Another way to look at the classic archetypes is that they are facets of the hero's (or the writer's) personality. The other characters represent possibilities for the hero, for good or ill. A hero sometimes proceeds through the story gathering and incorporating the energy and traits of the other characters. She learns from the other characters, fusing them into a complete human being who has picked up something from everyone she has met along the way.

The Archetypes
as Emanations of the Hero

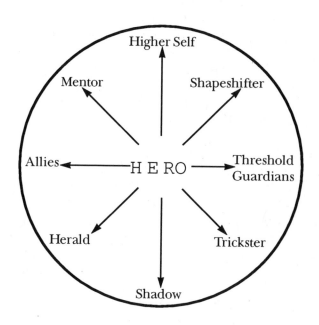

The archetypes can also be regarded as personified symbols of various human qualities. Like the major arcana cards of the Tarot, they stand for the aspects of a complete human personality. Every good story reflects the total human story, the universal human condition of being born into this world, growing, learning, struggling to become an individual, and dying. Stories can be read as metaphors for the general human situation, with characters who embody universal, archetypal qualities, comprehensible to the group as well as the individual.

THE MOST COMMON AND USEFUL ARCHETYPES

For the storyteller, certain character archetypes are indispensable tools of the trade. You can't tell stories without them. The archetypes that occur most frequently in stories, and that seem to be the most useful for the writer to understand are:

HERO
MENTOR (Wise Old Man or Woman)
THRESHOLD GUARDIAN
HERALD
SHAPESHIFTER
SHADOW
TRICKSTER

There are, of course, many more archetypes; as many as there are human qualities to dramatize in stories. Fairy tales are crowded with archetypal figures: the Wolf, the Hunter, the Good Mother, the Wicked Stepmother, the Fairy Godmother, the Witch, the Prince or Princess, the Greedy Innkeeper, and so forth, who perform highly specialized functions. Jung and others have identified many psychological archetypes, such as the *Puer Aeternus* or eternal boy, who can be found in myths as the ever-youthful Cupid, in stories as characters such as Peter Pan, and in life as men who never want to grow up.

Particular genres of modern stories have their specialized character types, such as the "Whore With the Heart of Gold" or the "Arrogant West Point Lieutenant" in Westerns, the "Good Cop-Bad Cop" pairing in buddy pictures, or the "Tough but Fair Sergeant" in war movies.

However these are only variants and refinements of the archetypes discussed in the following chapters. The archetypes we will discuss are the most basic patterns, from which all others are shaped to fit the needs of specific stories and genres.

Two questions are helpful for a writer trying to identify the nature of an archetype: 1) What psychological function or part of the personality does it represent? and 2) What is its dramatic function in a story? Keep these questions in mind as we look at seven of the basic archetypes, the people or energies we are likely to meet on the Hero's Journey.

HERO

HERO

"We're on a mission from God."

from *The Blues Brothers,*
Screenplay by Dan Aykroyd and John Landis

The word **hero** is Greek, from a root that means "to protect and to serve" (incidentally the motto of the Los Angeles Police Department). A Hero is someone who is willing to sacrifice his own needs on behalf of others, like a shepherd who will sacrifice to protect and serve his flock. At the root the idea of **Hero** is connected with self-sacrifice. (Note that I use the word Hero to describe a central character or protagonist of either sex.)

PSYCHOLOGICAL FUNCTION

In psychological terms, the archetype of the Hero represents what Freud called the ego — that part of the personality that separates from the mother, that considers itself distinct from the rest of the human race. Ultimately, a Hero is one who is able to transcend the bounds and illusions of the ego, but at first, Heroes are all ego; the I, the one, that personal identity which thinks it is separate from the rest of the group. The journey of many Heroes is the story of that separation from the family or tribe, equivalent to a child's sense of separation from the mother.

The Hero archetype represents the ego's search for identity and wholeness. In the process of becoming complete, integrated human beings, we are all Heroes facing internal guardians, monsters, and helpers. In the quest to explore our own minds we find teachers, guides, demons, gods, mates, servants, scapegoats, masters, seducers, betrayers, and allies, as aspects of our personalities and characters in our dreams. All the villains, tricksters, lovers, friends, and foes of the

Hero can be found inside ourselves. The psychological task we all face is to integrate these separate parts into one complete, balanced entity. The ego, the Hero thinking she is separate from all these parts of herself, must incorporate them to become the Self.

DRAMATIC FUNCTIONS

AUDIENCE IDENTIFICATION

The dramatic purpose of the Hero is to give the audience a window into the story. Each person hearing a tale or watching a play or movie is invited, in the early stages of the story, to **identify** with the Hero, to merge with him and see the world of the story through his eyes. Storytellers do this by giving their Heroes a combination of qualities, a mix of universal and unique characteristics.

Heroes have qualities that we all can identify with and recognize in ourselves. They are propelled by universal drives that we can all understand: the desire to be loved and understood, to succeed, survive, be free, get revenge, right wrongs, or seek self-expression.

Stories invite us to invest part of our personal identity in the Hero for the duration of the experience. In a sense we become the Hero for awhile. We project ourselves into the Hero's psyche, and see the world through her eyes. Heroes need some admirable qualities, so that we want to be like them. We want to experience the self-confidence of Katherine Hepburn, the elegance of Fred Astaire, the wit of Cary Grant, the sexiness of Marilyn Monroe.

Heroes should have universal qualities, emotions, and motivations that everyone has experienced at one time or another: revenge, anger, lust, competition, territoriality, patriotism, idealism, cynicism, or despair. But Heroes must also be unique human beings, rather than stereotypical creatures or tin gods without flaws or unpredictability. Like any effective work of art they need both universality and originality. Nobody wants to see a movie or read a story about abstract qualities in human form. We want stories about real people. A real character, like a real person, is not just a single trait but a unique combination of many qualities and drives, some of them conflicting. And the more conflicting, the better. A character torn by warring allegiances to love and duty is inherently interesting to an audience. A character who has a unique combination of contradictory impulses, such as trust and suspicion or hope and despair, seems more realistic and human than one who displays only one character trait.

A well-rounded Hero can be determined, uncertain, charming, forgetful, impatient, and strong in body but weak at heart, all at the same time. It's the particular combination of qualities that gives an audience the sense that the Hero is one of a kind, a real person rather than a type.

GROWTH

Another story function of the Hero is learning or growth. In evaluating a script sometimes it's hard to tell who is the main character, or who should be. Often the best answer is: the one who learns or grows the most in the course of the story. Heroes overcome obstacles and achieve goals, but they also gain new knowledge and wisdom. The heart of many stories is the learning that goes on between a Hero and a mentor, or a Hero and a lover, or even between a Hero and a villain. We are all each other's teachers.

ACTION

Another heroic function is acting or doing. The Hero is usually the most active person in the script. His will and desire is what drives most stories forward. A frequent flaw in screenplays is that the Hero is fairly active throughout the story, but at the most critical moment becomes passive and is rescued by the timely arrival of some outside force. At this moment above all, a Hero should be fully active, in control of his own fate. The Hero should perform the decisive action of the story, the action that requires taking the most risk or responsiblity.

SACRIFICE

People commonly think of Heroes as strong or brave, but these qualities are secondary to **sacrifice** — the true mark of a Hero. Sacrifice is the Hero's willingness to give up something of value, perhaps even her own life, on behalf of an ideal or a group. Sacrifice means "making holy". In ancient times people made sacrifices, even of human beings, to acknowledge their debt to the spirit world, the gods, or nature, to appease those mighty forces, and to make holy the processes of daily life. Even death became sanctified, a holy act.

DEALING WITH DEATH

At the heart of every story is a confrontation with death. If the Hero doesn't face actual death, then there is the threat of death or symbolic death in the form of a high-stakes game, love affair, or adventure in which the Hero may succeed (live) or fail (die).

Heroes show us how to deal with death. They may survive it, proving that death is not so tough. They may die (perhaps only symbolically) and be reborn, proving that death can be transcended. They may die a Hero's death, transcending death by offering up their lives willingly for a cause, an ideal, or a group.

True heroism is shown in stories when Heroes offer themselves on the altar of chance, willing to take the risk that their quest for adventure may lead to danger, loss, or death. Like soldiers who know that by enlisting they have agreed to give their lives if their country asks them to, Heroes accept the possibility of sacrifice.

The most effective Heroes are those who experience sacrifice. They may give up a loved one or friend along the way. They may give up some cherished vice or eccentricity as the price of entering into a new way of life. They may return some of their winnings or share what they have gained in the Special World. They may return to their starting point, the tribe or village, and bring back boons, elixirs, food, or knowledge to share with the rest of the group. Great culture Heroes like Martin Luther King or Gandhi gave their lives in pursuit of their ideals.

HEROISM IN OTHER ARCHETYPES

Sometimes the Hero archetype is not just manifested in the main character, the protagonist who bravely fights the bad guys and wins. The archetype can be manifested in other characters, when they act heroically. An unheroic character can grow to be heroic. The title character of *Gunga Din* begins as another archetype altogether, a trickster or clown, but by striving to be a Hero, and by sacrificing himself at a crucial moment on behalf of his friends, he earns the right to be called a Hero. In *Star Wars*, Obi Wan Kenobi clearly manifests the archetype of the mentor through most of the story. However he **acts** heroically and temporarily wears the mask of the Hero when he sacrifices himself to allow Luke to escape the Death Star.

It can be very effective to have a villainous or antagonistic character unexpectedly manifest heroic qualities. On the sitcom level, when a character like Danny De Vito's despicable "Taxi" dispatcher Louie suddenly reveals he has a soft heart or has done something noble, the episode wins an Emmy. A gallant villain, heroic in some ways and despicable in others, can be very appealing. Ideally, every well-rounded character should manifest a touch of every archetype, because the archetypes are expressions of the parts that make up a complete personality.

CHARACTER FLAWS

Interesting flaws humanize a character. We can recognize bits of ourselves in a Hero who is challenged to overcome inner doubts, errors in thinking, guilt or trauma from the past, or fear of the future. Weaknesses, imperfections, quirks, and vices immediately make a Hero or any character more real and appealing. It seems the more neurotic characters are, the more the audience likes them and identifies with them.

Flaws also give a character somewhere to go — the so-called "character arc" in which a character develops from condition A. to condition Z. through a series of steps. Flaws are a starting point of imperfection or incompleteness from which a character can grow. They may be deficiencies in a character. Perhaps a Hero has no romantic partner, and is looking for the "missing piece" to complete her life. This is often symbolized in fairy tales by having the Hero experience a loss or a death in the family. Many fairy tales begin with the death of a parent or the kidnapping of a brother or sister. This subtraction from the family unit sets the nervous energy of the story in motion, not to stop until the balance has been restored by the creation of a new family or the reuniting of the old.

In most modern stories it is the Hero's personality that is being recreated or restored to wholeness. The missing piece may be a critical element of personality such as the ability to love or trust. Heroes may have to overcome some problem such as lack of patience or decisiveness. Audiences love watching Heroes grapple with personality problems and overcome them. Will Edward, the rich but cold-hearted businessman of *Pretty Woman*, warm up under the influence of the life-loving Vivian and become her Prince Charming? Will Vivian gain some self-respect and escape her life of prostitution? Will Conrad, the guilt-ridden teenager in *Ordinary People*, regain his lost ability to accept love and intimacy?

VARIETIES OF HERO

Heroes come in many varieties, including willing and unwilling Heroes, group-oriented and loner Heroes, Anti-heroes, tragic Heroes, and catalyst Heroes. Like all the other archetypes, the Hero is a flexible concept that can express many kinds of energy. Heroes may combine with other archetypes to produce hybrids like the Trickster Hero, or they may temporarily wear the mask of another archetype, becoming a Shapeshifter, a Mentor to someone else, or even a Shadow.

Although usually portrayed as a positive figure, the Hero may also express dark or negative sides of the ego. The Hero archetype generally represents the human spirit in positive action, but may also show the consequences of weakness and reluctance to act.

WILLING AND UNWILLING HEROES

It seems Heroes are of two types: 1) willing, active, gung-ho, committed to the adventure, without doubts, always bravely going ahead, self-motivated, or 2) unwilling, full of doubts and hesitations, passive, needing to be motivated or pushed into the adventure by outside forces. Both make equally entertaining stories, although a Hero who is passive throughout may make for an uninvolving dramatic experience. It's usually best for an unwilling Hero to change at some point, to become committed to the adventure after some necessary motivation has been supplied.

ANTI-HEROES

Anti-hero is a slippery term that can cause a lot of confusion. Simply stated, an Anti-hero is not the opposite of a Hero, but a specialized kind of Hero, one who may be an outlaw or a villain from the point of view of society, but with whom the audience is basically in sympathy. We identify with these outsiders because we have all felt like outsiders at one time or another.

Anti-Heroes may be of two types: 1) characters who behave much like conventional Heroes, but are given a strong touch of cynicism or who have a wounded quality, like Bogart's characters in *The Big Sleep* and *Casablanca*, or 2) tragic Heroes, central figures of a story who may not be likeable or admirable, whose actions we may even deplore, like "Macbeth" or Scarface or the Joan Crawford of *Mommie Dearest.*

The wounded Anti-hero may be a heroic knight in tarnished armor, a loner who has rejected society or been rejected by it. These characters may win at the end and may have the audience's full sympathy at all times, but in society's eyes they are outcasts, like

45

Robin Hood, roguish pirate or bandit Heroes, or many of Bogart's characters. They are often honorable men who have withdrawn from society's corruption, perhaps ex-cops or soldiers who became disillusioned and now operate in the shadow of the law as private eyes, smugglers, gamblers, or soldiers of fortune. We love these characters because they are rebels, thumbing their noses at society as we would all like to do. Another archetype of this kind is personified in James Dean in *Rebel Without a Cause* and *East of Eden,* or the young Marlon Brando, whose character in *The Wild Ones* acted out a new and quite different generation's dissatisfaction with the old. Actors like Mickey Rourke, Matt Dillon, and Sean Penn carry on the tradition today.

The second type of Anti-hero is more like the classical idea of the tragic Hero. These are flawed Heroes who never overcome their inner demons and are brought down and destroyed by them. They may be charming, they may have admirable qualities, but the flaw wins out in the end. Some tragic Anti-heroes are not so admirable, but we watch their downfall with fascination because "there, but for the grace of God, go I". Like the ancient Greeks who watched Oedipus fall, we are purged of our emotions and we learn to avoid the same pitfalls as we watch the destruction of Al Pacino's character in *Scarface,* Sigourney Weaver as Diane Fossey in *Gorillas in the Mist,* or Diane Keaton's character in *Looking for Mr. Goodbar.*

GROUP-ORIENTED HEROES

Another distinction must be made about Heroes with respect to their orientation to society. Like the first storytellers, the earliest humans who went out hunting and gathering on the plains of Africa, most Heroes are group-oriented: They are part of a society at the beginning of the story, and their journey takes them to an unknown land far from home. When we first meet them, they are part of a clan, tribe, village, town, or family. Their story is one of separation from that group (Act One); lone adventure in the wilderness away from the group (Act Two); and usually, eventual reintegration with the group (Act Three).

Group-oriented Heroes often face a choice between returning to the Ordinary World of the first act, or remaining in the Special World of the second act. Heroes who choose to remain in the Special World are rare in Western culture but fairly common in classic Asian and Indian tales.

LONER HEROES

In contrast to the group-oriented Hero is the loner Western Hero such as *Shane*, Clint Eastwood's Man with No Name, John Wayne's Ethan in *The Searchers*, or The Lone Ranger. With this Hero type, the stories begin with the Heroes estranged from society. Their natural habitat is the wilderness, their natural state is solitude. Their journey is one of reentry into the group (Act One); adventure within the group, on the group's normal turf (Act Two); and return to isolation in the wilderness (Act Three). For them the Special World of Act Two is the tribe or village, which they visit briefly but in which they are always uncomfortable. The wonderful shot of John Wayne at the end of *The Searchers* sums up the energy of this Hero type. Wayne is framed in a cabin doorway as an outsider forever cut off from the joys and comforts of the family. This kind of Hero need not be limited to Westerns. It can be used effectively in dramas or action movies where a loner detective is tempted back into adventure, where a hermit or retired person is called back into society, or where an emotionally isolated person is challenged to re-enter the world of relationships.

As with group-oriented Heroes, the loner Heroes have the final choice of returning to their initial state (solitude), or remaining in the Special World of Act Two. Some Heroes begin as loners and end as group-oriented Heroes who elect to stay with the group.

CATALYST HEROES

A certain class of Hero is an exception to the rule that the Hero is usually the character who undergoes the most change. These are catalyst Heroes, central figures who may act heroically, but who do not change much themselves because their main function is to bring about transformation in others. Like a true catalyst in chemistry, they bring about a change in a system without being changed themselves.

A good example is Eddie Murphy's character Axel Foley from *Beverly Hillls Cop*. His personality is already fully formed and distinctive at the story's beginning. He doesn't have much of a character arc because he has nowhere to go. He doesn't learn or change much in the course of the story, but he does bring about change in his Beverly Hills cop buddies, Taggart and Rosewood. By comparison they have relatively strong character arcs, from being uptight and by-the-book to being hip and streetwise, thanks to Axel's influence. In fact, although Axel is the central figure, the villain's main opponent, and the character with the best lines and the most screen time, it could be argued that he is not the true Hero, but the Mentor of the piece, while young Rosewood (Judge Reinhold) is the actual Hero because he learns the most.

Catalyst Heroes are especially useful in continuing stories such as episodic TV shows and sequels. Like The Lone Ranger or Superman, these Heroes undergo few internal changes, but primarily act to help others or guide them in their growth. Of course it's a good idea once in awhile to give even these characters some moments of growth and change to help keep them fresh and believable.

THE ROAD OF HEROES

Heroes are symbols of the soul in transformation, and of the journey each person takes through life. The stages of that progression, the natural stages of life and growth, make up the Hero's Journey. The Hero archetype is a rich field for exploration by writers and spiritual seekers. Carol S. Pearson's book *Awakening The Heroes Within* further breaks down the idea of the Hero into useful archetypes (Innocent, Orphan, Martyr, Wanderer, Warrior, Caregiver, Seeker, Lover, Destroyer, Creator, Ruler, Magician, Sage, and Fool) and graphs the emotional progress of each. It's a good guide to a deeper psychological understanding of the Hero in its many facets. The special avenues traveled by some female heroes are described in *The Heroine's Journey: Woman's Quest for Wholeness* by Maureen Murdock.

48

MENTOR

MENTOR : WISE OLD MAN OR WOMAN

"May the Force be with you!"

from *Star Wars* by George Lucas

An archetype found frequently in dreams, myths, and stories is the **Mentor**, usually a positive figure who aids or trains the hero. Campbell's name for this force is the **Wise Old Man** or **Wise Old Woman**. This archetype is expressed in all those characters who teach and protect heroes and give them gifts. Whether it's God walking with Adam in the Garden of Eden, Merlin guiding King Arthur, the Fairy Godmother helping Cinderella, or a veteran sergeant giving advice to a rookie cop, the relationship between hero and Mentor is one of the richest sources of entertainment in literature and film.

The word "Mentor" comes to us from *The Odyssey*. A character named Mentor guides the young hero, Telemachus, on his Hero's Journey. In fact it's the goddess Athena who helps Telemachus, by assuming the form of Mentor. (See Chapter 13 for a fuller discussion of Mentor's role.) Mentors often speak in the voice of a god, or are inspired by divine wisdom. Good teachers and Mentors are **enthused**, in the original sense of the word. "Enthusiasm" is from the Greek **en theos**, meaning god-inspired, having a god in you, or being in the presence of a god.

PSYCHOLOGICAL FUNCTION

In the anatomy of the human psyche, Mentors represent the Self, the god within us, the aspect of personality that is connected with all things. This higher Self is the wiser, nobler, more godlike part of us. Like Jiminy Cricket in the Disney version of *Pinocchio*, the Self acts as a conscience to guide us on the road of life when no Blue Fairy or kindly Gepetto is there to protect us and tell us right from wrong.

51

Mentor figures, whether encountered in dreams, fairy tales, myths, or screenplays, stand for the hero's highest aspirations. They are what the hero may become if she persists on the Road of Heroes. Mentors are often former heroes who have survived life's early trials and are now passing on the gift of their knowledge and wisdom.

The Mentor archetype is closely related to the image of the parent. The fairy godmother in stories such as "Cinderella" can be be interpreted as the protecting spirit of the girl's dead mother. Merlin is a surrogate parent to the young King Arthur, whose father is dead. Many heroes seek out Mentors because their own parents are inadequate role models.

DRAMATIC FUNCTIONS

TEACHING

Just as learning is an important function of the hero, teaching or training is a key function of the Mentor. Training sergeants, drill instructors, professors, trail bosses, parents, grandparents, crusty old boxing coaches, and all those who teach a hero the ropes, are manifesting this archetype. Of course the teaching can go both ways. Anyone who has taught knows that you learn as much from your students as they do from you.

GIFT-GIVING

Giving gifts is also an important function of this archetype. In Vladimir Propp's analysis of Russian fairy tales, *Morphology of the Folktale*, he identifies this function as that of a "donor" or provider: one who temporarily aids the hero, usually by giving some gift. It may be a magic weapon, an important key or clue, some magical medicine or food, or a life-saving piece of advice. In fairy tales the donor might be a witch's cat, grateful for a little girl's kindness, who gives her a towel and a comb. Later when the girl is being chased by the witch, the towel turns into a raging river and the comb turns into a forest to block the witch's pursuit.

Examples of these gifts are abundant in movies, from the small-time mobster Puttynose giving James Cagney his first gun in *The Public Enemy* to Obi Wan Kenobi giving Luke Skywalker his father's light-saber. Nowadays the gift is as likely to be a computer code as the key to a dragon's lair.

GIFTS IN MYTHOLOGY

Gift-giving, the donor function of the Mentor, has an important role in mythology. Many heroes received gifts from their Mentors, the gods. Pandora, whose name means "all-gifted", was showered with presents, including Zeus' vindictive gift of the box which she was not supposed to open. Heroes such as Hercules were given some gifts by their Mentors, but among the Greeks the most gifted of heroes was Perseus.

PERSEUS

The Greek ideal of heroism was expressed in Perseus, the monster-slayer. He has the distinction of being one of the best equipped of heroes, so loaded down with gifts from higher powers that it's a wonder he could walk. In time, with the help of Mentors such as Hermes and Athena, he acquired winged sandals, a magic sword, a helmet of invisibility, a magic sickle, a magic mirror, the head of Medusa that turned all who look on it to stone, and a magic satchel to stow the head in. As if this were not enough, the movie version of the Perseus tale, *Clash of the Titans*, gives him the flying horse Pegasus as well.

In most stories, this would be overdoing it a bit. But Perseus is meant to be a paragon of heroes, so it's fitting he should be so well provided for by the gods, his Mentors in the quest.

GIFTS SHOULD BE EARNED

In Propp's dissection of Russian fairy tales, he observes that donor characters give magical presents to heroes, but usually only after the heroes have passed a test of some kind. This is a good rule of thumb: **The gift or help of the donor should be earned, by learning, sacrifice, or commitment.** Fairy tale heroes eventually earn the aid of animals or magical creatures by being kind to them in the beginning, sharing food with them, or protecting them from harm.

MENTOR AS INVENTOR

Sometimes the Mentor functions as a scientist or inventor, whose gifts are his devices, designs, or inventions. The great inventor of classical myth is Daedalus, who designed the Labyrinth and other wonders for the rulers of Crete. As the master artisan of the Theseus and the Minotaur story, he had a hand in creating the monster Minotaur and designed the Labyrinth as a cage for it. As a Mentor, Daedalus gave Ariadne the ball of thread that allowed Theseus to get in and out of the Labyrinth alive.

Imprisoned in his own maze as punishment for helping Theseus, Daedalus also invented the famous wax-and-feather wings that allowed him and his son Icarus to escape. As a Mentor to Icarus, he advised his son not to fly too close to the sun. Icarus, who had grown up in the pitch dark of the Labyrinth, was irresistibly attracted to the sun, ignored his father's advice, and fell to his death when the wax melted. The best advice is worthless if you don't take it.

THE HERO'S CONSCIENCE

Some Mentors perform a special function as a conscience for the hero. Characters like Jiminy Cricket in *Pinocchio* or Walter Brennan's Groot in *Red River* try to remind an errant hero of an important moral code. However, a hero may rebel against a nagging conscience. Would-be Mentors should remember that in the original Collodi story Pinocchio squashed the cricket to shut him up. The angel on a hero's shoulder can never offer arguments as colorful as those of the devil on the opposite side.

MOTIVATION

Another important function of the Mentor archetype is to motivate the hero, and help her overcome fear. Sometimes the gift alone is sufficient reassurance and motivation. In other cases the Mentor shows the hero something or arranges things to motivate her to take action and commit to the adventure.

In some cases a hero is so unwilling or fearful that he must be pushed into the adventure. A Mentor may need to give a hero a swift kick in the pants in order to get the adventure rolling.

PLANTING

A function of the Mentor archetype is often to **plant** information or a prop that will become important later. The James Bond films have a mandatory scene in which the weapons master "Q", one of Bond's recurring Mentors, describes the workings of some new briefcase gadget to a bored OO7. This information is a **plant**, meant for the audience to note but forget about until the climactic moment where the gadget becomes a life-saver. Such constructions help tie the beginning and end of the story together, and show that at some point everything we've learned from our Mentors comes in handy.

SEXUAL INITIATION

In the realm of love, the Mentor's function may be to initiate us into the mysteries of love or sex. In India they speak of the *shakti* — a sexual initiator, a partner who helps you experience the power of sex as a vehicle of higher consciousness. A shakti is a manifestation of God, a Mentor leading the lover to experience the divine.

Seducers and thieves of innocence teach heroes lessons the hard way. There may be a shadow side to Mentors who lead a hero down a dangerous road of obsessive love or loveless, manipulative sex. There are many ways to learn.

TYPES OF MENTOR

Like heroes, Mentors may be willing or unwilling. Sometimes they teach in spite of themselves. In other cases they teach by their bad example. The downfall of a weakened, tragically flawed Mentor can show the hero pitfalls to avoid. As with heroes, dark or negative sides may be expressed through this archetype.

DARK MENTORS

In certain stories the power of the Mentor archetype can be used to mislead the audience. In thrillers the mask of a Mentor is sometimes a decoy used to lure the hero into danger. Or in an anti-heroic gangster picture such as *The Public Enemy* or *Goodfellas*, where every conventional heroic value is inverted, an anti-Mentor appears to guide the anti-hero on the road to crime and destruction.

Another inversion of this archetype's energy is a special kind of **Threshold Guardian** (an archetype discussed in chapter 5). An example is found in *Romancing the Stone*, where Joan Wilder's witchy, sharp-tongued agent is to all appearances a Mentor, guiding her career and giving her advice about men. But when Joan is about to cross the threshold to adventure, the agent tries to stop her, warning her of the dangers and casting doubt in her mind. Rather than motivating her like a true Mentor, the agent becomes an obstacle in the hero's path. This is psychologically true to life, for often we must overcome or outgrow the energy of our best teachers in order to move to the next stage of development.

FALLEN MENTORS

Some Mentors are still on a Hero's Journey of their own. They may be experiencing a crisis of faith in their calling. Perhaps they are dealing with the problems of aging and approaching the threshold of death, or have fallen from the hero's road. The hero needs the Mentor to pull himself together one more time, and there's serious doubt that he can do it. Tom Hanks in *A League of Their Own* plays a former sports hero sidelined by injury and making a poor transition into Mentor-hood. He has fallen far from grace, and the audience is rooting for him to straighten up and honor his task of helping the heroes. Such a Mentor may go through all the stages of a hero's journey, on his own path to redemption.

CONTINUING MENTORS

Mentors are useful for giving assignments and setting stories in motion. For this reason they are often written into the cast of continuing stories. Recurring Mentors include Mr. Waverly on "The Man From U.N.C.L.E.", "M" in the Bond pictures, "The Chief" on "Get Smart", Will Geer and Ellen Corby as the grandparents on "The Waltons", Alfred in "Batman", James Earl Jones' CIA official in *Patriot Games* and *The Hunt for Red October*, etc.

MULTIPLE MENTORS

A hero may be trained by a series of Mentors who teach specific skills. Hercules is surely among the best trained of heroes, mentored by experts on wrestling, archery, horsemanship, weapon-handling, boxing, wisdom, virtue, song, and music. He even took a driver-training course in charioteering from one Mentor. All of us have learned from a series of Mentors, including parents, older brothers and sisters, friends, lovers, teachers, bosses, co-workers, therapists, and other role models.

Multiple Mentors may be needed to express different functions of the archetype. In the James Bond movies, OO7 always returns to his home base to confer with his main Wise Old Man, the spymaster "M" who gives him assignments, advice, and warnings. But the Mentor function of giving gifts to the hero is delegated to "Q", the weapons and gadget master. A certain amount of emotional support as well as advice and critical information is provided by Miss Moneypenny, representing another aspect of the Mentor.

COMIC MENTORS

A special type of Mentor occurs in romantic comedies. This person is often the friend or fellow office worker of the hero, and is usually of the same sex as the hero. She gives the hero some advice about love: go out more to forget the pain of a lost love; pretend to have an affair to make your husband jealous; feign interest in the beloved's hobbies; impress the beloved with gifts, flowers or flattery; be more aggressive; and so on. The advice often seems to lead the hero into temporary disaster, but it all turns out right in the end. These characters are a feature of romantic comedies, especially those of the 1950s when movies like *Pillow Talk* and *Lover Come Back* gave plenty of work for character actors like Thelma Ritter and Tony Randall who could portray this wise-cracking, sarcastic version of a Mentor.

MENTOR AS SHAMAN

Mentor figures in stories are closely related to the idea of the **shaman**: the healer, the medicine man or woman, of tribal cultures. Just as Mentors guide the hero through the special world, shamans guide their people through life. They travel to other worlds in dreams and visions and bring back stories to heal their tribes. It's often the function of a Mentor to help the hero seek a guiding vision for a quest to another world.

FLEXIBILITY OF THE MENTOR ARCHETYPE

Like the other archetypes, the Mentor or donor is not a rigid character type, but rather a **function**, a job which several different characters might perform in the course of a story. A character primarily manifesting one archetype — the hero, the shapeshifter, the trickster, even the villain — may temporarily slip on the mask of the Mentor in order to teach or give something to the hero.

In Russian fairy tales, the wonderful character of the witch Baba Yaga is a Shadow figure who sometimes wears the Mentor mask. On the surface she's a horrible, cannibalistic witch representing the dark side of the forest, its power to devour. But like the forest, she can be appeased and can shower gifts on the traveler. Sometimes if Prince Ivan is kind and complimentary to her, Baba Yaga gives him the magical treasure he needs to rescue the Princess Vasilisa.

Although Campbell called these Mentor figures Wise Old Men or Women, they are sometimes neither wise nor old. The young, in their innocence, are often wise and capable of teaching the old. The most foolish person in a story might be the one we learn the most from. As with the other archetypes, the function of a Mentor is more important than mere physical description. What the character **does** will often determine what archetype is being manifested at the moment.

Many stories have no specific character who can be identified as a Mentor. There's no white-bearded, wizardly figure who wanders around acting like a Wise Old Man. Nevertheless almost every story calls on the energy of this archetype at some point.

INNER MENTORS

In some Westerns or film noir stories the hero is an experienced, hardened character who has no need for a Mentor or guide. He has internalized the archetype and it now lives within him as an inner code of behavior. The Mentor may be the unspoken code of the gunfighter, or the secret notions of honor harbored by Sam Spade or Philip Marlowe. A code of ethics may be a disembodied manifestation of the Mentor archetype guiding the hero's actions. It's not uncommon for a hero to make reference to a Mentor who meant something to him earlier in life, even if there's no actual Mentor character in the story. A hero may remember, "My mother / father / grandfather/drill sergeant used to say...", and then call to mind the bit of wisdom that will become critical in solving the problem of the story. The energy of the Mentor archetype also may be invested in a prop such as a book or other artifact that guides the hero in the quest.

PLACEMENT OF MENTORS

Although the Hero's Journey often finds the Mentor appearing in Act One, the placement of a Mentor in a story is a practical consideration. A character may be needed at any point who knows the ropes, has the map to the unknown country, or can give the hero key information at the right time. Mentors may show up early in a story, or wait in the wings until needed at a critical moment in Act Two or Act Three.

Mentors provide heroes with motivation, inspiration, guidance, training, and gifts for the journey. Every hero is guided by something, and a story without some acknowledgement of this energy is incomplete. Whether expressed as an actual character or as an internalized code of behavior, the Mentor archetype is a powerful tool at the writer's command.

THRESHOLD
GUARDIAN

THRESHOLD GUARDIAN

"...I, for one, have an idea that he will never bring this journey off.."
from *The Odyssey* of Homer

All heroes encounter obstacles on the road to adventure. At each gateway to a new world there are powerful guardians at the threshold, placed to keep the unworthy from entering. They present a menacing face to the hero, but if properly understood, they can be overcome, bypassed, or even turned into allies. Many heroes (and many writers) encounter **Threshold Guardians**, and understanding their nature can help determine how to handle them.

Threshold Guardians are usually not the main villains or antagonists in stories. Often they will be lieutenants of the villain, lesser thugs or mercenaries hired to guard access to the chief's headquarters. They may also be neutral figures who are simply part of the landscape of the special world. In rare cases they may be secret helpers placed in the hero's path to test her willingness and skill.

There is often a symbiotic relationship between a villain and a Threshold Guardian. In nature, a powerful animal such as a bear will sometimes tolerate a smaller animal such as a fox nesting at the entrance of its lair. The fox, with its strong smell and sharp teeth, tends to keep other animals from wandering into the cave while the bear is sleeping. The fox also serves as an early warning system for the bear by making a racket if something tries to enter the cave. In similar fashion, villains of stories often rely on underlings such as doorkeepers, bouncers, bodyguards, sentries, gunslingers, or mercenaries to protect and warn them when a hero approaches the Threshold of the villain's stronghold.

PSYCHOLOGICAL FUNCTION: NEUROSES

These Guardians may represent the ordinary obstacles we all face in the world around us: bad weather, bad luck, prejudice, oppression, or hostile people like the waitress who refuses to grant Jack Nicholson's simple request in *Five Easy Pieces*. But on a deeper psychological level they stand for our internal demons: the neuroses, emotional scars, vices, dependencies, and self-limitations that hold back our growth and progress. It seems that every time you try to make a major change in your life, these inner demons rise up to their full force, not necessarily to stop you, but to test if you are really determined to accept the challenge of change.

DRAMATIC FUNCTION: TESTING

Testing of the hero is the primary dramatic function of the Threshold Guardian. When heroes confront one of these figures, they must solve a puzzle or pass a test. Like the Sphinx who presents Oedipus with a riddle before he can continue his journey, Threshold Guardians challenge and test heroes on the path.

How to deal with these apparent obstacles? Heroes have a range of options. They can turn around and run, attack the opponent head on, use craft or deceit to get by, bribe or appease the Guardian, or make an **Ally** of a presumed enemy. (Although we will not discuss the Ally as a separate archetype, heroes are aided by a variety of archetypes known collectively as Allies.)

One of the most effective ways of dealing with a Threshold Guardian is to "get into the skin" of the opponent, like a hunter entering into the mind of a stalked animal. The Plains Indians wore buffalo skins to sneak within bow-shot of the bison herd. The hero may get past a Threshold Guardian by entering into its spirit or taking on its appearance. A good example is in Act Two of *The Wizard of Oz*, when Tin Woodman, Cowardly Lion, and Scarecrow come to the Wicked Witch's castle to rescue the kidnapped Dorothy. The situation looks bleak. Dorothy's inside a strong castle defended by a regiment of

64

fierce-looking soldiers who march up and down singing "Oh-Ee-Oh". There's no possible way for the three friends to defeat such a large force.

However our heroes are ambushed by three sentries and overcome them, taking their uniforms and weapons. Disguised as soldiers, they join the end of a column and march right into the castle. They have turned an attack to their advantage by literally climbing into the skins of their opponents. Instead of uselessly trying to defeat a superior enemy, they have temporarily **become** the enemy.

It's important for a hero to recognize and acknowledge these figures as Threshold Guardians. In daily life, you have probably encountered resistance when you try to make a positive change in your life. People around you, even those who love you, are often reluctant to see you change. They are used to your neuroses and have found ways to benefit from them. The idea of your changing may threaten them. If they resist you, it's important to realize they are simply functioning as Threshold Guardians, testing you to see if you are really resolved to change.

SIGNALS OF NEW POWER

Successful heroes learn to recognize Threshold Guardians not as threatening enemies, but as useful Allies and early indicators that new power or success is coming. Threshold Guardians who appear to be attacking may in fact be doing the hero a huge favor.

Heroes also learn to recognize resistance as a source of strength. As in bodybuilding, the greater the resistance, the greater the strength. Rather than attacking the power of Threshold Guardians head on, heroes learn to use it so it doesn't harm them. In fact it makes them stronger. The martial arts teach that an opponent's strength can be used against him. Ideally, Threshold Guardians are not to be defeated but **incorporated** (literally, taken into the body). Heroes learn the Guardians' tricks, absorb them, and go on. Ultimately, fully evolved heroes feel compassion for their apparent enemies and transcend rather than destroy them.

65

Heroes must learn to read the signals of their Threshold Guardians. In *The Power of Myth*, Joseph Campbell illustrated this idea beautifully with an example from Japan. Ferocious-looking demon statues sometimes guard the entrances to Japanese temples. The first thing you notice is one hand held up like that of a policeman gesturing "Stop!" But when you look more closely, you see that the other hand invites you to enter. The message is: Those who are put off by outward appearances cannot enter the Special World, but those who can see past surface impressions to the inner reality are welcome.

In stories, Threshold Guardians take on a fantastic array of forms. They may be border guards, sentinels, night watchmen, lookouts, bodgyguards, bandidos, editors, doormen, bouncers, entrance examiners, or anyone whose function is to temporarily block the way of the hero and test her powers. The energy of the Threshold Guardian may not be embodied as a character, but may be found as a prop, architectural feature, animal, or force of nature that blocks and tests the hero. Learning how to deal with Threshold Guardians is one of the major tests of the Hero's Journey.

HERALD

HERALD

"If you build it, they will come."

> The Voice in *Field of Dreams*
> Screenplay by Phil Alden Robinson from the
> novel *Shoeless Joe* by W.P. Kinsella

Often a new force will appear in Act One to bring a challenge to the hero. This is the energy of the **Herald** archetype. Like the heralds of medieval chivalry, Herald characters issue challenges and announce the coming of significant change.

The heralds of knighthood were responsible for keeping track of lineages and coats of arms, and had an important role in identifying people and relationships in battle, tournaments, and on great state occasions such as weddings. They were the protocol officers of their day. At the commencement of war a herald might be called upon to recite the causes of the conflict; in effect, to provide the motivation. In Shakespeare's *Henry V*, the Ambassadors from the Dauphin (crown prince) of France act as Heralds when they bring the young English king an insulting gift of tennis balls, which implies King Henry is fit for nothing but a frivolous game of tennis. The appearance of these Heralds is the spark that sets off a war. Later the character of Mountjoy, the Dauphin's Herald, bears messages between King Henry and his master during the crucial battle of Agincourt.

Typically, in the opening phase of a story, heroes have "gotten by" somehow. They have handled an imbalanced life through a series of defenses or coping mechanisms. Then all at once some new energy enters the story that makes it impossible for the hero to simply get by any longer. A new person, condition, or information shifts the hero's balance, and nothing will ever be the same. A decision must be made, action taken, the conflict faced. A Call to Adventure has been delivered, often by a character who manifests the archetype of the Herald. Heralds are so necessary in mythology that the Greek god Hermes (Roman Mercury) is devoted to expressing this function. Hermes appears everywhere as the messenger or Herald of the gods, performing some errand or bearing a message from Zeus. At the beginning of *The Odyssey* Hermes, at Athena's urging, bears a message from Zeus to the nymph Calypso that she must release Odysseus. The appearance of Hermes as Herald gets the story rolling.

PSYCHOLOGICAL FUNCTION: CALL FOR CHANGE

Heralds have the important pscyhological function of announcing the need for change. Something deep inside us knows when we are ready to change and sends us a messenger. This may be a dream figure, a real person, or a new idea we encounter. In Field of Dreams it's the mysterious Voice that the hero hears saying "If you build it, they will come." The Call might come from a book we read, or a movie we see. But something inside us has been struck like a bell, and the resulting vibrations spread out through our lives until change is inevitable.

DRAMATIC FUNCTION : MOTIVATION

Heralds provide motivation, offer the hero a challenge, and get the story rolling. They alert the hero (and the audience) that change and adventure are coming.

An example of the Herald archetype as a motivator in movies can be found in Alfred Hitchcock's *Notorious*. Cary Grant plays a secret agent trying to enlist Ingrid Bergman, the playgirl daughter of a Nazi spy, in a noble cause. He offers her both a challenge and an opportunity: She can overcome her bad reputation and the family shame by dedicating herself to Cary's noble cause. (The cause turns out to be not so noble later on, but that's another story.)

Like most heroes, Bergman's character is fearful of change and reluctant to accept the challenge, but Grant, like a medieval herald, reminds her of the past and gives her motivation to act. He plays her a recording of an argument she had with her father, in which she renounced his spying and declared her loyalty to the United States. Confronted by the evidence of her own patriotism, she accepts the call to adventure. She is motivated.

The Herald may be a person or a force. The coming of a storm or the first tremors of the earth, as in *Hurricane* or *Earthquake*, may be the Herald of adventure. The crash of the stock market or the declaration of war have set many a story in motion.

Often the Herald is simply a means of bringing news to the hero of a new energy that will change the balance. It could be a telegram or a phone call. In *High Noon*, the Herald is a telegraph clerk who brings Gary Cooper word that his enemies are out of jail and headed for town to kill him. In *Romancing the Stone*, the Herald for Joan Wilder is a treasure map that arrives in the mail, and a phone call from her sister, who is being held hostage in Colombia.

TYPES OF HERALD

The Herald may be a positive, negative, or neutral figure. In some stories the Herald is the villain or his emissary, perhaps issuing a direct challenge to the hero, or trying to dupe the hero into getting involved. In the thriller *Arabesque*, the Herald is the private secretary of the villain who tries to lure the hero, a college professor of modest means, into danger with a tempting offer of work. In some cases, a villainous Herald may announce the challenge not to the hero but to the audience. In *Star Wars* the first appearance of Darth Vader, as he captures Princess Leia, proclaims to the audience that something is out of balance before the hero, Luke Skywalker, has even appeared.

In other stories the Herald is an agent of the forces of good, calling the hero to a positive adventure. The Herald's mask may be worn temporarily by a character who mainly embodies some other archetype. A Mentor frequently acts as a Herald who issues a challenge to the hero. The Herald may be a hero's loved one or Ally, or someone neutral to the hero, such as a Trickster or Threshold Guardian.

The Herald archetype may come into play at almost any point in a story, but is most frequently employed in Act One to help bring the hero into the adventure. Whether it is an inner call, an external development, or a character bringing news of change, the energy of the Herald is needed in almost every story.

SHAPESHIFTER

SHAPESHIFTER

"You can expect the unexpected."
          Publicity for the film *Charade*

People often have trouble grasping the elusive archetype of the **Shapeshifter**, perhaps because its very nature is to be shifting and unstable. Its appearance and characteristics change as soon as you examine it closely. Nonetheless, the Shapeshifter is a powerful archetype and understanding its ways can be helpful in storytelling and in life.

Heroes frequently encounter figures, often of the opposite sex, whose primary characteristic is that they appear to change constantly from the hero's point of view. Often the hero's love interest or romantic partner will manifest the qualities of a Shapeshifter. We have all experienced relationships in which our partner is fickle, two-faced, or bewilderingly changeable. In *Fatal Attraction* the hero is confronted with a Shapeshifting woman who changes from a passionate lover to an insane, murderous harpy.

Shapeshifters change appearance or mood, and are difficult for the hero and the audience to pin down. They may mislead the hero or keep her guessing, and their loyalty or sincerity is often in question. An Ally or friend of the same sex as the hero may also act as a Shapeshifter in a buddy comedy or adventure. Wizards, witches, and ogres are traditional Shapeshifters in the world of fairy tales.

PSYCHOLOGICAL FUNCTION

An important psychological purpose of the Shapeshifter archetype is to express the energy of the **animus** and **anima**, terms from the psychology of Carl Jung. The animus is Jung's name for the male element in the female unconscious; the bundle of positive and negative images of masculinity in a woman's dreams and fantasies. The anima is the corresponding female element in the male unconscious. In this theory, people have a complete set of both male and female qualities which are necessary for survival and internal balance.

Historically, the female characteristics in men and the male characteristics in women have been sternly repressed by society. Men learn at an early age to show only the macho, unemotional side of themselves. Women are taught by society to play down their masculine qualities. This can lead to emotional and even physical problems. Men are now working to regain some of their suppressed feminine qualities — sensitivity, intuition, and the ability to feel and express emotion. Women sometimes spend their adult lives trying to reclaim the male energies within them which society has discouraged, such as power and assertiveness.

These repressed qualities live within us and are manifested in dreams and fantasies as the animus or anima. They may take the form of dream characters such as opposite sex teachers, family members, classmates, gods or monsters who allow us to express this unconscious but powerful force within. An encounter with the anima or animus in dreams or fantasy is considered an important step in psychological growth.

PROJECTION

We may also confront the animus and anima in reality. By nature we look for people who match our internal image of the opposite sex. Often we imagine the resemblance and **project** our desire to join with the anima or animus onto some unsuspecting person. We may fall into relationships in which we have not seen the partner clearly. Instead we have seen the anima or animus, our own internal notion of the ideal partner, projected onto the other person. We often go through relationships trying to force the partner to match our **projection**. Hitchcock created a powerful expression of this phenomenon in *Vertigo*. James Stewart forces Kim Novak to change her hair and clothing to match the image of his feminine ideal Carlota, a woman who ironically never existed in the first place.

It's natural for each sex to regard the other as ever-changing, mysterious. Many of us don't understand our own sexuality and psychology very well, let alone that of the opposite sex. Often our main experience of the opposite sex is their changeability and their tendency to shift attitudes, appearances, and emotions for no apparent reason.

Women complain that men are vague, vacillating, and unable to commit. Men complain that women are moody, flighty, fickle, and unpredictable. Anger can turn gentle men into beasts. Women change dramatically during their monthly cycle, shifting with the phases of the moon. During pregnancy they drastically shift shape and mood. At some time most of us have been perceived by others as "two-faced" Shapeshifters.

The animus and anima may be positive or negative figures who may be helpful to the hero or destructive to him. In some stories it's the task of the hero to figure out which side, positive or negative, he is dealing with.

The Shapeshifter archetype is also a catalyst for change, a symbol of the psychological urge to transform. Dealing with a Shapeshifter may cause the hero to change attitudes about the opposite sex or come to terms with the repressed energies that this archetype stirs up.

These projections of our hidden opposite sides, these images and ideas about sexuality and relationships, form the archetype of the Shapeshifter.

DRAMATIC FUNCTION

The Shapeshifter serves the dramatic function of bringing doubt and suspense into a story. When heroes keep asking, "Is he faithful to me? Is she going to betray me? Does he truly love me? Is he an ally or

77

an enemy?", a Shapeshifter is generally present.

Shapeshifters appear with great frequency and variety in the film noir and thriller genres. *The Big Sleep, The Maltese Falcon,* and *Chinatown* feature detectives confronting shape-shifting women whose loyalty and motives are in doubt. In other stories such as Hitchcock's *Suspicion* or *Shadow of a Doubt,* a good woman must figure out if a Shapeshifting man is worthy of her trust.

A common type of Shapeshifter is called the **femme fatale**, the woman as temptress or destroyer. The idea is as old as the Bible, with its stories of Eve in the Garden of Eden, the scheming Jezebel, and Delilah cutting off Samson's hair to rob him of his strength. The femme fatale finds expression today in stories of cops and detectives betrayed by killer women, such as Sharon Stone's character in *Basic Instinct* or Kathleen Turner's in *Body Heat. Black Widow* and *Single White Female* are interesting variants in which a *female* hero confronts a deadly, Shapeshifting femme fatale.

The Shapeshifter, like the other archetypes, can be manifested by male or female characters. There are as many **hommes fatale** in myth, literature, and movies as there are femmes. In Greek mythology, Zeus was a great Shapeshifter, changing forms to cavort with human maidens who usually ended up suffering for it. *Looking for Mr. Goodbar* is about a woman seeking a perfect lover, but finding instead a Shapeshifting man who brings her death. The film *The Stranger* depicts a good woman (Loretta Young) who is about to marry a monstrous Shapeshifter, a closet Nazi played by Orson Welles.

The *fatale* aspect is not always essential to this archetype. Shapeshifters may only dazzle and confuse the hero, rather than trying to kill her. Shapeshifting is a natural part of romance. It's common to be blinded by love, unable to see the other person clearly through the many masks they wear. The character played by Michael Douglas in *Romancing the Stone* appears to be a Shapeshifter to hero Kathleen Turner, who is kept guessing until the last moment about the loyalty of her male counterpart.

Shapeshifting may manifest in changes of appearance. In many films a woman's change of costume or hairstyle indicates that her identity is shifting and her loyalty is in doubt. This archetype may also be expressed through changes in behavior or speech, such as assuming different accents or telling a succession of lies. In the thriller *Arabesque*, Shapeshifter Sophia Loren tells unwilling hero Gregory Peck a bewildering series of stories about her background, all of which turn out be untrue. Many heroes have to deal with Shapeshifters, male and female, who assume disguises and tell lies to confuse them.

A famous Shapeshifter from *The Odyssey* is the sea god Proteus, "the Old Man of the Sea". Menelaus, one of the heroes returning from the Trojan War, traps Proteus to force information out of him. Proteus changes into a lion, a snake, a panther, a boar, running water, and a tree in his attempt to escape. But Menelaus and his men hold on tight until Proteus returns to his true form and yields up the answers to their questions. The story teaches that if heroes are patient with Shapeshifters the truth may eventually come out. "Protean", our adjective meaning "readily taking many forms", comes from the story of Proteus.

MASK OF THE SHAPESHIFTER

As with the other archetypes, Shapeshifting is a function or a mask that may be worn by any character in a story. A hero may wear the mask in a romantic situation. Richard Gere, in *An Officer and a Gentleman,* puts on airs and tells a hatful of lies to impress Debra Winger. He temporarily acts as a Shapeshifter although he is the hero of the piece.

Sometimes a hero must become a Shapeshifter to escape a trap or get past a Threshold Guardian. In *Sister Act,* Whoopi Goldberg's character, a Las Vegas lounge singer, disguises herself as a Catholic nun to keep from being killed as a witness to a mob murder.

Villains or their allies may wear the Shapeshifter mask to seduce or confuse a hero. The wicked queen in *Snow White* assumes the form of an old crone to trick the hero into eating a poisoned apple.

Shapeshifting is also a natural attribute of other archetypes such as Mentors and Tricksters. Merlin, Mentor of the King Arthur stories, frequently changes shape to aid Arthur's cause. The goddess Athena in *The Odyssey* assumes the appearance of many different humans to help Odysseus and his son.

Shapeshifters can also be found in so-called "buddy movies" in which the story centers on two male or two female characters who share the role of hero. Often one is more conventionally heroic and easier for the audience to identify with. The second character, while of the same sex as the main hero, will often be a Shapeshifter, whose loyalty and true nature are always in question. In the comedy *The In-Laws*, the "straight" hero, Alan Arkin, is nearly driven crazy by the Shapeshifting of his buddy, Peter Falk, a CIA agent.

The Shapeshifter is one of the most flexible archetypes and serves a protean variety of functions in modern stories. It's found most often in male-female relationships, but it may also be useful in other situations to portray characters whose appearance or behavior changes to meet the needs of the story.

SHADOW

SHADOW

"You can't keep a good monster down!"
                    Publicity for *Ghost of Frankenstein*

The archetype known as the **Shadow** represents the energy of the dark side, the unexpressed, unrealized, or rejected aspects of something. Often it's the home of the suppressed monsters of our inner world. Shadows can be all the things we don't like about ourselves, all the dark secrets we can't admit, even to ourselves. The qualities we have renounced and tried to root out still lurk within, operating in the Shadow world of the unconscious. The Shadow can also shelter positive qualities that are in hiding or that we have rejected for some reason.

The negative face of the Shadow in stories is projected onto characters called villains, antagonists, or enemies. Villains and enemies are usually dedicated to the death, destruction or defeat of the hero. Antagonists may not be quite so hostile — they may be Allies who are after the same goal but who disagree with the hero's tactics. Antagonists and heroes in conflict are like horses in a team pulling in different directions, while villains and heroes in conflict are like trains on a head-on collision course.

PSYCHOLOGICAL FUNCTION

The Shadow can represent the power of repressed feelings. Deep trauma or guilt can fester when exiled to the darkness of the unconscious, and emotions hidden or denied can turn into something monstrous that wants to destroy us. If the Threshold Guardian represents neuroses, then the Shadow archetype stands for psychoses that not only hamper us, but threaten to destroy us. The Shadow may simply be that shady part of ourselves that we are always wrestling with in struggles over bad habits and old fears. This energy can be a powerful internal force with a life of its own and its own set of interests and priorities. It can be a destructive force, especially if not acknowledged, confronted, and brought to light.

Thus in dreams, Shadows may appear as monsters, demons, devils, evil aliens, vampires, or other fearsome enemies. Note that many Shadow figures are also shapeshifters, such as vampires and werewolves.

DRAMATIC FUNCTION

The function of the Shadow in drama is to challenge the hero and give her a worthy opponent in the struggle. Shadows create conflict and bring out the best in a hero by putting her in a life-threatening situation. It's often been said that a story is only as good as its villain, because a strong enemy forces a hero to rise to the challenge.

The challenging energy of the Shadow archetype can be expressed in a single character, but it may also be a mask worn at different times by any of the characters. Heroes themselves can manifest a Shadow side. When the protagonist is crippled by doubts or guilt, acts in self-destructive ways, expresses a death wish, gets carried away with his success, abuses his power, or becomes selfish rather than self-sacrificing, the Shadow has overtaken him.

MASK OF THE SHADOW

The Shadow can combine in powerful ways with other archetypes. Like the other archetypes, the Shadow is a **function** or **mask** which can be worn by any character. The primary Mentor of a story may wear the Shadow mask at times. In *An Officer and A Gentleman* the drill sergeant played by Louis Gossett, Jr. wears the masks of both Mentor and Shadow. He is Richard Gere's Mentor and second father, guiding him through the rigorous Navy training. But in terms of the life-and-death heart of the story, Gossett is also a Shadow who is trying to destroy Gere by driving him out of the program. He tests the young man to the limit to find out if he has what it takes, and almost kills him in the process of bringing out the best in him.

Another strong combination of archetypes is found in the fatal Shapeshifter figures discussed earlier. In some stories, the person who starts out as the hero's love interest shifts shape so far that she becomes the Shadow, bent on the hero's destruction. Femmes fatale are often called "shady ladies". This might represent a struggle between a person's male and female sides, or obsession with the opposite sex turned into a psychotic state of mind. Orson Welles created a classic story on this theme in *The Lady from Shanghai*, in which Rita Hayworth dazzles Welles' character, shifts shape, and tries to destroy him.

A Shadow may also wear the masks of other archetypes. Anthony Hopkins' "Hannibal the Cannibal" character from *Silence of the Lambs* is primarily a Shadow, a projection of the dark side of human nature, but he also functions as a helpful Mentor to Jodi Foster's FBI agent, providing her with information that helps her catch another insane killer.

Shadows may become seductive Shapeshifters to lure the hero into danger. They may function as Tricksters or Heralds, and may even manifest heroic qualities. Villains who fight bravely for their cause or experience a change of heart may even be redeemed and become heroes themselves, like the Beast in *Beauty and the Beast.*

HUMANIZING THE SHADOW

Shadows need not be totally evil or wicked. In fact, it's better if they are humanized by a touch of goodness, or by some admirable quality. The Disney animated cartoons are memorable for their villains, such as Captain Hook in *Peter Pan*, the demon in *Fantasia*, the beautiful but wicked queen from *Snow White*, the glamorous fairy Maleficent in *The Sleeping Beauty*, and Cruelle D'Eville in *One Hundred and One Dalmatians*. They are even more deliciously sinister because of their dashing, powerful, beautiful, or elegant qualities.

Shadows can also be humanized by making them vulnerable. The novelist Graham Greene masterfully makes his villains real, frail people. He often has the hero on the verge of killing a villain, only to discover the poor fellow has a head cold or is reading a letter from his little daughter. Suddenly the villain is not just a fly to be swatted but a real human being with weaknesses and emotions. Killing such a figure becomes a true moral choice rather than a thoughtless reflex.

It's important to remember in designing stories that most Shadow figures do not think of themselves as villains or enemies. From his point of view, a villain is the hero of his own myth, and the audience's hero is his villain. A dangerous type of villain is "the right man", the person so convinced his cause is just that he will stop at nothing to achieve it. Beware the man who believes the end justifies the means. Hitler's sincere belief that he was right, even heroic, allowed him to order the most villainous atrocities to achieve his aims.

A Shadow may be a character or force external to the hero, or it may be a deeply repressed part of the hero. *Dr. Jekyll and Mr. Hyde* vividly depicts the power of the dark side in a good man's personality.

External Shadows must be vanquished or destroyed by the hero. Shadows of the internal kind may be disempowered like vampires, simply by bringing them out of the Shadows and into the light of consciousness. Some Shadows may even be redeemed and turned into positive forces. One of the most impressive Shadow figures in movie history, Darth Vader of the *Star Wars* series, is revealed in *Return of the Jedi* to be the hero's father. All his wickedness is finally forgiven, making him a benign, ghostly figure, watching over his son. The Terminator also grows from being a killing machine bent on destroying the heroes in *The Terminator* to being a protective Mentor to the heroes in *Terminator 2: Judgement Day*.

Like the other archetypes, Shadows can express positive as well as negative aspects. The Shadow in a person's psyche may be anything that has been suppressed, neglected, or forgotten. The Shadow shelters the healthy, natural feelings we believe we're not supposed to show. But healthy anger or grief, if suppressed in the territory of the Shadow, can turn to harmful energy that strikes out and undermines us in unexpected ways. The Shadow may also be unexplored potential, such as affection, creativity, or psychic ability, that goes unexpressed. "The road not taken", the possibilities of life that we eliminate by making choices at various stages, may collect in the Shadow, biding their time until brought into the light of consciousness.

The psychological concept of the Shadow archetype is a useful metaphor for understanding villains and antagonists in our stories, as well as for grasping the unexpressed, ignored, or deeply hidden aspects of our heroes.

TRICKSTER

TRICKSTER

"That makes no sense and so do I."
Daffy Duck

The Trickster archetype embodies the energies of mischief and desire for change. All the characters in stories who are primarily clowns or comical sidekicks express this archetype. The specialized form called the Trickster Hero is the leading figure in many myths and is very popular in folklore and fairy tales.

PSYCHOLOGICAL FUNCTION

Tricksters serve several important psychological functions. They cut big egos down to size, and bring heroes and audiences down to earth. By provoking healthy laughter they help us realize our common bonds, and they point out folly and hypocrisy. Above all, they bring about healthy change and transformation, often by drawing attention to the imbalance or absurdity of a stagnant psychological situation. They are the natural enemies of the status quo. Trickster energy can express itself through impish accidents or slips of the tongue that alert us to the need for change. When we are taking ourselves too seriously, the Trickster part of our personalities may pop up to bring back needed perspective.

DRAMATIC FUNCTION: COMIC RELIEF

In drama, Tricksters serve all these psychological functions, plus the dramatic function of **comic relief**. Unrelieved tension, suspense, and conflict can be emotionally exhausting, and in even the heaviest drama an audience's interest is revived by moments of laughter. An old rule of drama points out the need for balance: **Make 'em cry a lot; let 'em laugh a little.**

Tricksters may be servants or Allies working for the hero or Shadow, or they may be independent agents with their own skewed agendas.

The Tricksters of mythology provide many examples of the workings of this archetype. One of the most colorful is Loki, the Norse god of trickery and deceit. A true Trickster, he serves the other gods as legal counselor and advisor, but also plots their destruction, undermining the status quo. He is fiery in nature, and his darting, elusive energy helps heat up the petrified, frozen energy of the gods, moving them to action and change. He also provides much-needed comic relief in the generally dark Norse myths.

Loki is sometimes a comical sidekick character in stories featuring the gods Odin or Thor as heroes. In other stories he is a hero of sorts, a **Trickster Hero** who survives by his wits against physically stronger gods or giants. At last he turns into a deadly adversary or Shadow, leading the hosts of the dead in a final war against the gods.

TRICKSTER HEROES

Trickster Heroes have bred like rabbits in the folktales and fairy tales of the world. Indeed, some of the most popular Tricksters are rabbit heroes: the B'rer Rabbit of the American South, the Hare of African tales, the many rabbit heroes from Southeast Asia, Persia, India, etc. These stories pit the defenseless but quick-thinking rabbit against much larger and more dangerous enemies: folktale Shadow figures like wolves, hunters, tigers, and bears. Somehow the tiny rabbit always manages to outwit his hungry opponent, who usually suffers painfully from dealing with a Trickster Hero.

The modern version of the rabbit Trickster is of course Bugs Bunny. The Warner Brothers animators made use of folktale plots to pit Bugs against hunters and predators who didn't stand a chance against his quick wits. Other cartoon Tricksters of this type include Warner's Daffy Duck, Speedy Gonzales, the Roadrunner, and Tweety Bird; Walter Lantz's Woody Woodpecker and Chilly Willy the penguin; and MGM's ubiquitous dog Droopy, who always outwits the befuddled

Wolf. Mickey Mouse started as an ideal animal Trickster, although he has matured into a sober master of ceremonies and corporate spokesman.

Native Americans have a particular fondness for Tricksters such as Coyote and Raven. The clown Kachina gods of the Southwest are Tricksters of great power as well as comic ability.

Once in awhile it's fun to turn the tables and show that Tricksters themselves can be outwitted. Sometimes a Trickster like the Hare will try to take advantage of a weaker, slower animal like Mr. Tortoise. In folktales and fables such as "The Tortoise and the Hare", the slowest outwits the fastest by dogged persistence or by cooperating with others of its kind to outwit the faster animal.

Tricksters like to stir up trouble for its own sake. Joseph Campbell relates a Nigerian story in which the Trickster god Edshu walks down a road in a hat that's red on one side and blue on the other. When people comment "Who was that going by in a red hat?" they get into fights with people on the other side of the road who insist the hat was blue. The god takes credit for the trouble, saying "Spreading strife is my greatest joy".

Tricksters are often **catalyst characters**, who affect the lives of others but are unchanged themselves. Eddie Murphy in *Beverly Hills Cop* displays Trickster energy as he stirs up the existing system without changing much himself.

The heroes of comedy, from Charlie Chaplin to the Marx Brothers to the cast of "In Living Color", are Tricksters who subvert the status quo and make us laugh at ourselves. Heroes of other genres must often put on the Trickster mask in order to outwit a Shadow or get around a Threshold Guardian.

The archetypes are an infinitely flexible language of character. They offer a way to understand what function a character is performing at a given moment in a story. Awareness of the archetypes can help to free writers from stereotyping, by giving their characters greater psychological verity and depth. The archetypes can be used to make characters who are both unique individuals and universal symbols of the qualities that form a complete human being. They can help make our characters and stories psychologically realistic and true to the ancient wisdom of myths.

Now that we've met the denizens of the story world, let's return to the Road of Heroes for a closer look at the twelve stages and how the archetypes play their parts in the Hero's Journey.

BOOK TWO:

STAGES OF
THE JOURNEY

STAGE ONE : THE ORDINARY WORLD

"A beginning is a very delicate time."

from *Dune,* a screenplay by David Lynch,
based on the novel by Frank Herbert

In *The Hero with a Thousand Faces,* Joseph Campbell describes the beginning of the typical hero's journey. "A hero ventures forth from the world of common day into a region of supernatural wonder..." In this chapter, we'll explore that "world of common day", the **Ordinary World,** and see how it frames the hero and sets modern-day stories in motion.

The opening of any story, be it myth, fairy tale, screenplay, novel, short story, or comic book, has some special burdens to bear. It must hook the reader or viewer, set the tone of the story, suggest where it's going, and get across a mass of information without slowing the pace. A beginning is, indeed, a delicate time.

A GUIDE TO THE JOURNEY

As a guide through the labyrinth of story, let's imagine ourselves as a tribe of people who live by hunting and gathering, as our ancestors did a hundred thousand years ago, or as people still do in remote parts of the world today. We'll check in with these Seekers at each stage of the hero's journey, and try to put ourselves in their skins.

> *Look around, sister, brother of the Home Tribe. You can see the people are barely getting by, surviving on a dwindling supply of last season's food. Times are bad and the country all around seems lifeless. The people grow weak before our eyes, but a few of us are filled with restless energy.*

Like you. You're uncomfortable, feeling you no longer fit in with this drab, exhausted place. You may not know it, but you're soon to be selected as a hero, to join the select company of the Seekers, those who have always gone out to face the unknown. You'll undertake a journey to restore life and health to the entire Home Tribe, an adventure in which the only sure thing is that you'll be changed. You're uneasy, but there's a thrill running through you. You're poised to break free from this world, ready to enter the world of adventure.

BEFORE THE BEGINNING

Before a story even begins, a storyteller faces creative choices. What's the first thing your audience will experience? The title? The first line of dialogue? The first image? Where in the lives of your characters will the story actually begin? Do you need a prologue or introduction, or should you jump right into the middle of the action? The opening moments are a powerful opportunity to set the tone and create an impression. You can conjure up a mood, an image, or a metaphor that will give the audience a frame of reference to better experience your work. **The mythological approach to story boils down to using metaphors or comparisons to get across your feelings about life.**

The great German stage and film director Max Reinhardt believed that you can create an atmosphere in a theatre well before an audience sits down or the curtain goes up. A carefully selected title can strike a metaphor that intrigues the audience and attunes them to the coming experience. Good promotion can engage them with images and slogans that are metaphors for the world of your story. By controlling music and lighting as the audience enters the space, and consciously directing such details as the attitudes and costumes of the ushers, a specific mood can be created. The audience can be put in the ideal frame of mind for the experience they will share, prepared for comedy, romance, horror, drama, or whatever effect you wish to create.

Oral storytellers begin their tales with ritualized phrases ("Once upon a time") and personalized gestures to get the attention of the audience. These signals can cue the listeners to the funny, sad, or ironic mood of the story they will hear.

Today many elements go into making those first impressions before the book or the movie ticket is bought; the title, the book cover art, publicity and advertising, posters and trailers, and so forth. The story is cooked down to a few symbols or metaphors that begin to put the audience in the right mood for the journey.

TITLE

A title is an important clue to the nature of the story and the writer's attitude. A good title can become a multi-leveled metaphor for the condition of the hero or his world. The title of *The Godfather*, for example, suggests that Don Corleone is both god and father to his people. The graphic design of the logo for the novel and movie lays out another metaphor, the hand of a puppeteer working the strings of an unseen marionette. Is Don Corleone the puppeteer, or is he the puppet of a higher force? Are we all puppets of God, or do we have free will? The metaphoric title and imagery allow many interpretations and help to make the story a coherent design.

OPENING IMAGE

The opening image can be a powerful tool to create mood and suggest where the story will go. It can be a visual metaphor that, in a single shot or scene, conjures up the Special World of Act Two and the conflicts and dualities that will be confronted there. It can suggest the theme, alerting the audience to the issues your characters will face. The opening shot of Clint Eastwood's *Unforgiven* shows a man outside a farmhouse, digging a grave for his wife who has just died. His relationship with his wife and the way she changed him are major themes in the story. The image of a man digging a grave outside his house can be read as an apt metaphor for the plot: The hero leaves home and journeys to the land of death, where he

99

witnesses death, causes death, and almost dies himself. Eastwood the director returns to the same setup at the end of the film, using the image to give a sense of closure as we see the man leave the grave and return to his home.

PROLOGUE

Some stories begin with a prologue section that precedes the main body of the story, perhaps before the introduction of the main characters and their world. The fairy tale of "Rapunzel" begins with a scene before the birth of the hero, and Disney's *Beauty and the Beast* begins with a prologue illustrated in stained glass, giving the back-story of the Beast's enchantment. Myths take place within a context of mythical history that goes back to the Creation, and events leading up to the entrance of the main character may have to be portrayed first. Shakespeare and the Greeks often gave their plays a prologue, spoken by a narrator or a chorus, to set the tone and give the context of the drama. Shakespeare's *Henry V* begins with an eloquent passage, intoned by a Chorus character who invites us to use our "imaginary forces" to create the kings, horses, and armies of his story. "Admit me Chorus to this history" he requests, "Who, prologue-like, your humble patience pray/Gently to hear, kindly to judge, our play."

A prologue can serve several useful functions. It may give an essential piece of backstory, cue the audience to what kind of movie or story this is going to be, or start the story with a bang and let the audience settle into their seats. In *Close Encounters of the Third Kind*, a prologue shows the discovery of a mysterious squadron of World War II airplanes, perfectly preserved in the desert. This precedes the introduction of the hero, Roy Neary, and his world. It serves to intrigue the audience with a host of riddles, and gives a foretaste of the thrills and wonder ahead.

In *The Last Boy Scout* a prologue shows a pro football player going berserk and shooting his teammates under the pressure of drugs and gambling. The sequence precedes the first appearance of the hero and intrigues or "hooks" the audience. It signals that this is going to be an exciting action story involving life-and-death matters.

This prologue and the one in *Close Encounters* are a little disorienting. They hint that these movies are going to be about extraordinary events that may strain credibility. In secret societies, an old rule of initiation is: **Disorientation leads to suggestibility.** That's why initiates are often blindfolded and led around in the dark, so they will be more psychologically open to suggestion from the rituals staged by the group. In storytelling, getting the audience a little off-base and upsetting their normal perceptions can put them into a receptive mood. They begin to suspend their disbelief and enter more readily into a Special World of fantasy.

Some prologues introduce the villain or threat of the story before the hero appears. In *Star Wars,* the evil Darth Vader is shown kidnapping Princess Leia before the hero, Luke Skywalker, is introduced in his mundane world. Some detective films begin with a murder before the hero is introduced in his office. Such prologues cue the audience that the balance of a society has been disturbed. A chain of events is set in motion, and the forward drive of the story cannot cease until the wrong has been righted and the balance restored.

A prologue is not necessary or desirable in every case. **The needs of the story will always dictate the best approach to structure.** You may want to begin, as many stories do, by introducing the hero in her normal environment: The "Ordinary World".

THE ORDINARY WORLD

Because so many stories are journeys that take heroes and audiences to Special Worlds, most begin by establishing an Ordinary World as a baseline for comparison. The Special World of the story is only special if we can see it in contrast to a mundane world of everyday affairs from which the hero issues forth. The Ordinary World is the context, home base, and background of the hero.

The Ordinary World in one sense is the place you came from last. In life we pass through a succession of Special Worlds which slowly become ordinary as we get used to them. They evolve from strange, foreign territory to familiar bases from which to launch a drive into the next Special World.

CONTRAST

It's a good idea for writers to make the Ordinary World as different as possible from the Special World, so audience and hero will experience a dramatic change when the threshold is finally crossed. In *The Wizard of Oz* the Ordinary World is depicted in black and white, to make a stunning contrast with the Technicolor Special World of Oz. In the thriller *Dead Again,* the Ordinary World of modern day is shot in color to contrast with the nightmarish black and white Special World of the 1940s flashbacks. *City Slickers* contrasts the drab, restrictive environment of the city with the more lively arena of the West where most of the story takes place.

Compared to the Special World, the Ordinary World may seem boring and calm, but the seeds of excitement and challenge can usually be found there. The hero's problems and conflicts are already present in the Ordinary World, waiting to be activated.

FORESHADOWING: A MODEL OF THE SPECIAL WORLD

Writers often use the Ordinary World section to create a small model of the Special World, **foreshadowing** its battles and moral dilemmas. In *The Wizard of Oz*, Dorothy clashes with ornery Miss Gulch and is rescued from danger by three farmhands. These early scenes foretell Dorothy's battles with the Witch and her rescue by the Tin Woodman, Cowardly Lion, and Scarecrow.

Romancing the Stone begins with a clever foreshadowing technique. The first thing the audience sees is an elaborate fantasy of a noble heroine battling sleazy villains and finally riding off to romance with a comically idealized hero. The scene is a model of the Special World

Joan Wilder will encounter in the second act. The fantasy is revealed to be the conclusion of Joan Wilder's romance novel, which she is writing in her cluttered New York apartment. The opening fantasy sequence serves a dual purpose. It tells us a great deal about Joan Wilder and her unrealistic notions of romance, and also predicts the problems and situations she will face in the Special World of Act Two, when she encounters real villains and a less than ideal man. Foreshadowing can help unify a story into a rhythmic or poetic design.

RAISING THE DRAMATIC QUESTION

Another important function of the Ordinary World is to suggest the dramatic question of the story. **Every good story poses a series of questions about the hero.** Will she achieve the goal, overcome her flaw, learn the lesson she needs to learn? Some questions relate primarily to the action or plot. Will Dorothy get home from Oz? Will E. T. get home to his planet? Will the hero get the gold, win the game, beat the villains?

Other questions are dramatic and have to do with the hero's emotions and personality. Will Patrick Swayze's character in *Ghost* learn to express love? In *Pretty Woman*, will the uptight businessman Edward learn from the prostitute Vivian how to relax and enjoy life? The action questions may propel the plot, but the dramatic questions hook the audience and involve them with the emotions of the characters.

INNER AND OUTER PROBLEMS

Every hero needs both an inner and an outer problem. In developing fairy tales for Disney Feature Animation, we often find that writers can give the heroes a good outer problem: Can the princess manage to break an enchantment on her father who has been turned to stone? Can the hero get to the top of a glass mountain and win a princess' hand in marriage? Can Gretel rescue Hansel from the Witch? But sometimes writers neglect to give the characters a compelling inner problem to solve as well.

103

Characters without inner challenges seem flat and uninvolving, however heroically they may act. They need an inner problem, a personality flaw or a moral dilemma to work out. They need to learn something in the course of the story: how to get along with others, how to trust themselves, how to see beyond outward appearances. Audiences love to see characters learning, growing, and dealing with the inner and outer challenges of life.

MAKING AN ENTRANCE

How the audience first experiences your hero is another important condition you control as a storyteller. What is he doing the first time we see him, when he makes his **entrance**? What is he wearing, who is around him, and how do they react to him? What is his attitude, emotion, and goal at the moment? Does he enter alone or join a group, or is he already on stage when the story begins? Does he narrate the story, is it told through the eyes of another character, or is it seen from the objective eye of conventional narrative?

Every actor likes to "make an entrance", an important part of building a character's relationship with the audience. Even if a character is written as already on stage when the lights come up, the actor will often make an entrance out of it by how she first impresses an audience with her appearance and behavior. As writers we can give our heroes an entrance by thinking about how the audience first experiences them. What are they doing, saying, feeling? What is their context when we first see them? Are they at peace or in turmoil? Are they at full emotional power or are they holding back for a burst of expression later?

Most important is: What is the character *doing* at the moment of entrance?. The character's first action is a wonderful opportunity to speak volumes about his attitude, emotional state, background, strengths, and problems. The first action should be a model of the hero's characteristic attitude and the future problems or solutions that will result. The first behavior we see should be characteristic. It should define and reveal character, unless your intent is to mislead the audience and conceal the character's true nature.

Tom Sawyer makes a vivid entrance into our imaginations because Samuel Clemens has painted such a character-revealing first look at his Missouri boy hero. The first time we see Tom he is performing a characteristic action, turning the rotten job of whitewashing the fence into a wonderful mind game. Tom is a con artist, but the con is thoroughly enjoyed by his victims. Tom's character is revealed through all his actions, but most clearly and definitively in his entrance, which defines his attitude toward life.

Actors stepping onto a stage and writers introducing a character are also trying to *entrance* the audience, or produce in them a trance-like state of identification and recognition. One of the magic powers of writing is its ability to lure each member of the audience into projecting a part of their ego into the character on the page, screen, or stage.

As a writer you can build up an atmosphere of anticipation or provide information about an important character by having other characters talk about her before she shows up. But more important and memorable will be her own first action upon entering the story — her entrance.

INTRODUCING THE HERO TO THE AUDIENCE

Another important function of the Ordinary World is to **introduce** the hero to the audience. Like a social introduction, the Ordinary World establishes a bond between people and points out some common interests so that a dialogue can begin. In some way we should recognize that the hero is like us. In a very real sense, a story invites us to step into the hero's shoes, to see the world through his eyes. As if by magic we project part of our consciousness into the hero. To make this magic work you must establish a strong bond of sympathy or common interest between the hero and the audience.

This is not to say that heroes must always be good or wholly sympathetic. They don't even have to be likeable, but they must be *relatable*, a word used by movie executives to describe the quality of compassion and understanding that an audience must have for a hero. Even if the hero is underhanded or despicable, we can still understand her plight and imagine ourselves behaving in much the same way, given the same background, circumstances, and motivation.

IDENTIFICATION

The opening scenes should create an **identification** between audience and hero, a sense that they are equals in some ways.

How do you achieve this? Create identification by giving heroes universal goals, drives, desires, or needs. We can all relate to basic drives such as the need for recognition, affection, acceptance, or understanding. The screenwriter Waldo Salt, speaking of his script for *Midnight Cowboy*, said that his hero Joe Buck was driven by a universal human need to be touched. Even though Joe Buck engaged in some pretty sleazy behavior, we sympathize with his need because we have all experienced it at some time. Identification with universal needs establishes a bond between audience and hero.

THE HERO'S LACK

Fairy tale heroes have a common denominator, a quality that unites them across boundaries of culture, geography and time. They are **lacking** something, or something is taken away from them. Often they have just lost a family member. A mother or father has died, or a brother or sister has been kidnapped. Fairy tales are about searching for completeness and striving for wholeness, and often it's a subtraction from the family unit that sets the story in motion. The need to fill in the missing piece drives the story toward the final perfection of "They lived happily ever after".

Many movies begin by showing an incomplete hero or family. Joan Wilder in *Romancing the Stone* or Roger Thornhill in *North by Northwest* are incomplete because they need ideal mates to balance their lives. Fay Wray's character in *King Kong* is an orphan who knows only "There's supposed to be an uncle someplace."

These missing elements help to create sympathy for the hero, and draw the audience into desiring her eventual wholeness. Audiences abhor the vacuum created by a missing piece in a character.

Other stories show the hero as essentially complete until a close friend or relative is kidnapped or killed in the first act, setting in motion a story of rescue or revenge. John Ford's *The Searchers* begins with news that a young woman has been kidnapped by Indians, launching a classic saga of search and rescue.

Sometimes the hero's family may be complete, but something is missing from the hero's personality — a quality such as compassion, forgiveness, or the ability to express love. The hero of *Ghost* is unable to say "I love you" at the beginning of the film. Only after he has run the course of the journey from life to death is he able to say those magic words.

It can be very effective to show that a hero is unable to perform some simple task at the beginning of the story. In *Ordinary People* the young hero Conrad is unable to eat French toast his mother has prepared for him. It signifies, in symbolic language, his inability to accept being loved and cared for, because of the terrible guilt he bears over the accidental death of his brother. It's only after he undertakes an emotional hero's journey, and relives and processes the death through therapy, that he is able to accept love. At the end of the story Conrad's girlfriend offers to make him breakfast, and this time he finds he has an appetite. In symbolic language, his appetite for life has returned.

TRAGIC FLAWS

The Greek theory of tragedy, expressed twenty-four centuries ago by Aristotle, describes a common fault of tragic heroes. They may possess many admirable qualities, but among them is one tragic flaw or *hamartia* that puts them at odds with their destiny, their fellow men, or the gods. Ultimately it leads to their destruction.

Most commonly this tragic flaw was a kind of pride or arrogance called *hubris*. Tragic heroes are often superior people with extraordinary powers but they tend to see themselves as equal to or better than the gods. They ignore fair warnings or defy the local moral codes, thinking they are above the laws of gods and men. This fatal arrogance inevitably unleashes a force called *Nemesis*, originally a goddess of retribution. Her job was to set things back into balance, usually by bringing about the destruction of the tragic hero.

Every well-rounded hero has a trace of this tragic flaw, some weakness or fault that makes him thoroughly human and real. Perfect, flawless heroes aren't very interesting, and are hard to relate to. Even Superman has weak spots which humanize him and make him sympathetic: his vulnerability to Kryptonite, his inability to see through lead, and his secret identity which is always in danger of being exposed.

WOUNDED HEROES

Sometimes a hero may seem to be well-adjusted and in control, but that control masks a deep psychic **wound**. Most of us have some old pain or hurt that we don't think about all the time, but which is always vulnerable on some level of awareness. These wounds of rejection, betrayal, or disappointment are personal echoes of a universal pain that everyone has suffered from: the pain of the child's physical and emotional separation from its mother. In a larger sense, we all bear the wound of separation from God or the womb of existence — that place from which we are born and to which we will return when we die. Like Adam and Eve cast out of Eden, we are forever separate from our source, isolated and wounded.

To humanize a hero or any character, give her a wound, a visible, physical injury or a deep emotional wound. The hero of *Lethal Weapon*, played by Mel Gibson, is sympathetic because he has lost a loved one. The wound makes him edgy, suicidal, unpredictable, and interesting. Your hero's wounds and scars mark the areas in which he is guarded, defensive, weak, and vulnerable. A hero may also be extra-strong in some areas as a defense for the wounded parts.

The movie *The Fisher King* is a thorough study of two men and their psychic wounds. The story is inspired by the Arthurian legend of the Holy Grail and the Fisher King, whose physical wound symbolized a wound of the spirit. This legend tells of a king who was wounded in the thigh and was therefore unable to rule his land or find any pleasure in life. Under his weakened kingship, the land was dying, and only the powerful spiritual magic of the Holy Grail could revive it. The quest by the Knights of the Round Table to find the Grail is the great adventure to restore health and wholeness to a system that has been almost fatally wounded. The Jungian psychologist Robert A. Johnson brings insight to the meaning of the Fisher King wound in his book on masculine psychology, *He.*

Another wounded, almost tragic hero is Tom Dunston, played by John Wayne in the classic Western *Red River.* Dunston makes a terrible moral error early in his career as a cattleman, by choosing to value his mission more than his love, and following his head rather than his heart. This choice leads to the death of his lover, and for the rest of the story he bears the psychic scars of that wound. His suppressed guilt makes him more and more harsh, autocratic, and judgmental, and almost brings him and his adopted son to destruction before the wound is healed by letting love back into his life.

A hero's wounds may not be visible. People put a great deal of energy into protecting and hiding these weak and vulnerable spots. But in a fully developed character they will be apparent in the areas where she is touchy, defensive, or a little too confident. The wound may never be openly expressed to the audience — it can be a secret between the writer and the character. But it will help give the hero a sense of personal history and realism, for we all bear some scars from past humiliations, rejections, disappointments, abandonments, and failures. Many stories are about the journey to heal a wound and to restore a missing piece to a broken psyche.

ESTABLISHING WHAT'S AT STAKE

For readers and viewers to be involved in the adventure, to care about the hero, they have to know at an early stage exactly what's at stake. In other words, what does the hero stand to gain or lose in the adventure? What will be the consequences for the hero, society, and the world if the hero succeeds or fails?

Myths and fairy tales are good models for establishing what's at stake. They often set up a threatening condition that makes the stakes of the game very clear. Perhaps the hero must pass a series of tests or his head will be cut off. The Greek hero Perseus, portrayed in the movie *Clash of the Titans*, must undergo many ordeals or his beloved princess Andromeda will be devoured by a sea monster. Other tales put family members in jeopardy like the father who is threatened in *Beauty and the Beast*. The hero Belle has a strong motivation to put herself in a dangerous position at the mercy of the Beast. Her father will languish and die unless she does the Beast's bidding. The stakes are high and clear.

Scripts often fail because the stakes simply aren't high enough. A story in which the hero will only be slightly embarrassed or inconvenienced if he fails is likely to get the "So what?" reaction from readers. Make sure the stakes are high — life and death, big money, or the hero's very soul.

BACKSTORY AND EXPOSITION

The Ordinary World is the most appropriate place to deal with exposition and backstory. **Backstory** is all the relevant information about a character's history and background — what got her to the situation at the beginning of the story. **Exposition** is the art of gracefully revealing the backstory and any other pertinent information about the plot: The hero's social class, upbringing, habits, experiences, as well as the prevailing social conditions and opposing forces that may affect the hero. Exposition is everything the audience needs to know to understand the hero and the story. Backstory and exposition are among the hardest writing skills to master. Clumsy exposition tends to stop the story cold. Blunt exposition draws attention to itself, giving the backstory in the form of a voiceover or a "Harry the Explainer" character who comes on solely for the purpose of telling the audience what the author wants them to know. It's usually better to put the audience right into the action and let them figure things out as the story unfolds.

The audience will feel more involved if they have to work a little to piece together the backstory from visual clues or exposition blurted out while characters are emotionally upset or on the run. Backstory can be doled out gradually over the course of the story or yielded up grudgingly. Much is revealed by what people **don't** do or say.

Many dramas are about secrets being slowly and painfully revealed. Layer by layer the defenses protecting a hurtful secret are torn away. This makes the audience participants in a detective story, an emotional puzzle.

THEME

The Ordinary World is the place to state the theme of your story. What is the story really about? If you had to boil down its essence to a single word or phrase, what would it be? What single idea or quality is it about? Love? Trust? Betrayal? Vanity? Prejudice? Greed? Madness? Ambition? Friendship? What are you trying to say? Is your theme "Love conquers all", "You can't cheat an honest man", "We must work together to survive", or "Money is the root of all evil"?

Theme, a word derived from Greek, is close in meaning to the Latin-based **premise**. Both words mean "something set before", something laid out in advance that helps determine a future course. The theme of a story is an underlying statement or assumption about an aspect of life. Usually it's set out somewhere in Act One, in the Ordinary

World. It could be an offhand remark by one of the characters, expressing a belief which is then rigorously tested in the course of the story. The real theme of the piece may not emerge or announce itself until you have worked with the story for awhile, but sooner or later you must become aware of it. Knowing the theme is essential to making the final choices in dialogue, action and set dressing that turn a story into a coherent design. In a good story, everything is related somehow to the theme, and the Ordinary World is the place to make the first statement of the main idea.

THE WIZARD OF OZ

I refer often to *The Wizard of Oz* because it's a classic movie that most people have seen, and because it's a fairly typical hero's journey with clearly delineated stages. It also has a surprising degree of psychological depth, and can be read not only as a fairy story of a little girl trying to get back home, but as a metaphor of a personality trying to become complete.

> *As the story unfolds, the hero Dorothy has a clear outer problem. Her dog Toto has dug up Miss Gulch's flowerbed and Dorothy is in trouble. She tries to elicit sympathy for her problem from her aunt and uncle, but they are too busy preparing for a coming storm. Like the heroes of myth and legend before her, Dorothy is restless, out of place, and doesn't know where to light.*

> *Dorothy also has a clear inner problem. She doesn't fit in anymore, she doesn't feel "at home". Like the incomplete heroes of fairy tales, she has a big piece missing from her life – her parents are dead. She doesn't yet know it, but she's about to set out on a quest for completion; not through a marriage and the beginning of a new ideal family, but through meeting a series of magical forces that represent parts of a complete and perfect personality.*

> *To foreshadow these meetings, Dorothy encounters a small model of the Special World adventure. Bored, she tries to balance on the thin railing of a pig pen, and falls in. Three friendly*

112

farmhands rescue her from danger, predicting the roles the same actors will play in the Special World. The scene says, in the language of symbol, that Dorothy has been walking a tightrope between warring sides of her personality, and sooner or later she will need all the help she can get, from every part of her being, to survive the inevitable fall into conflict.

→▭ ▭←

Heroes may have no obvious missing piece, flaw, or wound. They may merely be restless, uneasy, and out of sync with their environment or culture. They may have been getting by, trying to adjust to unhealthy conditions by using various coping mechanisms or crutches such as emotional or chemical dependencies. They may have deluded themselves that everything is all right. But sooner or later, some new force enters the story to make it clear they can no longer mark time. That new energy is the Call to Adventure.

QUESTIONING THE JOURNEY

1. What is the Ordinary World of *Big*? *Fatal Attraction*? *The Fisher King*? Look at a film, play, or story of your choice. How does the author introduce the hero? Reveal character? Give exposition? Suggest the theme? Does the author use an image to foreshadow or suggest where the story is going?

2. In your own writing, how well do you know your hero? Do a complete biographical sketch, specifying personal history, physical description, education, family background, job experiences, romances, dislikes and prejudices, preferences in food, clothes, hair, cars, etc.

3. Do a timeline, specifying what the character was doing and where he was at every stage of life. Find out what was going on in the world at these times. What ideas, events and people have been the greatest influences on your character?

4. How is your story's hero incomplete? Get specific about the character's needs, desires, goals, wounds, fantasies, wishes, flaws, quirks, regrets, defenses, weaknesses, and neuroses. What single characteristic could lead to your hero's destruction or downfall? What single characteristic could save her? Does your character have both an inner and an outer problem? Does she have a universal human need? How does she characteristically go about getting that need met?

5. Make a list of all the points of backstory and exposition that the audience needs to know to get the story started. How can those be revealed indirectly, visually, on the run, or through conflict?

6. Do different cultures need different kinds of stories? Do men and women need different kinds of stories? How are the heroic journeys of men and women different?

CALL TO ADVENTURE

STAGE TWO : THE CALL TO ADVENTURE

"It's money and adventure and fame! It's the thrill of a lifetime!...and a long sea voyage that starts at six o'clock tomorrow!"
From the screenplay *King Kong* by James Creelman and Ruth Rose

---

The Ordinary World of most heroes is a static but unstable condition. The seeds of change and growth are planted, and it takes only a little new energy to germinate them. That new energy, symbolized in countless ways in myths and fairy tales, is what Joseph Campbell termed the **Call to Adventure**.

> *Trouble shadows the Home Tribe. You hear its call, in the grumbling of our stomachs and the cries of our hungry children. The land for miles around is tapped out and barren and clearly someone must go out beyond the familiar territory. That unknown land is strange and fills us with fear, but pressure mounts to do something, to take some risks, so that life can continue.*

> *A figure emerges from the campfire smoke, an elder of the Home Tribe, pointing to you. Yes, you have been chosen as a Seeker and called to begin a new quest. You'll venture your life so that the greater life of The Home Tribe may go on.*

GET THE STORY ROLLING

Various theories of screenwriting acknowledge the Call to Adventure by other names such as the inciting or initiating incident, the catalyst, or the trigger. All agree that some event is necessary to get a story rolling, once the work of introducing the main character is done.

The Call to Adventure may come in the form of a message or a messenger. It may be a new event like a declaration of war, or the arrival of a telegram reporting that the outlaws have just been released from prison and will be in town on the noon train to gun down the sheriff. Serving a writ or warrant and issuing a summons are ways of giving Calls in legal proceedings.

The Call may simply be a stirring within the hero, a messenger from the unconscious, bearing news that it's time for change. These signals sometimes come in the form of dreams, fantasies or visions. Roy Neary in *Close Encounters of the Third Kind* gets his Call in the form of haunting images of Devil's Tower drifting up from his subconscious. Prophetic or disturbing dreams help us prepare for a new stage of growth by giving us metaphors that reflect the emotional and spiritual changes to come.

The hero may just get fed up with things as they are. An uncomfortable situation builds up until that one last straw sends him on the adventure. Joe Buck in *Midnight Cowboy* has simply had enough of washing dishes in a diner and feels the Call building up inside him to hit the road of adventure. In a deeper sense, his universal human need is driving him, but it takes that one last miserable day in the diner to push him over the edge.

SYNCHRONICITY

A string of accidents or coincidences may be the message that calls a hero to adventure. This is the mysterious force of **synchronicity** which C. G. Jung explored in his writings. The accidental recurrence of words, ideas, or events can take on meaning and draw attention to the need for action and change. Many thrillers such as Hitchcock's *Strangers on a Train* get rolling because an accident throws two people together as if by the hand of fate.

TEMPTATION

The Call to Adventure may summon a hero with **temptation**, such as the allure of an exotic travel poster or the sight of a potential lover. It could be the glint of gold, the rumor of treasure, the siren song of ambition. In the Arthurian legend of Percival (aka Parsifal), the innocent young hero is summoned to adventure by the sight of five magnificent knights in armor, riding off on some quest. Percival has never seen such creatures, and is stirred to follow them. He is compelled to find out what they are, not realizing it is his destiny to soon become one of them.

HERALDS OF CHANGE

The Call to Adventure is often delivered by a character in a story who manifests the archetype of the Herald. A character performing the function of Herald may be positive, negative, or neutral, but will always serve to get the story rolling by presenting the hero with an invitation or challenge to face the unknown. In some stories the Herald is also a Mentor for the hero, a wise guide who has the hero's best interests at heart. In others the Herald is an enemy, flinging a gauntlet of challenge in the hero's face or tempting the hero into danger.

Initially heroes often have trouble distinguishing whether a Enemy or an Ally lies behind the Herald's mask. Many a hero has mistaken a well-meaning mentor's Call for that of an enemy, or misinterpreted the overtures of a villain as a friendly invitation to an enjoyable adventure. In the thriller and film noir genres, writers may deliberately obscure the reality of the Call. Shadowy figures may make ambiguous offers, and heroes must use every skill to interpret them correctly.

Often heroes are unaware there is anything wrong with their Ordinary World and don't see any need for change. They may be in a state of denial. They have been just barely getting by, using an arsenal of crutches, addictions and defense mechanisms. The job of the

119

Herald is to kick away these supports, announcing that the world of the hero is unstable and must be put back into healthy balance by action, by taking risks, by undertaking the adventure.

RECONNAISSANCE

The Russian fairy tale scholar Vladimir Propp identified a common early phase in a story, called **reconnaissance**. A villain makes a survey of the hero's territory, perhaps asking around the neighborhood if there are any children living there, or seeking information about the hero. This information-gathering can be a Call to Adventure, alerting the audience and the hero that something is afoot and the struggle is about to begin.

DISORIENTATION AND DISCOMFORT

The Call to Adventure can often be unsettling and disorienting to the hero. Heralds sometimes sneak up on heroes, appearing in one guise to gain a hero's confidence and then shifting shape to deliver the Call. Alfred Hitchcock provides a potent example in *Notorious*. Here the hero is playgirl Ingrid Bergman, whose father has been sentenced as a Nazi spy. The Call to Adventure comes from a Herald in the form of Cary Grant, who plays an American agent trying to enlist her aid in infiltrating a Nazi spy ring.

First he charms his way into her life by pretending to be a playboy interested only in booze, fast cars, and her. But after she accidentally discovers he's a "copper", he shifts to the mask of Herald to deliver a deeply challenging Call to Adventure.

Bergman wakes up in bed, hung over from their night of partying. Grant, standing in the doorway, orders her to drink a bubbly bromide to settle her stomach. It doesn't taste good but he makes her drink it anyway. It symbolizes the new energy of the adventure, which tastes like poison compared to the addictions she's been used to, but which ultimately will be good medicine for her.

In this scene Grant leans in a doorway, silhouetted like some dark angel. From Bergman's point of view, this Herald could be an angel or a devil. The devilish possibility is suggested by his name, revealed for the first time as "Devlin". As he advances into the room to deliver the Call to Adventure, Hitchcock follows him in a dizzying point-of-view shot that reflects the hung-over state of the hero, Bergman, as she lies in bed. Grant seems to walk on the ceiling. In the symbolic language of film the shot expresses his change of position from playboy to Herald, and its disorienting effect on the hero. Grant gives the Call, a patriotic invitation to infiltrate a Nazi spy ring. As it is delivered, Grant is seen right side up and in full light for the first time, representing the Call's sobering effect on Bergman's character.

As they talk, a crown-like, artificial hairpiece slides from Bergman's head, showing that her fairy tale existence as a deluded, addicted princess must now come to an end. Simultaneously on the soundtrack can be heard the distant call of a train leaving town, suggesting the beginning of a long journey. In this sequence Hitchcock has used every symbolic element at his command to signal that a major threshold of change is approaching. The Call to Adventure is disorienting and distasteful to the hero, but necessary for her growth.

LACK OR NEED

A Call to Adventure may come in the form of a loss or subtraction from the hero's life in the Ordinary World. The adventure of the movie *Quest for Fire* is set in motion when a Stone Age tribe's last scrap of fire, preserved in a bone fire-cage, is extinguished. Members of the tribe begin to die of cold and hunger because of this loss. The hero receives his Call to Adventure when one of the women puts the fire-cage in front of him, signalling without words that the loss must be made up by undertaking the adventure.

The Call could be the kidnapping of a loved one or the loss of anything precious, such as health, security, or love.

121

NO MORE OPTIONS

In some stories, the Call to Adventure may be the hero simply running out of options. The coping mechanisms no longer work, other people get fed up with the hero, or the hero is placed in increasingly dire straits until the only way left is to jump into the adventure. In *Sister Act*, Whoopi Goldberg's character witnesses a mob murder and has to go into hiding as a nun. Her options are limited — pretend to be a nun or die. Other heroes don't even get that much choice — they are simply "shanghaied" into adventure, conked on the head to wake up far out at sea, committed to adventure whether they like it or not.

WARNINGS FOR TRAGIC HEROES

Not all Calls to Adventure are positive summons to high adventure. They may also be dire warnings of doom for tragic heroes. In Shakespeare's *Julius Caesar*, a character cries out the warning, "Beware the Ides of March." In *Moby Dick*, the crew is warned by a crazy old man that their adventure will turn into a disaster.

MORE THAN ONE CALL: CALL WAITING

Since many stories operate on more than one level, a story can have more than one Call to Adventure. A sprawling epic such as *Red River* has a need for several scenes of this type. John Wayne's character Tom Dunston receives a Call of the heart, when his lover urges him to stay with her or take her with him on his quest. Dunston himself issues another Call to physical adventure when he invites his cowboys to join him on the first great cattle drive after the Civil War.

Romancing the Stone issues a complex Call to Adventure to its hero Joan Wilder when she receives a phone call from her sister who has been kidnapped by thugs in Colombia. The simple Call of physical adventure is set up by the need to rescue the sister, but another Call is being made on a deeper level in this scene. Joan opens an envelope which her sister's husband has mailed to her and finds a map to the treasure mine of *El Corazon,* "The Heart", suggesting that Joan is also being called to an adventure of the heart.

THE WIZARD OF OZ

> *Dorothy's vague feelings of unease crystallize when Miss Gulch arrives and spitefully takes away Toto. A conflict is set up between two sides struggling for control of Dorothy's soul. A repressive Shadow energy is trying to bottle up the good-natured intuitive side. But the instinctive Toto escapes. Dorothy follows her instincts, which are issuing her a Call to Adventure, and runs away from home. She feels painted into a corner by a lack of sympathy from Aunt Em, her surrogate mother, who has scolded her. She sets out to respond to the Call, under a sky churning with the clouds of change.*

The Call to Adventure is a process of selection. An unstable situation arises in a society and someone volunteers or is chosen to take responsibility. Reluctant heroes have to be called repeatedly as they try to avoid responsibility. More willing heroes answer to inner calls and need no external urging. They have selected themselves for adventure. These gung-ho heroes are rare, and most heroes must be prodded, cajoled, wheedled, tempted, or shanghaied into adventure. Most heroes put up a good fight and entertain us by their efforts to escape the Call to Adventure. These struggles are the work of the reluctant hero or as Campbell called it, the Refusal of the Call.

QUESTIONING THE JOURNEY

1. What is the Call to Adventure in *Citizen Kane*? *High Noon*? *Fatal Attraction*? *Basic Instinct*? *Moby Dick*? Who or what delivers the Call? What archetypes are manifested by the deliverer?

2. What Calls to Adventure have you received, and how did you respond to them? Have you ever had to deliver a Call to Adventure to someone else?

3. Can a story exist without some kind of Call to Adventure? Can you think of stories that don't have a Call?

4. In your own story, would it make a difference if the Call were moved to another point in the script? How long can you delay the Call and is this desirable?

5. What is the ideal place for the Call? Can you do without it?

6. Have you found an interesting way to present the Call or twist it around so it's not a cliche?

7. Your story may require a succession of Calls. Who is being called to what level of adventure?

REFUSAL
OF THE CALL

STAGE THREE: REFUSAL OF THE CALL

"You're not cut out for this, Joan, and you know it."
From *Romancing The Stone*, a screenplay by Diane Thomas

The problem of the hero now becomes how to respond to the Call to Adventure. Put yourself in the hero's shoes and you can see that it's a difficult passage. You're being asked to say yes to a great unknown, to an adventure that will be exciting but also dangerous and even life-threatening. It wouldn't be a real adventure otherwise. You stand at a threshold of fear, and an understandable reaction would be to hesitate or even refuse the Call, at least temporarily.

> *Gather your gear, fellow Seeker. Think ahead to possible dangers, and reflect on past disasters. The specter of the unknown walks among us, halting our progress at the threshold. Some of us turn down the quest, some hesitate, some are tugged at by families who fear for our lives and don't want us to go. You hear people mutter that the journey is foolhardy, doomed from the start. You feel fear constricting your breathing and making your heart race. Should you stay with the Home Tribe, and let others risk their necks in the quest? Are you cut out to be a Seeker?*

This halt on the road before the journey has really started serves an important dramatic function of signalling the audience that the adventure is risky. It's not a frivolous undertaking but a danger-filled, high stakes gamble in which the hero might lose fortune or life. The pause to weigh the consequences makes the commitment to the adventure a real choice in which the hero, after this period of hesitation or refusal, is willing to stake her life against the possibility of winning the goal. It also forces the hero to examine the quest carefully and perhaps redefine its objectives.

AVOIDANCE

It's natural for heroes to first react by trying to dodge the adventure. Even Christ, in the Garden of Gethsemane on the eve of the Crucifixion, prayed "Let this cup pass from me." He was simply checking to see if there was any way of avoiding the ordeal. Is this trip really necessary?

Even the most heroic of movie heroes will sometimes hesitate, express reluctance, or flatly refuse the Call. Rambo, Rocky, and innumerable John Wayne characters turn away from the offered adventure at first. A common grounds for Refusal is past experience. Heroes claim to be veterans of past adventures which have taught them the folly of such escapades. You won't catch them getting into the same kind of trouble again. The protest continues until the hero's Refusal is overcome, either by some stronger motivation (such as the death or kidnapping of a friend or relative) which raises the stakes, or by the hero's inborn taste for adventure or sense of honor.

Detectives and lovers may refuse the Call at first, referring to experiences which have made them sadder but wiser. There is charm in seeing a hero's reluctance overcome, and the stiffer the Refusal, the more an audience enjoys seeing it worn down.

EXCUSES

Heroes most commonly Refuse the Call by stating a laundry list of weak excuses. In a transparent attempt to delay facing their inevitable fate, they say they *would* undertake the adventure, if not for a pressing series of engagements. These are temporary roadblocks, usually overcome by the urgency of the quest.

PERSISTENT REFUSAL LEADS TO TRAGEDY

Persistent Refusal of the Call can be disastrous. In the Bible, Lot's wife is turned to a pillar of salt for denying God's Call to leave her home in Sodom and never look back. Looking backward, dwelling in the past, and denying reality are forms of Refusal.

Continued denial of a high Calling is one of the marks of a tragic hero. At the beginning of *Red River*, Tom Dunston refuses a Call to an adventure of the heart and begins a slide into almost certain doom. He continues to refuse Calls to open his heart, and is on the path of a tragic hero. It's only when he finally accepts the Call in Act Three that he is redeemed and spared the tragic hero's fate.

CONFLICTING CALLS

Actually Tom Dunston faces two Calls to Adventure at once. The Call to the heart's adventure comes from his sweetheart, but the one he answers is the Call of his male ego, telling him to strike out alone on a macho path. Heroes may have to choose between conflicting Calls from different levels of adventure. The Refusal of the Call is a time to articulate the hero's difficult choices.

POSITIVE REFUSALS

Refusal of the Call is usually a negative moment in the hero's progress, a dangerous moment in which the adventure might go astray or never get off the ground at all. However, there are some special cases in which refusing the Call is a wise and positive move on the part of the hero. When the Call is a temptation to evil or a summons to disaster, the hero is smart to say no. The Three Little Pigs wisely refused to open the door to the Big Bad Wolf's powerful arguments. In *Death Becomes Her*, Bruce Willis' character receives several powerful Calls to drink a magic potion of immortality. Despite an alluring sales pitch by Isabella Rosselini, he Refuses the Call and saves his own soul.

ARTIST AS HERO

Another special case in which Refusal of the Call can be positive is that of the artist as hero. We writers, poets, painters, and musicians face difficult, contradictory Calls. We must fully immerse ourselves in the world to find the material for our art. But we must also at times withdraw from the world, going alone to actually make the art. Like many heroes of story, we receive conflicting Calls, one from the outer world, one from our own insides, and we must choose or make compromises. To answer a higher Call to express ourselves, we artists may have to refuse the Call of what Joseph Campbell terms "the blandishments of the world."

When you are getting ready to undertake a great adventure, the Ordinary World knows somehow and clings to you. It sings its sweetest, most insistent song, like the Sirens trying to draw Odysseus and his crew onto the rocks. Countless distractions tempt you off track as you begin to work. Odysseus had to stop up the ears of his men with wax so they wouldn't be lured onto the rocks by the Sirens' bewitching song.

However Odysseus first had his men tie him to the mast, so he could hear the Sirens but would be unable to steer the ship into danger. Artists sometimes ride through life like Odysseus lashed to the mast, with all senses deeply experiencing the song of life, but also voluntarily bound to the ship of their art. They are refusing the powerful Call of the world, in order to follow the wider Call of artistic expression.

WILLING HEROES

While many heroes express fear, reluctance, or refusal at this stage, others don't hesitate or voice any fear. They are **willing heroes** who have accepted or even sought out the Call to Adventure. Propp calls them "seekers" as opposed to "victimized heroes". However the fear and doubt represented by The Refusal of the Call will find expression even in the stories of willing heroes. Other characters will express the fear, warning the hero and the audience of what may happen on the road ahead.

A willing hero like John Dunbar from *Dances With Wolves* may be past the fear of personal death. He has already sought out death in the first sequence of the movie as he rides suicidally in front of Rebel rifles and is miraculously spared. He seeks out the adventure of the

West willingly, without refusal or reluctance. But the danger and harshness of the prairie is made clear to the audience through the fate of other characters who represent Refusal of the Call. One is the mad, pathetic Army officer who gives Dunbar his scribbled "orders". He shows a possible fate for Dunbar. The frontier is so strange and challenging that it can drive some people insane. The officer has been unable to accept the reality of this world, has retreated into denial and fantasy, and refuses the frontier's Call by shooting himself.

The other character who bears the energy of Refusal is the scroungy wagon driver who escorts Dunbar to his deserted post. He expresses nothing but fear of the Indians and the prairie, and wants Dunbar to Refuse the Call, abandon his enterprise, and return to civilization. The driver ends up being brutally killed by the Indians, showing the audience another possible fate for Dunbar. Though there is no Refusal by the hero himself, the danger of the adventure is acknowledged and dramatized through another character.

THRESHOLD GUARDIANS

Heroes who overcome their fear and commit to an adventure may still be tested by powerful figures who raise the banner of fear and doubt, questioning the hero's very worthiness to be in the game. They are Threshold Guardians, blocking the heroes before the adventure has even begun.

In *Romancing the Stone,* Joan Wilder accepts the Call and is totally committed to the adventure for the sake of her sister in Colombia. However the moment of fear, the way station of Refusal, is still elaborately acknowledged in a scene with her agent, who wears the fearful mask of a Threshold Guardian. A tough, cynical woman, she forcefully underlines the dangers and tries to talk Joan out of going. Like a witch pronouncing a curse, she declares that Joan is not up to the task of being a hero. Joan even agrees with her, but is now motivated by the danger to her sister. She is committed to the adventure. Though Joan herself does not Refuse the Call, the fear, doubt, and danger have still been made clear to the audience.

131

Joan's agent demonstrates how a character may switch masks to show aspects of more than one archetype. She appears at first to be a Mentor and friend to Joan, an ally in her profession and her dealings with men. But this Mentor turns into a fierce Threshold Guardian, blocking the way into the adventure with stern warnings. She's like an overprotective parent, not allowing the daughter to learn through her own mistakes. Her function at this point is to test the hero's commitment to the adventure.

This character serves another important function. She poses a dramatic question for the audience. Is Joan truly heroic enough to face and survive the adventure? This doubt is more interesting than knowing that the hero will rise to every occasion. Such questions create emotional suspense for the audience who watch the hero's progress with uncertainty hanging in the back of their minds. Refusal of the Call often serves to raise such doubts.

It's not unusual for a Mentor to change masks and perform the function of a Threshold Guardian. Some Mentors guide the hero deeper into the adventure; others block the hero's path on an adventure society might not approve of — an illicit, unwise, or dangerous path. Such a Mentor/Threshold Guardian becomes a powerful embodiment of society or culture, warning the hero not to go outside the accepted bounds. In *Beverly Hills Cop*, Eddie Murphy's Detroit police boss stands in his way, orders him off the case, and draws a line which Murphy is not supposed to cross. Of course Murphy does cross the line, immediately.

THE SECRET DOOR

Heroes inevitably violate limits set by Mentors or Threshold Guardians, due to what we might call the Law of the Secret Door. When Belle in *Beauty and the Beast* is told she has the run of the Beast's household, except for one door which she must never enter, we know that she will be compelled at some point to open that secret door. If Pandora is told she must not open the box, she won't rest until she's had a peek inside. If Psyche is told she must never look upon her

132

lover Cupid, she will surely find a way to lay eyes on him. These stories are symbols of human curiosity, the powerful drive to know all the hidden things, all the secrets.

THE WIZARD OF OZ

Dorothy runs away from home and gets as far as the carnival wagon of Professor Marvel, a Wise Old Man whose function, in this incarnation, is to block her at the threshold of a dangerous journey. At this point Dorothy is a willing hero, and it's left for the Professor to express the danger of the road for the audience. With a bit of shamanic magic, he convinces her to return home. He has convinced her to Refuse the Call, for now.

But in effect Professor Marvel is issuing a higher Call to go home, make peace with her embattled feminine energy, reconnect with Aunt Em's love, and deal with her feelings rather than run away from them.

Although Dorothy turns back for the time being, powerful forces have been set in motion in her life. She finds that the frightful power of the tornado, a symbol of the feelings she has stirred up, has driven her loved ones and allies underground, out of reach. No one can hear her. She is alone except for Toto, her intuition. Like many a hero she finds that once started on a journey, she can never go back to the way things were. Ultimately, Refusal is pointless. She has already burned some bridges behind her and must live with the consequences of taking the first step on the Road of Heroes.

Dorothy takes refuge in the empty house, the common dream symbol for an old personality structure. But the whirling forces of change, which she herself has stirred up, come sweeping towards her and no structure can protect against its awesome power.

⊶⊳ ⊲⊷

Refusal may be a subtle moment, perhaps just a word or two of hesitation between receiving and accepting a Call. (Often several stages of the journey may be combined in a single scene. Folklorists call this "conflation".) Refusal may be a single step near the beginning of the journey, or it may be encountered at every step of the way, depending on the nature of the hero.

Refusal of the Call can be an opportunity to redirect the focus of the adventure. An adventure taken on a lark or to escape some unpleasant consequence may be nudged into a deeper adventure of the spirit.

A hero hesitates at the threshold to experience the fear, to let the audience know the formidability of the challenges ahead. But eventually fear is overcome or set aside, often with the help of wise, protective forces or magical gifts, representing the energy of the next stage, Meeting with the Mentor.

QUESTIONING THE JOURNEY

1. How does the hero Refuse the Call in *Fatal Attraction? Pretty Woman? A League of Their Own?* Is Refusal of the Call or reluctance a necessary stage for every story? For every hero?

2. What are the heroes of your story afraid of? Which are false fears or paranoia? Which are real fears? How are they expressed?

3. In what ways have they refused Calls to Adventure, and what are the consequences of Refusal?

4. If the protagonists are willing heroes, are there characters or forces that make the dangers clear for the audience?

5. Have you refused Calls to Adventure, and how would your life be different if you had accepted them?

6. Have you accepted Calls to Adventure that you wish you had refused?

MEETING THE MENTOR

STAGE FOUR : MEETING WITH THE MENTOR

"She (Athene) assumed the appearance of Mentor and seemed so like him as to deceive both eye and ear..."

The Odyssey of Homer

Sometimes it's not a bad idea to refuse a Call until you've had time to prepare for the "zone unknown" that lies ahead. In mythology and folklore that preparation might be done with the help of the wise, protective figure of the **Mentor**, whose many services to the hero include protecting, guiding, teaching, testing, training, and providing magical gifts. In his study of Russian folktales, Vladimir Propp calls this character type the "donor" or "provider" because its precise function is to supply the hero with something needed on the journey. Meeting with the Mentor is the stage of the Hero's Journey in which the hero gains the supplies, knowledge, and confidence needed to overcome fear and commence the adventure.

> *You Seekers, fearful at the brink of adventure, consult with the elders of the Home Tribe. Seek out those who have gone before. Learn the secret lore of watering holes, game trails, and berry patches, and what badlands, quicksand, and monsters to avoid. An old one, too feeble to go out again, scratches a map for us in the dirt. The shaman of the tribe presses something into your hand, a magic gift, a potent talisman that will protect us and guide us on the quest. Now we can set out with lighter hearts and greater confidence, for we take with us the collected wisdom of the Home Tribe.*

HEROES AND MENTORS

Movies and stories of all kinds are constantly elaborating the relationship between the two archetypes of hero and Mentor.

The *Karate Kid* films, *The Prime of Miss Jean Brodie*, and *Stand and Deliver* are stories devoted entirely to the process of mentors teaching students. Countless films such as *Red River, Ordinary People, Star Wars,* and *Fried Green Tomatoes* reveal the vital force of Mentors at key moments in the lives of heroes.

SOURCES OF WISDOM

Even if there is no actual character performing the many functions of the Mentor archetype, heroes almost always make contact with some source of wisdom before committing to the adventure. They may seek out the experience of those who have gone before, or they may look inside themselves for wisdom won at great cost in former adventures. Either way, they are smart to consult the map of the adventure, looking for the records, charts, and ship's logs of that territory. It's only prudent for wayfarers to stop and check the map before setting out on the challenging, often disorienting, Road of Heroes.

For the storyteller, Meeting with the Mentor is a stage rich in potential for conflict, involvement, humor, and tragedy. It's based in an emotional relationship, usually between a hero and a Mentor or advisor of some kind, and audiences seem to enjoy relationships in which the wisdom and experience of one generation is passed on to the next. Everyone has had a relationship with a Mentor or role model.

MENTORS IN FOLKLORE AND MYTH

Folklore is filled with descriptions of heroes meeting magical protectors who bestow gifts and guide them on the journey. We read of the elves who help the shoemaker; the animals who help and protect little girls in Russian fairy tales; the seven dwarves who give Snow White shelter; or Puss-in-Boots, the talking cat who helps his poor master win a kingdom. All are projections of the powerful archetype of the Mentor, helping and guiding the hero.

Heroes of mythology seek the advice and help of the witches, wizards, witch doctors, spirits, and gods of their worlds. The heroes of

Homer's stories are guided by patron gods and goddesses who give them magical aid. Some heroes are raised and trained by magical beings that are somewhere between gods and men, such as centaurs.

CHIRON: A PROTOYPE

Many of the Greek heroes were mentored by the centaur Chiron, a prototype for all Wise Old Men and Women. A strange mix of man and horse, Chiron was foster-father and trainer to a whole army of Greek heroes including Hercules, Actaeon, Achilles, Peleus, and Aesculapius, the greatest surgeon of antiquity. In the person of Chiron, the Greeks stored many of their notions about what it means to be a Mentor.

As a rule, centaurs are wild and savage creatures. Chiron was an unusually kind and peaceful one, but he still kept some of his wild horse nature. As a half man/half animal creature, he is linked to the shamans of many cultures who dance in the skins of animals to get in touch with animal power. Chiron is the energy and intuition of wild nature, gentled and harnessed to teaching. Like the shamans, he is a bridge between humans and the higher powers of nature and the universe. Mentors in stories often show that they are connected to nature or to some other world of the spirit.

As a Mentor, Chiron led his heroes-in-training through the thresholds of manhood by patiently teaching them the skills of archery, poetry, surgery, and so on. He was not always well rewarded for his efforts. His violence-prone pupil Hercules wounded him with a magic arrow which made Chiron beg the gods for the mercy of death. But in the end, after a truly heroic sacrifice in which he rescued Prometheus from the underworld by taking his place, Chiron received the highest distinction the Greeks could bestow. Zeus made him a constellation and a sign of the zodiac — Sagittarius, a centaur firing a bow. Clearly the Greeks had a high regard for teachers and Mentors.

MENTOR HIMSELF

The term **Mentor** comes from the character of that name in *The Odyssey*. Mentor was the loyal friend of Odysseus, entrusted with raising his son Telemachus while Odysseus made his long way back from the Trojan War. Mentor has given his name to all guides and trainers, but it's really Athena, the goddess of wisdom, who works behind the scenes to bring the energy of the Mentor archetype into the story.

"The goddess with the flashing eyes" has a big crush on Odysseus, and an interest in getting him home safely. She also looks out for his son Telemachus. She finds the son's story stuck in the opening scenes (The Ordinary World) of *The Odyssey* when the household is overrun by arrogant young suitors for his mother's hand. Athena decides to unstick the situation by taking human form. An important function of the Mentor archetype is to get the story rolling.

First she assumes the appearance of a traveling warrior named Mentes, to issue a stirring challenge to stand up to the suitors and seek his father (Call to Adventure). Telemachus accepts the challenge but the suitors laugh him off and he is so discouraged he wants to abandon the mission (Refusal of the Call). Once again the story seems stuck, and Athena unsticks it by taking the form of Telemachus' teacher Mentor. In this disguise she drums some courage into him and helps him assemble a ship and crew. Therefore, even though Mentor is the name we give to wise counselors and guides, it is really the goddess Athena who acts here.

Athena is the full, undiluted energy of the archetype. If she appeared in her true form, it would probably blast the skin off the bones of the strongest hero. The gods usually speak to us through the filter of other people who are temporarily filled with a god-like spirit. A good teacher or Mentor is **enthused** about learning. The wonderful thing is that this feeling can be communicated to students or to an audience.

The names Mentes and Mentor, along with our word "mental", stem from the Greek word for mind, *menos*, a marvelously flexible word that can mean intention, force, or purpose as well as mind, spirit, or remembrance. Mentors in stories act mainly on the mind of the hero, changing her consciousness or redirecting her will. Even if physical gifts are given, Mentors also strengthen the hero's mind to face an ordeal with confidence. *Menos* also means courage.

AVOIDING MENTOR CLICHES

The audience is extremely familiar with the Mentor archetype. The behaviors, attitudes, and functions of Wise Old Women and Men are well-known from thousands of stories, and it's easy to fall into cliches and stereotypes — kindly fairy godmothers and white-bearded wizards in tall Merlin hats. To combat this and keep your writing fresh and surprising, defy the archetypes! Stand them on their heads, turn them inside out, purposely do without them altogether to see what happens. The absence of a Mentor creates special and interesting conditions for a hero. But be aware of the archetype's existence, and the audience's familiarity with it.

MISDIRECTION

Audiences don't mind being misled about a Mentor (or any character) from time to time. Real life is full of surprises about people who turn out to be nothing like we first thought. The mask of the Mentor can be used to trick a hero into entering a life of crime. This is how Fagin enlists little boys as pickpockets in *Oliver Twist*. The mask of Mentor can be used to get a hero involved in a dangerous adventure, unknowingly working for the villains. In *Arabesque*, Gregory Peck is tricked into helping a ring of spies by a fake Wise Old Man. You can make the audience think they are seeing a conventional, kindly, helpful Mentor, and then reveal that the character is actually something quite different. Use the audience's expectations and assumptions to surprise them.

MENTOR-HERO CONFLICTS

The Mentor-hero relationship can take a tragic or deadly turn if the hero is ungrateful or violence-prone. Despite the reputation of Hercules as a peerless hero, he has an alarming tendency to do harm to his Mentors. In addition to painfully wounding Chiron, Hercules got so frustrated at music lessons that he bashed in the head of his music teacher Lycus with the first lyre ever made.

Sometimes a Mentor turns villain or betrays the hero. The movie *The Eiger Sanction* shows an apparently benevolent Mentor (George Kennedy) who surprisingly turns on his student hero (Clint Eastwood) and tries to kill him. The dwarf Regin, in Nordic myth, is at first a Mentor to Sigurd the Dragonslayer and helpfully reforges his broken sword. But in the long run the helper turns out to be a doublecrosser. After the dragon is slain, Regin plots to kill Sigurd and keep the treasure for himself.

Rumpelstilstkin is initially a fairy tale Mentor who helps the heroine by making good on her father's boast that she can spin straw into gold. But the price he demands for his gift is too high — he wants her baby. These stories teach us that not all Mentors are to be trusted, and that it's healthy to question a Mentor's motives. It's one way to distinguish good from bad advice.

Mentors sometimes disappoint the heroes who have admired them during apprenticeship. In *Mr. Smith Goes to Washington,* Jimmy Stewart learns that his Mentor and role model, the noble Senator played by Claude Rains, is as crooked and cowardly as the rest of Congress.

Mentors, like parents, may have a hard time letting go of their charges. An over-protective Mentor can lead to a tragic situation. The character of Svengali from the novel *Trilby* is a chilling portrait of a Mentor who becomes so obsessed with his student that he dooms them both.

MENTOR-DRIVEN STORIES

Once in awhile an entire story is built around a Mentor. *Goodbye, Mr. Chips,* the novel and film, is a whole story built on teaching. Mr. Chips is the Mentor of thousands of boys *and* the hero of the story, with his own series of Mentors.

The movie *Barbarossa* is a wise and funny look at a Mentor relationship sustained throughout the story. Its focus is the training of a country boy (Gary Busey) by a legendary Western desperado (Willie Nelson). The young man's learning is so complete that when the movie ends, he is ready to take Barbarossa's place as a larger-than-life folk hero.

MENTOR AS EVOLVED HERO

Mentors can be regarded as heroes who have become experienced enough to teach others. They have been down the Road of Heroes one or more times, and they have acquired knowledge and skill which can be passed on. The progression of images in the Tarot deck shows how a hero evolves to become a Mentor. A hero begins as a Fool and at various stages of the adventure rises through ranks of magician, warrior, messenger, conqueror, lover, thief, ruler, hermit, and so on. At last the hero becomes a Hierophant, a worker of miracles, a Mentor and guide to others, whose experience comes from surviving many rounds of the Hero's Journey.

CRITICAL INFLUENCE

Most often, teaching, training, and testing are only transient stages of a hero's progress, part of a larger picture. In many movies and stories the Wise Old Woman or Man is a passing influence on the hero. But the Mentor's brief appearance is critical to get the story past the blockades of doubt and fear. Mentors may appear only two or three times in a story. Glinda the Good Witch appears only three times in *The Wizard of Oz*:

143

1) giving Dorothy the red shoes and a yellow path to follow, 2) intervening to blanket the sleep-inducing poppies with pure white snow, and 3) granting her wish to return home, with the help of the magic red shoes. In all three cases her function is to get the story unstuck by giving aid, advice, or magical equipment.

Mentors spring up in amazing variety and frequency because they are so useful to storytellers. They reflect the reality that we all have to learn the lessons of life from someone or something. Whether embodied as a person, a tradition, or a code of ethics, the energy of the archetype is present in almost every story, to get things rolling with gifts, encouragement, guidance, or wisdom.

THE WIZARD OF OZ

Dorothy, like many heroes, encounters a series of Mentors of varying shades. She learns something from almost everyone she meets, and all the characters from whom she learns are in a sense Mentors.

Professor Marvel is the Mentor who reminds her that she is loved, and sends her on her quest for "home", a term that means far more than a Kansas farmhouse. Dorothy has to learn to feel at home in her own soul, and going back to face her problems is a step in that direction.

But the tornado flings her to Oz, where Dorothy encounters Glinda, the good witch, a new Mentor for a new land. Glinda acquaints her with the unfamiliar rules of Oz, gives her the magic gift of the ruby slippers, and points her on the way of the Yellow Brick Road, the golden Road of Heroes. She gives Dorothy a positive feminine role model to balance the negativity of the Wicked Witch.

The three magical figures that Dorothy meets along the way, a man of straw, a man of tin, and a talking lion, are allies and Mentors who teach her lessons about brains, heart, and

144

courage. They are different models of masculine energy that she must incorporate in building her own personality.

The Wizard himself is a Mentor, giving her a new Call to Adventure, the impossible mission of fetching the witch's broomstick. He challenges Dorothy to face her greatest fear – the hostile feminine energy of the Witch.

The little dog Toto is a Mentor, too, in a way. Acting entirely on instinct, he is her intuition, guiding her deeper into the adventure and back out again.

⊷▭ ▭⊶

The concept of the Mentor archetype has many uses for the writer. In addition to offering a force that can propel the story forward and supply the hero with necessary motivation or equipment for the journey, Mentors can provide humor or deep, tragic relationships. Some stories don't need a special character solely dedicated to perform the functions of this archetype, but at some point in almost any story, the Mentor functions of helping the hero are performed by some character or force, temporarily wearing the mask of the Mentor.

When writers get stuck, they may seek the help of Mentors just as heroes do. They may consult writing teachers or seek inspiration from the works of great writers. They may delve deep inside themselves to the real sources of inspiration in the Self, the dwelling place of the Muses. The best Mentor advice may be so simple. Breathe. Hang in there. You're doing fine. You've got what it takes to handle any situation, somewhere inside you.

Writers should bear in mind that they are Mentors of a kind to their readers, shamans who travel to other worlds and bring back stories to heal their people. Like Mentors, they teach with their stories and give of their experience, passion, observation, and enthusiasm. Writers, like shamans and Mentors, provide metaphors by which people guide their lives – a most valuable gift and a grave responsibility for the writer.

It's often the energy of the Mentor archetype that gets a hero past fear and sends her to the brink of adventure, at the next stage of the Hero's Journey, the First Threshold.

QUESTIONING THE JOURNEY

1. Who or what is the Mentor in *Fatal Attraction*? *Pretty Woman*? *Silence of the Lambs*?

2. Think of three long-running TV series. Are there Mentors in these shows? What functions do these characters serve?

3. Is there a character in your story who is a full-blown Mentor? Do other characters wear the mask of the Mentor at some point?

4. Would it benefit the story to develop a Mentor character if there is none?

5. What Mentor functions can be found or developed in your story? Does your hero need a Mentor?

6. Does your hero have some inner code of ethics or model of behavior? Does your hero have a conscience and how does it manifest itself?

7. *Raiders of the Lost Ark* and *Indiana Jones and The Temple of Doom* portray a hero who has no apparent Mentor. He learns things from people along the way, but there is no special character set aside for that task. The third film in the series, *Indiana Jones and the Last Crusade*, introduces the character of Indy's father, played by Sean Connery. Is he a Mentor? Are all parents Mentors? Are yours? In your stories, what is the attitude of your hero to the Mentor energy?

CROSSING THE FIRST THRESHOLD

STAGE FIVE : CROSSING THE FIRST THRESHOLD

"Just follow the Yellow Brick Road."
> from *The Wizard of Oz*, screenplay by Noel Langley,
> Florence Ryerson and Edgar AllanWoolf

Now the hero stands at the very threshold of the world of adventure, the Special World of Act Two. The call has been heard, doubts and fears have been expressed and allayed, and all due preparations have been made. But the real movement, the most critical action of Act One, still remains. **Crossing the First Threshold** is an act of the will in which the hero commits whole-heartedly to the adventure.

The ranks of the Seekers are thinner now. Some of us have dropped out, but the final few are ready to cross the threshold and truly begin the adventure. The problems of the Home Tribe are clear to everyone, and desperate — something must be done, now! Ready or not, we lope out of the village leaving all things familiar behind. As you pull away you feel the jerk of the invisible threads that bind you to your loved ones. It's difficult to pull away from everything you know but with a deep breath you go on, taking the plunge into the abyss of the unknown.

We enter a strange no-man's-land, a world between worlds, a zone of crossing that may be desolate and lonely, or in places, crowded with life. You sense the presence of other beings, other forces with sharp thorns or claws, guarding the way to the treasure you seek. But there's no turning back now, we all feel it; the adventure has begun for good or ill.

APPROACHING THE THRESHOLD

Heroes typically don't just accept the advice and gifts of their Mentors and then charge into the adventure. Often their final commitment is brought about through some external force which changes the course or intensity of the story. This is equivalent to the famous "plot point" or "turning point" of the conventional three-act movie structure. A villain may kill, harm, threaten, or kidnap someone close to the hero, sweeping aside all hesitation. Rough weather may force the sailing of a ship, or the hero may be given a deadline to achieve an assignment. The hero may run out of options, or discover that a difficult choice must be made. Some heroes are "shanghaied" into the adventure or pushed over the brink, with no choice but to commit to the journey. In *Thelma and Louise*, Louise's impulsive killing of a man who is assaulting Thelma is the action that pushes the women to Cross the First Threshold into a new world of being on the run from the law.

An example of the externally imposed event is found in Hitchcock's *North by Northwest*. Advertising man Roger Thornhill, mistaken for a daring secret agent, has been trying his best to avoid his Call to Adventure all through the first act. It takes a murder to get him committed to the journey. A man he's questioning at the U.N. building is killed in front of witnesses in such a way that everyone thinks Roger did it. Now he is truly a "man on the run", escaping both from the police and from the enemy agents who will stop at nothing to kill him. The murder is the external event that pushes the story over the First Threshold into the Special World, where the stakes are higher.

Internal events might trigger a Threshold Crossing as well. Heroes come to decision points where their very souls are at stake, where they must decide "Do I go on living my life as I always have, or will I risk everything in the effort to grow and change?" In *Ordinary People* the deteriorating life of the young hero Conrad gradually pressures him into making a choice, despite his fears, to see a therapist and explore the trauma of his brother's death.

Often a combination of external events and inner choices will boost the story towards the second act. In *Beverly Hills Cop* Axel Foley sees a childhood friend brutally executed by thugs, and is motivated to find the man who hired them. But it takes a separate moment of decision for him to overcome resistance and fully commit to the adventure. In a brief scene in which his boss warns him off the case, you see him make the inner choice to ignore the warning and enter the Special World at any cost.

THRESHOLD GUARDIANS

As you approach the threshold you're likely to encounter beings who try to block your way. They are called Threshold Guardians, a powerful and useful archetype. They may pop up to block the way and test the hero at any point in a story, but they tend to cluster around the doorways, gates and narrow passages of threshold crossings. Axel Foley's Detroit police captain, who firmly forbids him from getting involved in the investigation of the murder, is one such figure.

Threshold Guardians are part of the training of any hero. In Greek myth, the three-headed monster dog Cerberus guards the entrance to the underworld, and many a hero has had to figure out a way past his jaws. The grim ferryman Charon who guides souls across the River Styx is another Threshold Guardian who must be appeased with a gift of a penny.

The task for heroes at this point is often to figure out some way around or through these guardians. Often their threat is just an illusion, and the solution is simply to ignore them or to push through them with faith. Other Threshold Guardians must be absorbed or their hostile energy must be reflected back onto them. The trick may be to realize that what seems like an obstacle may actually be the means of climbing over the threshold. Threshold Guardians who seem to be enemies may be turned into valuable allies.

Sometimes the guardians of the First Threshold simply need to be acknowledged. They occupy a difficult niche and it wouldn't be polite to pass through their territory without recognizing their power and their important role of keeping the gate. It's a little like tipping a doorman or paying a ticket-taker at a theatre.

THE CROSSING

Sometimes this step merely signifies we have reached the border of the two worlds. We must take the leap of faith into the unknown or else the adventure will never really begin.

Countless movies illustrate the border between two worlds with the crossing of physical barriers such as doors, gates, arches, bridges, deserts, canyons, walls, cliffs, oceans, or rivers. In many Westerns thresholds are clearly marked by river or border crossings. In the adventure *Gunga Din,* the heroes must leap off a high cliff to escape a horde of screaming cult members at the end of Act One. They are bonded by this leap into the unknown, a Threshold Crossing signifying their willingness to explore the Special World of the Act Two together.

In the olden days of film, the transition between Act One and Act Two was often marked by a brief fade-out, a momentary darkening of the screen which indicated passage of time or movement in space. The fade-out was equivalent to the curtain coming down in the theatre so the stagehands can change the set and props to create a new locale or show elapse of time.

Nowadays it's common for editors to cut sharply from Act One to Act Two. Nevertheless the audience will still experience a noticeable shift in energy at the Threshold Crossing. A song, a music cue or a drastic visual contrast may help signal the transition. The pace of the story may pick up. Entering a new terrain or structure may signal the change of worlds. In *A League of Their Own* the Crossing is the moment the women enter a big-league baseball stadium, a marked contrast from the country ball fields where they've been playing.

The actual Crossing of the Threshold may be a single moment, or it may be an extended passage in a story. In *Lawrence of Arabia*, T. E. Lawrence's ordeals in crossing "the Sun's Anvil", a treacherous stretch of desert, are an elaboration of this stage into a substantial sequence.

The Crossing takes a certain kind of courage from the hero. He is like the Fool in the Tarot deck: one foot out over a precipice, about to begin freefall into the unknown.

That special courage is called making the **leap of faith**. Like jumping out of an airplane, the act is irrevocable. There's no turning back now. The leap is made on faith, the trust that somehow we'll land safely.

ROUGH LANDING

Heroes don't always land gently. They may crash in the other world, literally or figuratively. The leap of faith may turn into a crisis of faith as romantic illusions about the Special World are shattered by first contact with it. A bruised hero make pick herself up and ask "Is that all there is?" The passage to the Special World may be exhausting, frustrating, or disorienting.

THE WIZARD OF OZ

> *A tremendous natural force rises up to hurl Dorothy over the First Threshold. She is trying to get home but the tornado sends her on a detour to a Special World where she will learn what "home" really means. Dorothy's last name, Gale, is a word play that links her to the storm. In symbolic language, it's her own stirred-up emotions that have generated this twister. Her old idea of home, the house, is wrenched up by the tornado and carried to a far-off land where a new personality structure can be built.*
>
> *As she passes through the transition zone, Dorothy sees familiar sights but in unfamiliar circumstances. Cows fly through the*

*air, men row a boat through the storm, and Miss Gulch on her
bicycle turns into the Wicked Witch. Dorothy has nothing she
can count on now but Toto — her instincts.*

*The house comes down with a crash. Dorothy emerges to find a
world startlingly different from Kansas, populated by the Little
Men and Women of fairy tales. A Mentor appears magically
when Glinda floats onto the scene in a transparent bubble. She
begins to teach Dorothy about the strange ways of the new land,
and points out that the crash of Dorothy's house has killed a bad
witch. Dorothy's old personality has been shattered by the
uprooting of her old notion of home.*

*Glinda gives a mentor's gifts, the ruby slippers, and new
direction for the quest. To get home, Dorothy must first see the
Wizard, that is, get in touch with her own higher Self. Glinda
gives a specific path, the Yellow Brick Road, and sends her over
another threshold, knowing she will have to make friends,
confront foes, and be tested before she can reach her ultimate
goal.*

→━▣ ▣━←

The First Threshold is the turning point at which the adventure
begins in earnest, at the end of Act One. According to a corporate
metaphor in use at Disney, a story is like an airplane flight, and Act
One is the process of loading, fueling, taxiing, and rumbling down
the runway towards takeoff. The First Threshold is the moment the
wheels leave the ground and the plane begins to fly. If you've never
flown before, it may take awhile to adjust to being in the air. We'll
describe that process of adjustment in the next phase of the Hero's
Journey; Tests, Allies, Enemies.

QUESTIONING THE JOURNEY

1. What is the First Threshold of *City Slickers? Rain Man? Dances with Wolves?* How does the audience know we've gone from one world to another? How does the energy of the story feel different?

2. Is your hero willing to enter the adventure or not? How does this affect the Threshold Crossing?

3. Are there guardian forces at the Threshold and how do they make the hero's leap of faith more difficult?

4. How does the hero deal with Threshold Guardians? What does the hero learn by Crossing the Threshold?

5. What have been the Thresholds in your own life? How did you experience them? Were you even aware you were crossing a threshold into a Special World at the time?

6. By Crossing a Threshold, what options is a hero giving up? Will these unexplored options come back to haunt the hero later?

TESTS, ALLIES, ENEMIES

STAGE SIX : TESTS, ALLIES, ENEMIES

"See, you got three or four good pals, why then you got yourself a tribe – there ain't nothin' stronger than that."

from *Young Guns*, screenplay by John Fusco

Now the hero fully enters the mysterious, exciting Special World which Joseph Campbell called "a dream landscape of curiously fluid, ambiguous forms, where he must survive a succession of trials." It's a new and sometimes frightening experience for the hero. No matter how many schools he has been through, he's a freshman all over again in this new world.

> *We Seekers are in shock – this new world is so different from the home we've always known. Not only are the terrain and the local residents different, the rules of this place are strange as they can be. Different things are valued here and we have a lot to learn about the local currency, customs, and language. Strange creatures jump out at you! Think fast! Don't eat that, it could be poison!*
>
> *Exhausted by the journey across the desolate threshold zone, we're running out of time and energy. Remember our people back in the Home Tribe are counting on us. Enough sightseeing, let's concentrate on the goal. We must go where the food and game and information are to be found. There our skills will be tested, and we'll come one step closer to what we seek.*

CONTRAST

The audience's first impressions of the Special World should strike a sharp contrast with the Ordinary World. Think of Eddie Murphy's first look at the Special World of *Beverly Hills Cop*, which makes such a drastic contrast to his former world of Detroit. Even if the hero remains physically in the same place throughout the story, there is movement and change as new emotional territory is explored. A Special World, even a figurative one, has a different feel, a different rhythm, different priorities and values, and different rules. In *Father of the Bride* or *Guess Who's Coming to Dinner*, while there is no physical threshold, there's definitely a crossing into a Special World with new conditions.

When a submarine dives, a wagon train leaves St. Louis, or the starship Enterprise leaves the earth, the conditions and rules of survival change. Things are often more dangerous, and the price of mistakes is higher.

TESTING

The most important function of this period of adjustment to the Special World is **testing**. Storytellers use this phase to test the hero, putting her through a series of trials and challenges that are meant to prepare her for greater ordeals ahead.

Joseph Campbell illustrates this stage with the tale of Psyche, who is put through a fairy-tale-like series of Tests before winning back her lost love, Cupid (Eros). This tale has been wisely interpreted by Robert A. Johnson in his book on feminine psychology, *She*. Psyche is given three seemingly impossible tasks by Cupid's jealous mother Venus and passes the Tests with the help of beings to whom she has been kind along the way. She has made Allies.

The Tests at the beginning of Act Two are often difficult obstacles, but they don't have the maximum life-and-death quality of later events. If the adventure were a college learning experience, Act One would be a series of entrance exams, and the Test stage of Act Two would be a series of pop quizzes, meant to sharpen the hero's skill in specific areas and prepare her for the more rigorous midterm and final exams coming up.

The Tests may be a continuation of the Mentor's training. Many Mentors accompany their heroes this far into the adventure, coaching them for the big rounds ahead.

The Tests may also be built into the architecture or landscape of the Special World. This world is usually dominated by a villain or Shadow who is careful to surround his world with traps, barricades and checkpoints. It's common for heroes to fall into traps here or trip the Shadow's security alarms. How the hero deals with these traps is part of the Testing.

ALLIES AND ENEMIES

Another function of this stage is the making of Allies or Enemies. It's natural for heroes just arriving in the Special World to spend some time figuring out who can be trusted and relied upon for special services, and who is not to be trusted. This too is a kind of Test, examining if the hero is a good judge of character.

ALLIES

Heroes may walk into the Test stage looking for information, but they may walk out with new friends or Allies. In *Shane*, a shaky partnership between the gunfighter Shane (Alan Ladd) and the farmer (Van Heflin) is cemented into a real friendship by the shared ordeal of a saloon-shattering brawl. When John Dunbar in *Dances with Wolves* crosses the threshold into the Special World of the frontier, he gradually makes alliances with Kicking Bear (Graham Greene) and the wolf he names Two Socks.

SIDEKICKS

Westerns frequently make use of a long-standing bond between a hero and a **sidekick**, an Ally who generally rides with the hero and supports his adventures. The Lone Ranger has Tonto, Zorro has the servant Bernardo, the Cisco Kid has Pancho. These pairings of hero and sidekick can be found throughout myth and literature: Sherlock

Holmes and Dr. Watson, Don Quixote and Sancho Panza, Prince Hal and Falstaff, or the Sumerian hero Gilgamesh and his wild companion Enkidu.

These close Allies of the hero may provide comic relief as well as assistance. **Comical sidekicks**, played by character actors such as Walter Brennan, Gabby Hays, Fuzzy Knight, and Slim Pickens, provide humor lacking in the stalwart, serious heroes they accompany. Such figures may freely cross the boundaries between Mentor and Trickster, sometimes aiding the hero and acting as his conscience, sometimes comically goofing up or causing mischief.

TEAMS

The Testing stage may also provide the opportunity for the forging of a team. Many stories feature multiple heroes or a hero backed up by a team of characters with special skills or qualities. The early phases of Act Two may cover the recruiting of a team, or give an opportunity for the team to make plans and rehearse a difficult operation. The World War II adventure films *The Dirty Dozen* and *The Great Escape* show the heroes bonding into a coherent team before tackling the main event of the story. In the Testing stage the hero may have to struggle against rivals for control of the group. The strengths and flaws of the team members are revealed during Testing.

In a romance, the Testing stage might be the occasion for a first date or for some shared experience that begins to build the relationship, such as the tennis match between Diane Keaton and Woody Allen in *Annie Hall.*

ENEMIES

Heroes can also make bitter enmities at this stage. They may encounter the Shadow or his servants. The hero's appearance in the Special World may tip the Shadow to his arrival and trigger a chain of threatening events. The cantina sequence in *Star Wars* sets up a conflict with the villain Jabba the Hut which culminates in *The Empire Strikes Back.*

160

Enemies include both the villains or antagonists of stories and their underlings. Enemies may perform functions of other archetypes such as the Shadow, the Trickster, the Threshold Guardian, and sometimes the Herald.

THE RIVAL

A special type of Enemy is the **rival**, the hero's competition in love, sports, business, or some other enterprise. The rival is usually not out to kill the hero, but is just trying to defeat him in the competition. In the film of *The Last of the Mohicans*, Major Duncan Hayward is the rival of hero Nathaniel Poe because they both want the same woman, Cora Munro. The plot of *Honeymoon in Vegas* revolves around a similar rivalry between the hapless hero (Nicholas Cage) and his gambler opponent (James Caan).

NEW RULES

The new rules of the Special World must be learned quickly by the hero and the audience. As Dorothy enters the land of Oz, she is bewildered when Glinda the Good asks "Are you a good witch or a bad witch?" In Dorothy's Ordinary World of Kansas, there are only bad witches, but in the Special World of Oz, witches can also be good, and fly in pink bubbles instead of on broomsticks. Another Test of the hero is how quickly she can adjust to the new rules of the Special World.

At this stage a Western may impose certain conditions on people entering a town or a bar. In *Unforgiven*, guns cannot be worn in the sheriff's territory. This restriction can draw the hero into conflicts. A hero may enter a bar to discover that the town is totally polarized by two factions; the cattlemen vs. the farmers, the Earps vs. the Clantons, the bounty hunters vs. the sheriff, and so on. In the pressure cooker of the saloon, people size each other up and take sides for the coming showdown. The cantina sequence in *Star Wars* draws on the images we all have of Western saloons as places for reconnaissance, challenges, alliances, and the learning of new rules.

161

WATERING HOLES

Why do so many heroes pass through bars and saloons at this point in the stories? The answer lies in the hunting metaphor of the Hero's Journey. Upon leaving the Ordinary World of village or den, hunters will often head straight for a watering hole to look for game. Predators sometimes follow the muddy tracks left by game who come down to drink. The watering hole is a natural congregating place and a good spot to observe and get information. It's no accident that we call neighborhood saloons and cocktail lounges our "local watering holes".

The crossing of the First Threshold may have been long, lonely, and dry. Bars are natural spots to recuperate, pick up gossip, make friends, and confront Enemies. They also allow us to observe people under pressure, when true character is revealed. How Shane handles himself in a bar fight convinces a farmer to become his Ally and stand up to the bullying cattlemen. In the tense bar-room confrontations in *Star Wars*, Luke Skywalker sees flashes of Obi Wan Kenobi's spiritual power and Han Solo's "look out for Number One" mentality. The bar can be a microcosm of the Special World, a place through which everyone must pass, sooner or later, like the saloon in *The Life and Times of Judge Roy Bean*. "Everybody Comes to Rick's", says the title of the play on which *Casablanca* is based.

Bars also play host to a number of other activities including music, flirting, and gambling. This stage in a story, whether it takes place in a bar or not, is a good place for a musical sequence that announces the mood of the Special World. A nightclub act may allow the introduction of a romantic interest, as in Jessica Rabbit's sensational torch song in *Who Framed Roger Rabbit?* Music can express the dualities of the Special World as well. At this stage in *Casablanca* the polarities are movingly presented in a musical duel between the passionate "Marsellaise" sung by the French patriots and the brutal "Deutschland Uber Alles" sung by the Nazis.

In the lonely outposts of adventure, saloons or their equivalent may be the only places for sexual intrigue. Bars can be the arena for flirting, romance, or prostitution. A hero may strike up a relationship in a bar to get information, and incidentally acquire an Ally or a lover.

Gambling and saloons go together, and games of chance are a natural feature of the Testing stage. Heroes may want to consult the oracles to see how luck will favor them. They want to learn about the wheel of fortune, and how luck can be coaxed their way. Through a game the stakes can be raised or a fortune can be lost. In the Hindu epic *The Mahabharata*, a cosmic family feud is set in motion by a rigged game of chance between two sets of brothers. (The bad guys cheat.)

THE WIZARD OF OZ

Of course not all heroes go to bars at this stage of the journey. Dorothy encounters her Tests, Allies, and Enemies on the Yellow Brick Road. Like Psyche or the heroes of many fairy tales she is wise enough to know that requests for aid on the road should be honored with an open heart. She earns the loyalty of the Scarecrow by getting him unhooked from his post and by helping him learn to walk. Meanwhile she learns that her Enemy, the Wicked Witch, shadows her at every turn and waits for the chance to strike. The Witch influences some grumpy apple trees to become Enemies to Dorothy and the Scarecrow. The Scarecrow proves his worthiness to be on the team by outwitting the trees. He taunts them into throwing apples, which he and Dorothy pick up to eat.

Dorothy wins the affection of another Ally, the Tin Woodman, by oiling his joints and listening sympathetically to his sad story of having no heart. The Witch appears again, showing her enmity for Dorothy and her Allies by hurling a fireball at them.

To protect her dog Toto, Dorothy stands up to the blustering of the Cowardly Lion, a potential Enemy or Threshold Guardian, and ends up making him an Ally.

The battlelines are clearly drawn. Dorothy has learned the rules of the Special World and has passed many Tests. Protected by Allies and on guard against declared Enemies, she is ready to approach the central source of power in the land of Oz.

The phase of Tests, Allies, and Enemies in stories is useful for "getting to know you" scenes where the characters get acquainted with each other and the audience learns more about them. This stage also allows the hero to accumulate power and information in preparation for the next stage: Approach to the Inmost Cave.

QUESTIONING THE JOURNEY

1. What is the Testing phase of *Sister Act? A League of Their Own? Big?* Why do heroes pass through a period of Tests? Why don't they just go right to the main event after entering Act Two?

2. How does your story's Special World differ from the Ordinary World? How can you increase the contrast?

3. In what ways is your hero Tested, and when does she make Allies or Enemies? Keep in mind there is no "right" way. The needs of the story may dictate when alliances are made.

4. Are there loner heroes who have no Allies?

5. Is your hero a single character or a group such as a platoon, a crew, a family, or a gang? If it is an "ensemble piece" like *The Breakfast Club* or *The Big Chill,* when does the team become a coherent group?

6. How does your hero react to the Special World with its strange rules and unfamiliar people?

APPROACH TO THE INMOST CAVE

STAGE SEVEN: APPROACH TO THE INMOST CAVE

COWARDLY LION: *There's only one thing more I'd like you fellows to do.*
TIN WOODMAN, SCARECROW: *What's that?*
COWARDLY LION: *Talk me out of it!*

from *The Wizard of Oz*

Heroes, having made the adjustment to the Special World, now go on to seek its heart. They pass into an intermediate region between the border and the very center of the Hero's Journey. On the way they find another mysterious zone with its own Threshold Guardians, agendas, and tests. This is the **Approach to the Inmost Cave**, where soon they will encounter supreme wonder and terror. It's time to make final preparations for the central ordeal of the adventure. Heroes at this point are like mountaineers who have raised themselves to a base camp by the labors of Testing, and are about to make the final assault on the highest peak.

> *Our band of Seekers leaves the oasis at the edge of the new world, refreshed and armed with more knowledge about the nature and habits of the game we're hunting. We're ready to press on to the heart of the new world where the greatest treasures are guarded by our greatest fears.*

> *Look around at your fellow Seekers. We've changed already and new qualities are emerging. Who's the leader now? Some who were not suited for life in the Ordinary World are now thriving. Others who seemed ideal for adventure are turning out to be the least able. A new perception of yourself and others is forming. Based on this new awareness, you can make plans and direct yourself towards getting what you want from the Special World. Soon you will be ready to enter the Inmost Cave.*

FUNCTIONS OF APPROACH

In modern storytelling, certain special functions naturally fall into this zone of **Approach**. As heroes near the gates of a citadel deep within the Special World, they may take time to make plans, do reconnaissance on the enemy, reorganize or thin out the group, fortify and arm themselves, and have a last laugh and a final cigarette before going over the top into no-man's-land. The student studies for the midterm. The hunter stalks the game to its hiding place. Adventurers squeeze in a love scene before tackling the central event of the movie.

COURTSHIP

The Approach can be an arena for elaborate courtship rituals. A romance may develop here, bonding hero and beloved before they encounter the main ordeal. In *North by Northwest,* Cary Grant meets a beautiful woman (Eva Marie Saint) on a train as he escapes from the police and the enemy spies. He doesn't know she works for the evil spies and has been assigned to lure him into their trap. However, her seduction backfires and she finds herself actually falling in love with him. Later, thanks to this scene of bonding, she becomes his Ally.

THE BOLD APPROACH

Some heroes boldly stride up to the castle door and demand to be let in. Confident, committed heroes will take this Approach. Axel Foley in *Beverly Hills Cop* crashes into the precincts of his enemy a number of times at the Approach phase, conning his way past Threshold Guardians and flaunting his intention to upset his opponent's world. Cary Grant in *Gunga Din* marches into the Inmost Cave of his antagonists, a cult of assassins, singing an English drinking song at the top of his lungs. His bold Approach is not pure arrogance: He puts on the outrageous show to buy time for his friend Gunga Din to slip away and summon the British army. In true heroic fashion Grant's character is sacrificing himself and tempting death on behalf of the group.

The Approach of Clint Eastwood's character in *Unforgiven* is not arrogant so much as ignorant. He rides into the Inmost Cave of the town during a rainstorm, and is unable to see a sign forbidding firearms. This brings him to an ordeal, a beating by the sheriff (Gene Hackman) that almost kills him.

PREPARATION FOR THE ORDEAL

Approach may be a time of further reconnaissance and information-gathering, or a time of dressing and arming for an ordeal. Gunfighters check their weapons, bullfighters dress carefully in their suits of lights.

THE WIZARD OF OZ

The Wizard of Oz has such a well-developed Approach section that we'll use it throughout this chapter to illuminate some of the functions of this stage.

OBSTACLES

Having made some Allies in the Testing stage, Dorothy and friends leave the woods on the border of Oz and immediately see the glittering Emerald City of their dreams. They Approach in joy, but before they reach their goal, they face a series of obstacles and challenges that will bond them as a group, and prepare them for the life-and-death struggle yet to come.

BEWARE OF ILLUSIONS

First they are put to sleep by a field of poppies sown by the Wicked Witch's magic. They are brought back to consciousness by a blanket of snow, courtesy of Glinda the Good.

The message for the hero is clear: Don't be seduced by illusions and perfumes, stay alert, don't fall asleep on the march.

THRESHOLD GUARDIANS

Dorothy and friends reach the City, only to find their way blocked by a rude sentry, a perfect Threshold Guardian (who looks suspiciously like Professor Marvel from Act One). He is a satirical figure, an exaggerated image of a bureaucrat whose job is to enforce stupid, pointless rules. Dorothy identifies herself as the one who dropped a house on the Wicked Witch of the East, and she has the Ruby Slippers to prove it. This wins the respect of the sentry who admits them immediately, saying "Well that's a horse of a different color!"

Message: Past experience on the journey may be the hero's passport to new lands. Nothing is wasted, and every challenge of the past strengthens and informs us for the present. We win respect for having made it this far.

The satire of bureaucratic nonsense reminds us that few heroes are exempt from the tolls and rituals of the Special World. Heroes must either pay the price of admission or find a way around the obstacles, as Dorothy does.

ANOTHER SPECIAL WORLD

Dorothy and company enter the wonderland of the City, where everything is green except for a horse pulling a carriage, the famous Horse of a Different Color who changes hue every time you look at him. The Driver also looks like Professor Marvel.

Message: You've entered yet another little Special World, with different rules and values. You may encounter a series of these like Chinese boxes, one inside the other, a series of shells protecting some central source of power. The multi-colored horse is a signal that rapid change is coming. The detail of several characters looking alike, or the same character taking a variety of roles, is a reminder we are in a dream world ruled by forces of comparison, association, and transformation. The protean changes of Professor Marvel suggest that a single powerful mind is at work in Oz, or that Dorothy's dream, if that's what it is, has been deeply influenced by his personality. Professor Marvel has become an animus figure for Dorothy; a focus for her projections about mature male energy. Her father is dead or absent and the male figures around the farm, Uncle Henry and the three farm hands, are weak. She is seeking an image of what a father can be, and projects Professor Marvel's paternal energy onto every authority figure she sees. If the Good Witch Glinda is a surrogate mother or positive anima for her, these variations of Professor Marvel are surrogate fathers.

BE PREPARED

Dorothy and friends are primped, pampered and prepared for their meeting with the Wizard, in the beauty parlors and machine shops of the Emerald City.

Message: Heroes know they are facing a great ordeal, and are wise to make themselves as ready as they'll ever be, like warriors polishing and sharpening their weapons, or students doing final drills before a big exam.

WARNING

Our heroes, feeling pretty good now, go out singing about how the day is laughed away in the merry old land of Oz. Just then the Witch screeches over the city, sky-writing from her broomstick, "Surrender Dorothy!" The people back away in terror, leaving our heroes alone outside the Wizard's door.

Message: It's good for heroes to go into the main event in a state of balance, with confidence tempered by humility and awareness of the danger. No matter how hysterical the celebrations in Oz, they always seem to be damped by an appearance by the Witch, a real party pooper. She is a deep disturbance in Dorothy's psyche which will ruin every pleasurable moment until dealt with decisively. The isolation of the heroes is typical. Like Gary Cooper trying to line up support from cowardly townspeople in *High Noon*, heroes may find good-time companions fading away when the going gets tough.

171

ANOTHER THRESHOLD

Our heroes knock at the Wizard's door and an even ruder sentry, another ringer for Professor Marvel, sticks his head out. His orders are "Not nobody, not nohow" is to get in to see the Wizard. Only the information that he's dealing with "the Witch's Dorothy" convinces him to go confer with the Wizard. While he's gone, the Lion sings "If I Were King of the Forest", expressing his aspirations.

Message: The credentials of experience may have to be presented repeatedly at successive rings of power. When delayed by obstacles, heroes do well to get acquainted with their fellow adventurers and learn of their hopes and dreams.

EMOTIONAL APPEAL TO A GUARDIAN

The Sentry returns to report that the Wizard says "Go away." Dorothy and her companions break down and lament. Now they'll never have their wishes met and Dorothy will never get home. The sad story brings floods of tears to the Sentry's eyes, and he lets them in.

Message: Sometimes, when the passport of experience no longer works to get you past a gate, an emotional appeal can break down the defenses of Threshold Guardians. Establishing a bond of human feeling may be the key.

AN IMPOSSIBLE TEST

Our heroes cross yet another threshold, being ushered into the throneroom of Oz by the Sentry, now their friend. Oz himself is one of the most terrifying images ever put on film — the gigantic head of an angry old man, surrounded by flames and thunder. He can grant your wish, but like the kings of fairytales, is miserly with his power. He imposes impossible tests in hopes that you will go away and leave him alone. Dorothy and friends are given the apparently unachievable task of fetching the broomstick of the Wicked Witch.

Message: It's tempting to think you can just march into foreign territory, take the prize, and leave. The awesome image of Oz reminds us that heroes are challenging a powerful status quo, which may not share their dreams and goals. That status quo may even live inside them in strong habits or neuroses that must be overcome before facing the main ordeal. Oz, Professor Marvel in his most powerful and frightening form, is a negative animus figure, the dark side of Dorothy's idea of a father. Dorothy must deal with her confused feelings about male energy before she can confront her deeper feminine nature.

The status quo might be an aging generation or ruler, reluctant to give up power, or a parent unwilling to admit the child is grown. The Wizard at this point is like a harassed father, grouchy about being interrupted and having demands put on him by youth. This angry parental force must be appeased or dealt with in some way before the adventure can proceed. We must all pass tests to earn the approval of parental forces.

Parents sometimes set impossible conditions on winning their love and acceptance. You can't ever seem to please them. Sometimes the very people you naturally turn to in a crisis will push you away. You may have to face the big moment alone.

SHAMANIC TERRITORY

The heroes pass on to the eerie region surrounding the Wicked Witch's castle. Here they encounter more Threshold Guardians, in the witch's creepy servants, the flying monkeys. Dorothy is kidnapped and flown away by the monkeys, and her companions are beaten and scattered. Tin Woodman is dented and Scarecrow is torn limb from limb.

Message: As heroes Approach the Inmost Cave, they should know they are in shaman's territory, on the edge between life and death. The Scarecrow being torn to pieces and scattered by the monkeys recalls the visions and dreams that signal selection as a shaman.

Shamans-to-be often dream of being dismembered by heavenly spirits and reassembled into the new form of a shaman. Dorothy being flown away by the monkeys is just the sort of thing that happens to shamans when they travel to other worlds.

COMPLICATIONS

The terrorized heroes are discouraged and confused after the monkey attack. Scarecrow's scattered limbs are reassembled by the Tin Woodman and Cowardly Lion.

Heroes may have disheartening setbacks at this stage while approaching the supreme goal. Such reversals of fortune are called *dramatic complications*. Though they may seem to tear us apart, they are only a further test of our willingness to proceed. They also allow us to put ourselves back together in a more effective form for traveling in this unfamiliar terrain.

HIGHER STAKES

Dorothy is now trapped in the castle. The Witch, mirroring the action of her lookalike Miss Gulch, crams Toto into a basket and threatens to throw him in the river unless Dorothy turns over the Ruby Slippers. Dorothy agrees to hand them over but the Witch is zapped by Glinda's protective spell when she tries to take the shoes. The Witch realizes she'll never get the shoes while Dorothy's alive and sets before her the hourglass with its rushing red sand like dried blood. When the last grain runs out, Dorothy will die.

Message: Another function of the Approach stage is to up the stakes and rededicate the team to its mission. The audience may need to be reminded of the "ticking clock" or the "time bomb" of the story. The urgency and life-and-death quality of the issue need to be underscored.

Toto in the basket is a repeated symbol of intuition stifled by the negative anima of the Witch/Miss Gulch. Dorothy's fear of her own

174

intuitive side keeps stuffing away her creativity and confidence, but it keeps popping up again, like Toto.

The Ruby Slippers are a deep dream symbol, representing both Dorothy's means of getting around in Oz; and her identity, her unassailable integrity. The shoes are a reassuring Mentor's gift, the knowledge that you are a unique being with a core that cannot be shaken by outside events. They are like Ariadne's Thread in the story of Theseus and the Minotaur, a connection with a positive, loving anima that gets you through the darkest of labyrinths.

REORGANIZATION

Toto escapes from the basket as he did in Act One and runs out of the castle to join forces with the three friends who are still piecing together the Scarecrow. Toto leads them to the castle, where they are daunted at the task of getting the helpless Dorothy out of the forbidding, well-defended place. The responsibility of moving the adventure forward has fallen to Dorothy's three Allies; this place is so terrible that there's no help here from kindly wizards and witches. They have gotten by as clowns; now they must become heroes.

Message: Toto again acts as Dorothy's intuition, sensing that it's time to call on Allies and lessons learned to get her out of a trap. The Approach stage is also a time to reorganize a group: to promote some members, sort out living, dead, and wounded, assign special missions, and so on. Archetypal masks may need to be changed as characters are made to perform new functions.

With her freedom of action removed, Dorothy has switched archetypal masks here, trading the Hero mask for that of the Victim, the archetype of helplessness. The three companions have also traded masks, being promoted from Trickster clowns or Allies, to full-fledged Heroes who will carry the action for awhile. The audience may find that assumptions about the characters are being overturned as surprising new qualities emerge under the pressure of Approach.

175

The sense that the heroes must face some things without the help of protective spirits is reminiscent of many mythic tales of trips to the underworld. Human heroes often have to go it alone on a mission from the gods. They must travel to the land of the dead where the gods themselves are afraid to walk. We may consult doctors or therapists, friends or advisors, but there are some places where our Mentors can't go and we are on our own.

HEAVY DEFENSES

Scarecrow, Lion, and Tin Woodman now creep up to observe the threshold of the Inmost Cave itself, the drawbridge of the Wicked Witch's castle, defended by a whole army of ferocious-looking Threshold Guardians, wearing bearskin hats and gloves and growling their grim marching song.

Message: Heroes can expect the villain's headquarters to be defended with animal-like ferocity. The castle itself, with its barred gate and drawbridge like a devouring mouth and tongue, is a symbol of the elaborate fortifications around an all-consuming neurosis. The defenses around the Witch's negative anima make the Wizard's guards and palace look inviting by comparison.

WHO IS THE HERO AT THIS POINT?

The three reluctant heroes evaluate the situation. The Lion wants to run, but the Scarecrow has a plan which requires Lion to be the leader. This makes sense since he is the most ferocious-looking, but he still wants to be talked out of it.

Message: the Approach is a good time to recalibrate your team, express misgivings, and give encouragement. Team members make sure all are in agreement about goals, and determine that the right people are in the right jobs. There may even be bitter battles for dominance among the group at this stage, as pirates or thieves fight for control of the adventure.

However, here the Cowardly Lion's efforts to escape responsibility are comic, and point up another function of the Approach: comic relief. This may be the last chance to relax and crack a joke because things are about to get deadly serious in the Supreme Ordeal phase.

GET INTO YOUR OPPONENT'S MIND

As part of their Approach, the three heroes try to cook up a plan as they move closer to the gate. Three sentries attack them, and after a struggle in which costumes fly through the air, our heroes emerge wearing the uniforms and bearskin hats of their enemies. In this disguise, they join the platoon of marching sentries and stride right into the castle.

Message: Here the heroes employ the device of "getting into the skin" of the Threshold Guardians before them. Like the Plains Indians donning buffalo robes to creep close to their prey, the heroes literally put on the skins of their opponents and slip in among them. When in Rome, do as the Romans do. This aspect of the Approach teaches that we must get into the minds of those who seem to stand in our way. If we understand or empathize with them, the job of getting past them or absorbing their energy is much easier. We can turn their attacks into opportunities to get into their skin. Heroes may also put on disguises to conceal their real intentions as they get close to the Inmost Cave of the opponent.

BREAKTHROUGH

The three heroes now discard their disguises and make their way to the chamber of the castle where Dorothy is imprisoned. The Tin Woodman uses his axe to chop through the door.

Message: At some point it may be necessary to use force to break through the final veil to the Inmost Cave. The hero's own resistance and fear may have to be overcome by a violent act of will.

NO EXIT

With Dorothy rescued, and the foursome united again, they now turn their attention to escape. But they are blocked in all directions by the witch's guards.

Message: No matter how heroes try to escape their fate, sooner or later the exits are closed off and the life-and-death issue must be faced. With Dorothy and companions "trapped like rats", the Approach to the Inmost Cave is complete.

The Approach encompasses all the final preparations for the Supreme Ordeal. It often brings heroes to a stronghold of the opposition, a defended center where every lesson and Ally of the journey so far comes into play. New perceptions are put to the test, and the final obstacles to reaching the heart are overcome, so that the Supreme Ordeal may begin.

QUESTIONING THE JOURNEY

1. Campbell says that in myths, the crossing of the First Threshold is often followed by the hero passing through "the belly of the whale". He cites stories from many cultures of heroes being swallowed by giant beasts. In what sense are the heroes "in the belly of the whale" in the early stages of Act Two in *Thelma and Louise? Fatal Attraction? Unforgiven?*

2. Campbell describes several ideas or actions surrounding the major ordeal of a myth: "Meeting with the Goddess", "Woman as Temptress", "Atonement with the Father". In what ways are these ideas part of Approaching the Inmost Cave?

3. In your own story, what happens between entering the Special World and reaching a central crisis in that world? What special preparations lead up to the crisis?

4. Does conflict build, and do the obstacles get more difficult or interesting?

5. Do your heroes want to turn back at this stage, or are they fully committed to the adventure now?

6. In what ways is the hero, in facing external challenges, also encountering inner demons and defenses?

7. Is there a physical Inmost Cave or headquarters of the villain which the heroes Approach? Or is there some emotional equivalent?

SUPREME ORDEAL

STAGE EIGHT: THE SUPREME ORDEAL

AMES BOND: *What do you expect me to do, Goldfinger?*
GOLDFINGER: *Why Mr. Bond, I expect you to die.*

from *Goldfinger,* screenplay
Richard Maibaum and Paul Dehn

Now the hero stands in the deepest chamber of the Inmost Cave, facing the greatest challenge and the most fearsome opponent yet. This the real heart of the matter, what Joseph Campbell called the **Supreme Ordeal**. It is the mainspring of the heroic form and the key to its magic power.

> *Seeker, enter the Inmost Cave and look for that which will restore life to the Home Tribe. The way grows narrow and dark. You must go alone on hands and knees and you feel the earth press close around you. You can hardly breathe. Suddenly you come out into the deepest chamber and find yourself face to face with a towering figure, a menacing Shadow composed of all your doubts and fears and well armed to defend a treasure. Here, in this moment, is the chance to win all or die. No matter what you came for, it's Death that now stares back at you. Whatever the outcome of the battle, you are about to taste death and it will change you.*

DEATH AND REBIRTH

The simple secret of the Supreme Ordeal is this: **Heroes must die so that they can be reborn.** The dramatic movement that audiences enjoy more than any other is death and rebirth. In some way in every story, heroes face death or something like it: their greatest fears, the failure of an enterprise, the end of a relationship, the death of an old personality. Most of the time, they magically survive this death and are

181

literally or symbolically reborn to reap the consequences of having cheated death. They have passed the main test of being a hero.

Spielberg's E. T. dies before our eyes but is reborn through alien magic and a boy's love. Sir Lancelot, remorseful over having killed a gallant knight, prays him back to life. Clint Eastwood's character in *Unforgiven* is beaten senseless by a sadistic sheriff and hovers at the edge of death, thinking he's seeing angels. Sherlock Holmes, apparently killed with Professor Moriarity in the plunge over Reichenbach Falls, defies death and returns transformed and ready for more adventures. Patrick Swayze's character, murdered in *Ghost*, learns how to cross back through the veil to protect his wife and finally express his true love for her.

CHANGE

Heroes don't just visit death and come home. They return **changed**, transformed. No one can go through an experience at the edge of death without being changed in some way. In the center of *An Officer and a Gentleman*, Richard Gere survives a death-and-rebirth ordeal of the ego at the hands of drill instructor Lou Gossett. It dramatically changes Gere's character, making him more sensitive to the needs of others and more conscious that he's part of a group.

Axel Foley, with a villain's gun to his head in *Beverly Hills Cop*, seems sure to die, but is rescued by the bumbling, naive white detective Rosewood (Judge Reinhold). After this rescue from death Foley is more cooperative and willing to submerge his gigantic ego in the group.

THE CRISIS, NOT THE CLIMAX

The Supreme Ordeal is a major nerve ganglion of the story. Many threads of the hero's history lead in, and many threads of possibility and change lead out the other side. It should not be confused with the climax of the Hero's Journey — that's another nerve center further down near the end of the story (like the brain at the base of a dinosaur's tail). The Ordeal is usually the central event of the story, or the main event of the second act. Let's call it the **crisis** to differentiate it from the **climax** (the big moment of Act Three and the crowning event of the whole story).

A crisis is defined by Webster's as "the point in a story or drama at which hostile forces are in the tensest state of opposition." We also speak of a crisis in an illness; a point, perhaps a high spike of fever, after which the patient either gets worse or begins to recover. The message: Sometimes things have to get worse before they can get better. A Supreme Ordeal crisis, however frightening to the hero, is sometimes the only way to recovery or victory.

PLACEMENT OF THE ORDEAL

The placement of the crisis or Supreme Ordeal depends on the needs of the story and the tastes of the storyteller. The most common pattern is for the death-and-rebirth moment to come near the middle

Central Crisis

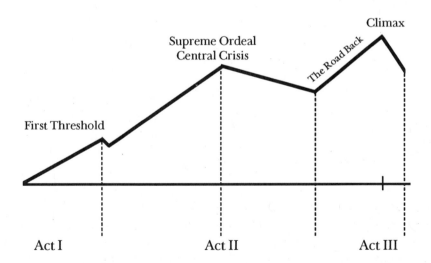

Major Dramatic High Points in a Story with a *Central* Crisis

183

of the story, as shown in the Central Crisis diagram.

A **central crisis** has the advantage of symmetry, and leaves plenty of time for elaborate consequences to flow from the ordeal. Note that this structure allows for another critical moment or turning point at the end of Act Two.

Delayed Crisis

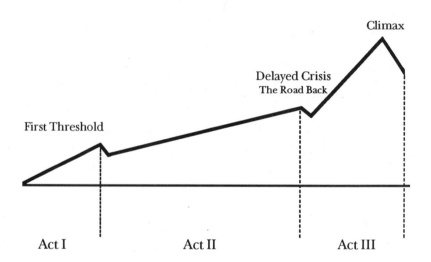

Major Dramatic High Points in a Story with a *Delayed* Crisis

However an equally effective structure can be built with a **delayed crisis** that comes near the end of Act Two, about two-thirds to three-quarters of the way into the story.

The delayed crisis structure matches closely with the ideal of the Golden Mean, that elegant proportion (approximately three to five) that seems to produce the most pleasing artistic results. A delayed crisis leaves more room for preparation and Approach and allows a slow buildup to a big moment at the end of Act Two.

Whether the crisis is at the center of the story or nearer the end of
Act Two, it's safe to say every story needs a crisis moment that conveys
the Supreme Ordeal's sense of death and revival.

POINTS OF TENSION

Act Two is a long stretch for the writer and the audience, up to an
hour in an average feature film. You can look at the three-act
structure as a dramatic line stretched across two major points of
tension, the act breaks. Like a circus tent hanging on its poles,
structure is subject to gravity — the waning of the audience's attention
in the time between these peaks of tension. A story that has no
central moment of tension may sag like a circus tent that needs an
extra support pole in the middle. Act Two is an hour-long chunk of
your movie, or a hundred pages of your novel. It needs some kind of
structure to hold it in tension.

The crisis at the halfway point is a watershed, a continental divide in
the hero's journey, that acknowledges the traveler has reached the
middle of the trip. Journeys naturally arrange themselves around a
central event: getting to the top of the mountain, the depth of the
cave, the heart of the forest, the most intimate interior of a foreign
country, or the most secret place in your own soul. Everything in the
trip has been leading up to this moment, and everything after it will
be just going home. There may be even greater adventures to come —
the final moments of a trip may be the most exciting or memorable —
but every journey seems to have a center; a bottom or a peak,
somewhere near the middle.

The words crisis, critic, and critical come from a Greek word that
means "to separate". A crisis is an event that separates the two halves
of the story. After crossing this zone, which is often the borderland of
death, the hero is literally or metaphorically reborn and nothing will
ever be the same.

WITNESS TO SACRIFICE

The reality of a death-and-rebirth crisis may depend upon point of view. A witness is often an important part of this stage, someone standing nearby who sees the hero *appear* to die, momentarily mourns the death, and is elated when the hero is revived. Some of the death-and-resurrection effects in *Star Wars* depend on the presence of witnesses, such as the two robot Allies, R2D2 and C3PO. In an elaborate Supreme Ordeal sequence, they are listening by intercom to the progress of their heroes, Skywalker and company. The robots are horrified to hear what sounds like the heroes being crushed to death in a giant trashmasher deep in the Inmost Cave of the Deathstar.

These witnesses stand for the audience who are identifying with the heroes and feeling the pain of death with them. It's not that audiences are sadistic and enjoy seeing their heroes killed. It's that we all relish a little taste of death every now and then. Its bitter flavor makes life taste sweeter. Anyone who has survived a true near-death experience, a sudden close call in a car or plane, knows that for awhile afterward colors seem sharper, family and friends are more important, and time is more precious. The nearness of death makes life more real.

A TASTE OF DEATH

People pay good money for a taste of death. Bungee-jumping, skydiving, and terrifying amusement park rides give people the jolt that awakens fuller appreciation of life. Adventure films and stories are always popular because they offer a less risky way to experience death and rebirth, through heroes we can identify with.

But wait a minute, we left poor Luke Skywalker being crushed to death in the heart, or rather the stomach, of the Deathstar. He's in the belly of the whale. The robot witnesses are distraught at hearing what sounds like their master's death. They grieve and the audience grieves with them, tasting death. All of the film-maker's artful technique is dedicated to making the audience think their heroes are

186

being ground to a paste. But then the robots realize that what they thought were screams of death were in fact cries of relief and triumph. The robots managed to shut off the trashmasher and the heroes have miraculously survived. The grief of the robots and the audience suddenly, explosively, turns to joy.

THE ELASTICITY OF EMOTION

Human emotions, it seems, have certain elastic properties, rather like basketballs. When thrown down hard, they bounce back high. In any story you are trying to lift the audience, raise their awareness, heighten their emotions. The structure of a story acts like a pump to increase the involvement of the audience. Good structure works by alternately lowering and raising the hero's fortunes and with them, the audience's emotions. Depressing an audience's emotions has the same effect as holding an inflated basketball under water: When the downward pressure is released, the ball flies up out of the water. Emotions depressed by the presence of death can rebound in an instant to a higher state than ever before. This can become the base on which you build to a still higher level. The Supreme Ordeal is one of the deepest "depressions" in a story and therefore leads to one of its highest peaks.

In an amusement park ride you are hurled around in darkness or on the edge of space until you think you're going to die, but somehow you come out elated that you have survived. A story without some hint of this experience is missing its heart. Screenwriters sometimes have a lot of trouble with the length of Act Two. It can seem monotonous, episodic, or aimless. This may be because they've conceived of it as simply a series of obstacles to the hero's final goal, rather than as a dynamic series of events leading up to and trailing away from a central moment of death and rebirth. Even in the silliest comedy or most light-hearted romance, Act Two needs a central life or death crisis, a moment when the hero is experiencing death or maximum danger to the enterprise.

HERO APPEARS TO DIE

The long second act of *Star Wars* is kept from sagging by a central crisis section in which the borders of death are thoroughly explored in not one, but a series of ordeals. At another point in the giant trash compactor sequence, Luke is pulled under the sewage by the tentacle of an unseen monster. It was this scene that really made me understand the mechanism of the Supreme Ordeal.

First, the audience and the witnesses at hand (Han Solo, Princess Leia, the Wookie) see a few bubbles come up, a sign that Luke is still struggling, alive, and breathing. So far, so good. But then the bubbles stop coming. The witnesses begin reacting as if he were dead. In a few seconds you begin to wonder if he's ever coming up. You know George Lucas is not going to kill off his hero halfway through the film and yet you begin to entertain the possibility.

I remember seeing a preview screening of *Star Wars* on the Fox lot and being completely taken in by the critical few seconds of this scene. I had invested something of myself in Luke Skywalker and when he appeared to be dead, I instantly became a disembodied presence in the screen. I began flitting from surviving character to character, wondering who I could identify with next. Would I ride through the rest of the story as the spoiled Princess Leia, the selfish opportunist Han Solo, or the beastly Wookie? I didn't feel comfortable in any of their skins. In these few seconds I experienced something like panic. The hero, for me, was truly in the belly of the whale, inaccessible, effectively dead. With the hero dead, who was I in this movie? What was my point of view? My emotions, like the basketball held under water, were depressed.

Just then Luke Skywalker explodes to the surface, slimy but alive. He has died to our eyes, but now he lives again, rebirthed by the companions who help him to his feet. At once the audience feels elated. The emotions ride higher for having been brought down so far. Experiences like this are the key to the popularity of the Star Wars movies. They fling heroes and audiences over the brink of death and snatch them back repeatedly. It's more than great special effects, funny dialogue, and sex that people are paying for. They love to see heroes cheat death. In fact they love to cheat death themselves. Identifying with a hero who bounces back from death is bungee-jumping in dramatic form.

HERO WITNESSES DEATH

Star Wars has not given us enough of a taste of death yet. Before the Supreme Ordeal section is over, Luke witnesses the physical death of his Mentor, Obi Wan, in a laser duel with the villain Darth Vader. Luke is devastated and feels the death as keenly as if it were his own. But in this mythical world, the borders of life and death are deliberately fuzzy. Obi Wan's body vanishes, raising the possibility he may survive somewhere to return when needed, like King Arthur and Merlin.

To a shaman like Obi Wan, death is a familiar threshold that can be crossed back and forth with relative ease. Obi Wan lives within Luke and the audience through his teachings. Despite physical death he is able to give Luke crucial advice at later points in the story: "Trust the Force, Luke".

HERO CAUSES DEATH

The hero doesn't have to die for the moment of death to have its effect. The hero may be a witness to death or the cause of death. In *Body Heat* the central event, William Hurt's Supreme Ordeal, is murdering Kathleen Turner's husband and disposing of his body. But it's a death for Hurt too, deep in his soul. His innocence has died, a victim of his own lust.

FACING THE SHADOW

By far the most common kind of Supreme Ordeal is some sort of battle or confrontation with an opposing force. It could be a deadly enemy, villain, antagonist, opponent, or even a force of nature. An

189

idea that comes close to encompassing all these possibilities is the archetype of the Shadow. A villain may be an external character, but in a deeper sense what all these words stand for is the negative possibilities of the hero himself. In other words, the hero's greatest opponent is his own Shadow.

As with all the archetypes, there are negative and positive manifestations of the Shadow. A dark side is needed sometimes to polarize a hero or a system, to give the hero some resistance to push against. Resistance can be your greatest source of strength. Ironically, what seem to be villains fighting for our death may turn out to be forces ultimately working for our good.

DEMONIZATION

Generally the Shadow represents the hero's fears and unlikeable, rejected qualities; all the things we don't like about ourselves and try to project onto other people. This form of projection is called **demonizing**. People in emotional crisis will sometimes project all their problems in a certain area onto another person or group who become the symbol of everything they hate and fear in themselves. In war and propaganda, the enemy becomes an inhuman devil, the dark Shadow of the righteous, angelic image we are trying to maintain for ourselves. The Devil himself is God's shadow, a projection of all the negative and rejected potential of the Supreme Being.

Sometimes we need this projection and polarization in order to see an issue clearly. A system can stay in unhealthy imbalance for a long time if the conflicts are not categorized, polarized, and made to duke it out in some kind of dramatic confrontation. Usually the Shadow can be brought out into the light. The unrecognized or rejected parts are acknowledged and made conscious despite all their struggling to remain in darkness. Dracula's abhorrence of sunlight is a symbol of the Shadow's desire to remain unexplored.

Villains can be looked at as the hero's Shadow in human form. No matter how alien the villain's values, in some way they are the dark reflection of the hero's own desires, magnified and distorted, her greatest fears come to life.

DEATH OF A VILLAIN

Sometimes the hero comes close to death at the Supreme Ordeal, but it is the villain who dies. However, the hero may have other forces, other Shadows, to deal with before the adventure is over. The action may move from the physical arena to a moral, spiritual, or emotional plane. Dorothy kills the Wicked Witch in Act Two, but faces an ordeal of the spirit: the death of her hopes of getting home in Act Three.

A villain's death should not be too easy for the hero to accomplish. In a Supreme Ordeal scene in Hitchcock's *Torn Curtain*, the hero tries to kill a spy in a farmhouse with no real weapons at hand. Hitchcock makes the point that killing someone can be much harder than the movies usually make it seem. Anyone's death has an emotional cost, as well, as the movie *Unforgiven* repeatedly shows. Clint Eastwood's bounty hunter kills but is painfully aware his targets are men just like him. Death should be real, and not a mere plot convenience.

THE VILLAIN ESCAPES

The hero may wound the villain at the Supreme Ordeal or kill the villain's underling. The chief villain escapes to be confronted once again in Act Three. Axel Foley has a death-and-rebirth confrontation with the criminal mastermind's lieutenants in Act Two of *Beverly Hills Cop*, but the final showdown with the main Shadow is held back for Act Three.

VILLAINS ARE HEROES OF THEIR OWN STORIES

Keep in mind that while some villains or Shadows exult in being bad, many don't think of themselves as evil at all. In their own minds they are right, the heroes of their own stories. A dark moment for the hero is a bright one for a Shadow. The arcs of their stories are mirror images: when the hero is up, the villain is down. It depends on point of view. By the time you are done writing a screenplay or novel, you should know your characters well enough that you can tell the story from the point of view of everyone: heroes, villains, sidekicks, lovers, allies, guardians, and lesser folk. Each is the hero of his own story. It's a good exercise to walk through the story at least once in the Shadow's skin.

HOW HEROES CHEAT DEATH

In the classic hero myths the Supreme Ordeal is set up as a moment in which the hero is expected to die. Many have come to this point before and none have survived. Perseus' Approach to the monster Medusa is choked with statues of heroes turned to stone by her glance. The labyrinth which Theseus enters is littered with the bones of those who were eaten by the monster inside or who starved trying to find their way out.

These mythic heroes face certain death but survive where others have failed because they have wisely sought supernatural aid in the earlier stages. They cheat death, usually with the help of the Mentor's gifts. Perseus uses the magic mirror, Athena's gift, to approach Medusa and avoid her direct gaze. He cuts off her head with his magic sword and keeps it from doing further harm by stowing it in his magic pouch, another Mentor's gift.

In the story of Theseus, the hero has won the love of Ariadne, daughter of the tyrant Minos of Crete, in the Approach phase. Now, when Theseus must go into the uncertain, deadly depths of the Labyrinth, he turns to Ariadne for aid. The princess goes to the Mentor of the story, the great inventor and architect Daedalus, designer of the Labyrinth. His magical help is of the simplest kind: a ball of thread. Ariadne holds one end while Theseus winds through the Labyrinth. He is able to find his way back from the house of death because of his connection to her — because of love, the thread that binds them.

ARIADNE'S THREAD

Ariadne's Thread is a potent symbol of the power of love, of the almost telepathic wiring that joins people in an intense relationship. It can tug at you like a physical connector at times. It's close kin to the "apron strings" that bind even adult children to their mothers — invisible wires but with greater tensile strength than steel.

Ariadne's Thread is an elastic band that connects a hero with loved ones. A hero may venture far out into madness or death, but is usually pulled back by such bonds. My mother tells me she had a medical emergency when I was a child that almost killed her. Her spirit left her body and flew around the room, feeling free and ready to leave, and only the sight of my sisters and I snapped her back into life. She had a reason to go on living, to take care of us.

The old English word for a ball of thread is a "clew". That's where we get our word clue. A clue is a thread that a seeker traces back to a center, looking for answers or order. The skeins of thread that connect one heart to another may be the vital clue that solves a mystery or resolves a conflict.

CRISIS OF THE HEART

The Supreme Ordeal can be a crisis of the heart. In a story of romance it might be the moment of greatest intimacy, something we all desire and yet fear. Perhaps what's dying here is a hero's defensiveness. In another story it might be a dark moment in the romance when the hero experiences betrayal or the apparent death of the relationship.

Joseph Campbell describes what we might call the romantic branches of the Supreme Ordeal in two chapters of *The Hero With a Thousand Faces* called "Meeting with the Goddess" and "Woman as Temptress". As he says, "the ultimate adventure...is commonly represented as a mystical marriage...the crisis at the nadir, the zenith, or at the uttermost edge of the earth, at the central point of the cosmos, in the

193

cosmos, in the tabernacle of the temple, or within the darkness of the deepest chamber of the heart." In stories of love, the crisis may be either a love scene or a separation from a loved one. Crisis, remember, comes from a Greek word meaning "to separate".

In *Romancing the Stone* the crisis is both a physical Supreme Ordeal and a separation of loved ones. Joan Wilder and her shapeshifting companion Jack Colton enter a literal Inmost Cave where they take possession of the giant emerald, *El Corazon*. But that's much too easy, and a few moments later they go through a real Supreme Ordeal as their car plunges over a waterfall and they dive out. Joan Wilder disappears under the water for several shots. The audience sees Jack Colton struggle ashore, and for scant seconds we are left wondering if Joan has died. Those few seconds are sufficient for the magic of the Supreme Ordeal to work. Joan then appears, struggling onto a rock in the foreground. That she has died and been reborn is clearly acknowledged in the dialogue. On the opposite bank, Colton cries out "I thought you drowned." Joan acknowledges "I did."

Colton is elated by their physical survival, but now the focus of the crisis for Joan shifts to the emotional plane. The untrustworthy Colton is on the opposite side of the raging river with the jewel. A real test of their love is coming. Will he keep his promise to meet her in the next town, or will he simply run away with *El Corazon* and break her heart? Will she be able to survive in the jungle of the Special World without him?

SACRED MARRIAGE

In stories with emotional and psychological depth, the Supreme Ordeal may bring a moment of mystic marriage within a person, a balancing of opposing inner forces. The fear and death aspect of the Ordeal may haunt the wedding: What if this doesn't work out? What if the part of myself I am walking to the altar with turns and overwhelms me? But despite these fears, heroes may acknowledge their hidden qualities, even their Shadows, and join with them in a sacred marriage. Heroes are ultimately seeking a confrontation with their anima, their soul, or the unrecognized feminine or intuitive parts of their personality.

Women may be seeking the animus, the masculine powers of reason and assertion that society has told them to hide. They may be trying to get back in touch with a creative drive or a maternal energy they've rejected. In a moment of crisis, a hero may get in touch with all sides of her personality, as her many selves are called forth en masse to deal with her life and death issues.

BALANCE

In a Sacred Marriage both sides of the personality are acknowledged to be of equal value. Such a hero, in touch with all the tools of being a human, is in a state of balance, centered, and not easily dislodged or upset. Campbell says the Sacred Marriage "represents the hero's total mastery of life," a balanced marriage between the hero and life itself.

Therefore the Supreme Ordeal may be a crisis in which the hero is joined with the repressed feminine or masculine side in a Sacred Marriage. But there may also be a Sacred Break-up! Open, deadly war may be declared by the dueling male and female sides.

THE LOVE THAT KILLS

Campbell touches on this destructive conflict in "The Woman as Temptress". The title is perhaps misleading — as with "The Meeting with the Goddess", the energy of this moment could be male or female. This Ordeal possibility takes the hero to a junction of betrayal, abandonment, or disappointment. It's a crisis of faith in the arena of love.

Every archetype has both a bright, positive side and a dark, negative side. The dark side of love is the mask of hate, recrimination, outrage, and rejection. This is the face of Medea as she kills her own children, the mask of Medusa herself, ringed with poison snakes of blame and guilt.

195

A crisis may come when a shapeshifting lover suddenly shows another side, leaving the hero feeling bitterly betrayed and dead to the idea of love. This is a favorite Hitchcock device. After a tender love scene in *North By Northwest* Cary Grant's character is betrayed to the spies by Eva Marie Saint. Grant goes into his mid-movie Ordeal feeling abandoned by her. The possibility of true love that she represented now seems dead, and it makes his Ordeal, in which he's almost gunned down by a cropdusting plane in a cornfield, all the more lonely.

NEGATIVE ANIMUS OR ANIMA

Sometimes in the journey of our lives we confront negative projections of the anima or animus. This can be a person who attracts us but isn't good for us, or a bitchy or bastardly part of ourselves that suddenly asserts itself like Mr. Hyde taking over from Dr. Jekyll. Such a confrontation can be a life-threatening Ordeal in a relationship or in a person's development. The hero of *Fatal Attraction* finds that a casual lover can turn into a lethal force if crossed or rejected. An ideal partner can turn into the Boston Strangler or a loving father can become a killer as in *The Shining*. The wicked stepmothers and queens of Grimms' fairy tales were, in the original versions, mothers whose love turned deadly.

GOING PSYCHO

One of the most disturbing and subversive uses of the Supreme Ordeal is Alfred Hitchcock's *Psycho*. The audience is made to identify and sympathize with Marion (Janet Leigh), even though she is an embezzler on the run. Through the first half of Act Two, there is no one else to identify with except the drippy innkeeper, Norman Bates (Anthony Perkins), and no audience wants to identify with him — he's weird. In a conventional film, the hero always survives the Supreme Ordeal, and lives to see the villain defeated in the climax. It's unimaginable that a star like Janet Leigh, an immortal heroine of the screen, will be sacrificed at the midpoint. But Hitchcock does the unthinkable and kills our hero halfway through the story. This is one

Supreme Ordeal that is final for the hero. No reprieve, no resurrection, no curtain call for Marion.

The effect is shattering. You get that odd feeling of being a disembodied ghost, floating around the frame as you watch Marion's blood pour down the drain. Who to identify with? Who to be? Soon it's clear: Hitchcock is giving you no one to identify with but Norman. Reluctantly, we enter Norman's mind, see the story through his eyes, and even begin to root for him as our new hero. At first we're supposed to think Norman is covering up for his insane mother, but later we discover Norman himself was the killer. We have been walking around in the skin of a psycho. Only a master like Hitchcock can pull off such a defiance of the rules about heroes, death, and Supreme Ordeals.

FACING THE GREATEST FEAR

The Supreme Ordeal can be defined as the moment the hero faces his greatest fear. For most people this is death, but in many stories it's just whatever the hero is most afraid of: facing up to a phobia, challenging a rival, or toughing out a storm or a political crisis. Indiana Jones inevitably must come face to face with what he fears most — snakes.

Of the many fears faced by heroes, the greatest dramatic power seems to come from the fear of standing up to a parent or authority figure. The family scene is the core of most serious drama, and a confrontation with a parent figure can provide a strong Supreme Ordeal.

STANDING UP TO A PARENT

In *Red River*, Montgomery Clift's character Matthew Garth faces this fear halfway through the story, when he tries to take away control of a cattle drive from his foster-father Tom Dunston (John Wayne) who has become a formidable Shadow. Dunston started the story as hero and Mentor, but traded those masks for that of a tyrant in the Approach phase. He's turned into a demented god, wounded, drunk, and cruel; an abusive father to his men, carrying duty too far. When Matt challenges his Mentor and role model he is facing his greatest fear in a Supreme Ordeal.

Dunston decrees he will play god and hang men who broke the laws of his little world. Matt stands up to him at the risk of being shot himself. Dunston, the Lord Death rising from his throne, draws to kill him; but Matt's Allies, earned in the Testing phase, step in and blow the gun out of Dunston's hand. Matt's power as a hero is now such that he doesn't need to lift a finger against his opponent. His will alone is strong enough to defeat death. In effect he dethrones Dunston and becomes king of the cattle drive himself, leaving his foster-father with nothing but a horse and a canteen. In stories like this, facing the greatest fear is depicted as youth standing up to the older generation.

YOUTH VERSUS AGE

The challenging of the older generation by the younger is a timeless drama, and the Supreme Ordeal of standing up to a forbidding parent is as old as Adam and Eve, Oedipus, or King Lear. This ageless conflict provides much of the power of playwrighting. The play *On Golden Pond* deals with a daughter's frantic effort to please her father, and its Ordeals are the daughter standing up to the father, and the father experiencing his own mortality.

This generational drama is sometimes played out on a world stage. The Chinese dissident students who took over Tiananmen Square and blocked the tanks with their bodies were challenging the status quo imposed by their parents and grandparents.

Fairy tale struggles with wolves and witches may be ways of expressing conflicts with parents. The witches are the dark aspect of the mother; the wolves, ogres, or giants the dark aspect of the father. Dragons and other monsters can be the Shadow side of a parent or a generation that has held on too long. Campbell spoke of the dragon as a Western symbol of a tyrant who has held fast to a kingdom or a family until all the life has been squeezed out of it.

The conflict between youth and age can be expressed internally as well as in external battles between children and parents. The smoldering combat that ignites in the Supreme Ordeal may be an inner struggle between an old, comfortable, well defended personality structure and a new one that is weak, unformed, but eager to be born. But the new Self can't be born until the old one dies or at least steps aside to leave more room on the center stage.

In rare cases a Supreme Ordeal can be the occasion for a healing of deep wounds between a hero and a parent. Campbell calls this possibility "Atonement with the Father". Sometimes a hero, by surviving an Ordeal or by daring to challenge the authority of a parental figure, will win the parent's approval and the seeming conflicts between them will be resolved.

DEATH OF THE EGO

The Supreme Ordeal in myths signifies the death of the ego. The hero is now fully part of the cosmos, dead to the old, limited vision of things and reborn into a new consciousness of connections. The old boundaries of the Self have been transcended or annihilated. In some sense the hero has become a god with the divine ability to soar above the normal limits of death and see the broader view of the connectedness of all things. The Greeks called this a moment of **apotheosis**, a step up from enthusiasm where you merely have the god in you. In a state of apotheosis you **are** the god. Tasting death lets you sit in God's chair for awhile.

The hero facing a Supreme Ordeal has moved her center from the ego to the Self, to the more god-like part of her. There may also be a movement from Self to group as a hero accepts more responsibility than just looking out for herself. A hero risks individual life for the sake of the larger collective life and wins the right to be called "hero".

199

THE WIZARD OF OZ

Dorothy and friends, trapped by the Wicked Witch and her Threshold Guardian army, now face their Supreme Ordeal. The Witch is enraged at them for having penetrated her Inmost Cave and stolen her greatest treasure, the Ruby Slippers. She descends on the foursome and threatens to kill them one by one, saving Dorothy until last.

The threat of death makes the stakes of the scene clear. The audience now knows it's going to be a battle between forces of life and death.

The Witch begins with the Scarecrow. She lights her broomstick and uses it as a torch to set him on fire. His straw blazes up and it looks like all is lost. Every child in the audience believes the Scarecrow is doomed and feels the horror of death with him.

Dorothy operates on instinct and does the only thing she can think of to save her friend: She grabs up a bucket of water and splashes it all over the Scarecrow. It puts out the fire, but it also wets down the Witch. Dorothy had no intention of killing the Witch, didn't even realize water would make her melt, but has killed her just the same. Death was in the room, and Dorothy merely deflected it onto another victim.

But the Witch does not just go "poof" and disappear. Her death is protracted, agonizing, and pathetic. "Oh, my beautiful wickedness! What a world, what a world!" By the time it's over you feel sorry for the Witch, and have had a real taste of death.

→▭ ▭←

Our heroes have gone face to face with death and can walk away to tell about it. After a moment of being stunned, they are elated. They go on to reap the consequences of defying death, in the next step, Reward, or Seizing the Sword.

QUESTIONING THE JOURNEY

1. What is the Supreme Ordeal in *Silence of the Lambs? Prince of Tides? Pretty Woman?*

2. What is the Supreme Ordeal in your story? Does your story truly have a villain? Or is there simply an antagonist?

3. In what way is the villain or antagonist the hero's Shadow?

4. Is the villain's power channeled through partners or underlings? What special functions do these parts perform?

5. Can the villain also be a Shapeshifter or Trickster? What other archetypes might a villain manifest?

6. In what way does your hero face death in the Supreme Ordeal? What is your hero's greatest fear?

REWARD
(SEIZING THE SWORD)

STAGE NINE : REWARD

"We came, we saw, we kicked its ass."

from *Ghostbusters,* screenplay by
Dan Aykroyd and Harold Ramis

With the crisis of the Supreme Ordeal passed, heroes now
experience the consequences of surviving death. With the dragon
that dwelt in the Inmost Cave slain or vanquished, they seize the
sword of victory and lay claim to their **Reward**. Triumph may be
fleeting but for now they savor its pleasures.

> *We Seekers look at one other with growing smiles. We've won the
> right to be called heroes. For the sake of the Home Tribe we faced
> death, tasted it, and yet lived. From the depths of terror we
> suddenly shoot up to victory. It's time to fill our empty bellies
> and raise our voices around the campfire to sing of our deeds.
> Old wounds and grievances are forgotten. The story of our
> journey is already being woven.*

> *You pull apart from the rest, strangely quiet. In the leaping
> shadows you remember those who didn't make it, and you notice
> something. You're different. You've changed. Part of you has died
> and something new has been born. You and the world will
> never seem the same. This too is part of the Reward for facing
> death.*

Encountering death is a big event and it will surely have
consequences. There will almost always be some period of time in
which the hero is recognized or rewarded for having survived death
or a great ordeal. A great many possibilities are generated by living
through a crisis, and Reward, the aftermath of the Supreme Ordeal,
has many shapes and purposes.

CELEBRATION

When hunters have survived death and brought down their game, it's natural to want to celebrate. Energy has been exhausted in the struggle, and needs to be replenished. Heroes may have the equivalent of a party or barbecue at this stage in which they cook and consume some of the fruits of victory. The heroes of the Odyssey always offered a sacrifice and had a meal to give thanks and celebrate after surviving some ordeal at sea. Strength is needed for the return to the upper world, so time is given for rest, recuperation and refueling. After the buffalo hunt (a Supreme Ordeal and brush with death) in *Dances With Wolves*, Dunbar and the tribe celebrate with a buffalo barbecue in which his Reward for saving a young man from death is greater acceptance by the Lakota.

CAMPFIRE SCENES

Many stories seem to have campfire type scenes in this region, where the hero and companions gather around a fire or its equivalent to review the recent events. It's also an opportunity for jokes and boasting. There is understandable relief at having survived death. Hunters and fishermen, pilots and navigators, soldiers and explorers all like to exaggerate their accomplishments. At the barbecue in *Dances With Wolves*, Dunbar is forced to retell the story of the buffalo hunt many times.

There may be conflict over the campfire, fighting over spoils. Dunbar gets into an argument over his hat which has been picked up by a Sioux warrior after Dunbar dropped it during the buffalo hunt.

A campfire scene may also be a chance for reminiscence or nostalgia. Having crossed the abyss of life and death, nothing will ever be the same. Heroes sometimes turn back and remember aloud what got them to this point. A loner hero might recall the events or people who influenced him, or speak about the unwritten code by which he runs his life.

These scenes serve important functions for the audience. They allow us to catch our breath after an exciting battle or ordeal. The characters might recap the story so far, giving us a chance to review the story and get a glimpse of how they perceive it. In *Red River*, Matthew Garth reviews the plot for a newcomer to the story, Tess (Joanne Dru), in a campfire scene. He reveals his feelings about his fosterfather and gives the audience a perspective on the complex, epic story.

In these quiet moments of reflection or intimacy we get to know the characters better. A memorable example is the scene in *Jaws* in which Robert Shaw's character Quint tells about his horrible World War II experiences with sharks in the Pacific. The men compare scars and sing a drinking song. It's a "getting-to-know-you" scene, built on the intimacy that comes from having survived an Ordeal together.

In Walt Disney's classic animated features such as *Pinocchio* or *Peter Pan*, the pace is usually frantic, but Disney was careful to slow them down from time to time and get in close on the characters in an emotional moment. These quieter or more lyric passages are important for making a connection with the audience.

LOVE SCENES

The aftermath of a Supreme Ordeal may be an opportunity for a love scene. Heroes don't really become heroes until the crisis; until then they are just trainees. They don't really deserve to be loved until they have shown their willingness to sacrifice. At this point a true hero has earned a love scene, or a "sacred marriage" of some kind. The *Red River* campfire scene described above is also a highly effective love scene.

In the thriller *Arabesque*, Gregory Peck and Sophia Loren, having survived an Ordeal together, are bonded in a love scene. She is a bewildering Shapeshifter who has told him a string of lies, but he has seen through to her essential core of goodness, and now trusts her.

The romantic waltz in *Beauty and the Beast* is the Beast's Reward for having survived an Ordeal with the townspeople and Belle's Reward for having seen past the Beast's monstrous appearance.

TAKING POSSESSION

One of the essential aspects of this step is the hero taking possession of whatever she came seeking. Treasure hunters take the gold, spies snatch the secret, pirates plunder the captured ship, an uncertain hero seizes her self-respect, a slave seizes control of his own destiny. A transaction has been made — the hero has risked death or sacrificed life, and now gets something in exchange. The Norse god Odin, in his Supreme Ordeal, gives up an eye and hangs on the World-Tree for nine days and nights. His Reward is the knowledge of all things and the ability to read the sacred runes.

SEIZING THE SWORD

I also call this unit of the journey **Seizing the Sword** because often it's an active movement of the hero who aggressively takes possession of whatever was being sought in the Special World. Sometimes a reward like love is given. But more frequently the hero takes possession of a treasure or even steals it, like James Bond taking the Lektor, a Soviet translating device, in *From Russia with Love.*

A moment of taking possession follows the death and rebirth crisis in *King Kong.* A transformation had occured in the monster ape during the Approach phase. King Kong shifted from being Fay Wray's abductor to being her protector, fighting off a tyrannosaur on the way to his Inmost Cave. By the time he reaches the Supreme Ordeal, defending her in a battle to the death with a giant serpent, he has become a full-fledged hero. Now he takes possession of his Reward. Like any good hero, he gets the girl.

In a tender but erotic scene, he takes her out onto the "balcony" of his cave and examines her, cradled in his enormous palm. He pulls off her clothes, strip by strip, sniffing her perfume curiously. He tickles her with his finger. The love scene is interrupted by another dinosaur threat, but it was definitely a Reward moment, a payback for having faced death head on during the crisis.

The idea of a hero Seizing the Sword comes from memories of stories in which heroes battle dragons and take their treasure. Among the treasures there may be a magic sword, perhaps the sword of the hero's father, broken or stolen by the dragon in previous battles. The image of the sword, as portrayed in the Tarot deck's suit of swords, is a symbol of the hero's will, forged in fire and quenched in blood, broken and remade, hammered and folded, hardened, sharpened, and focussed to a point like the light sabers of *Star Wars*.

But a sword is only one of many images for what is being seized by the hero at this step. Campbell's term for it is "The Ultimate Boon". Another concept is the Holy Grail, an ancient and mysterious symbol for all the unattainable things of the soul that knights and heroes quest after. A rose or a jewel may be the treasure in another story. The wily Monkey King of Chinese legends is seeking the sacred Buddhist sutras that have been taken to Tibet.

ELIXIR THEFT

Some heroes purchase the treasure in effect, buying it with their lives or the willingness to risk life. But other heroes steal the magic thing at the heart of the story. The prize is not always given, even if it has been paid for or earned. It must be taken. Campbell calls this motif "elixir theft".

Elixir means a medium or vehicle for medicine. It could be a harmless sweet liquid or powder to which other medicine is added. Administered alone or mixed with other useless chemicals, it might still work by what's known as the "placebo effect". Studies have shown that some people get better on a placebo, a substance with no medicinal value, even when they know it's just a sugar pill — testimony to the power of suggestion.

An elixir can also be a medicine that heals every ill, a magical substance that restores life. In alchemy the elixir is one of the steps towards the philosopher's stone which can transmute metals, create life, and transcend death. This ability to overcome the forces of death is the real Elixir most heroes seek.

The hero is often required to steal the Elixir. It is the secret of life and death, and much too valuable to be given up lightly. Heroes may turn Trickster or thief to make off with the treasure, like Prometheus stealing fire from the gods for mankind, or Adam and Eve tasting the apple. This theft may intoxicate the hero for a time, but there is often a heavy price to pay later.

INITIATION

Heroes emerge from their Ordeals to be recognized as special and different, part of a select few who have outwitted death. The Immortals of ancient Greece were a very exclusive club. Only the gods and a smattering of lucky humans were exempt from death, and only those humans who had done something remarkable or pleasing to the gods would be granted admittance by Zeus. Among these were Hercules, Andromeda, and Aesculapius.

Battlefield promotions and knighthood are ways of recognizing that heroes have passed an ordeal and entered a smaller group of special survivors. Joseph Campbell's overall name for what we are calling Act Two is "Initiation", a new beginning in a new rank. The hero after facing death is really a new creature. A woman who has gone through the life-threatening territory of childbirth belongs to a different order of being. She has been initiated into the company of motherhood, a select sorority.

Initiation into secret societies, sororities, or fraternities means that you are privy to certain secrets and sworn never to reveal them. You pass tests to prove your worthiness. You may be put through a ritual death-and-rebirth Ordeal and may be given a new name and rank to signify you are a newborn being.

NEW PERCEPTIONS

Heroes may find that surviving death grants new powers or better perceptions. In the previous chapter we spoke of death's ability to sharpen the perception of life. This is beautifully captured in the northern tale of Sigurd the dragon-killer. Sigurd's Supreme Ordeal is to slay a dragon named Fafnir. A drop of the dragon's blood happens to fall on Sigurd's tongue. He has truly tasted death, and for this is granted new powers of perception. He can understand the language of the the birds, and hears two of them warning him that his Mentor, the dwarf Regin, plans to kill him. He is saved from a second deadly danger because of his new-found power, the Reward for surviving death. New knowledge may be the sword that the hero seizes.

SEEING THROUGH DECEPTION

A hero may be granted a new insight or understanding of a mystery as her Reward. She may see through a deception. If she has been dealing with a shapeshifting partner, she may see through his disguises and perceive the reality for the first time. Seizing the Sword can be a moment of clarity.

CLAIRVOYANCE

After transcending death, a hero may even become clairvoyant or telepathic, sharing in the power of the immortal gods. Clairvoyant means simply "seeing clearly". A hero who has faced death is more aware of the connectedness of things, more intuitive. In *Arabesque*, after the love scene between Gregory Peck and Sophia Loren, the lovers are trying to figure out a secret code in ancient hieroglyphics. Peck suddenly realizes, with his newfound perceptive ability, that what the spies are after is not the code but a microfilm dot on the piece of paper. Surviving death has given him new power of insight. The realization is so exciting that it propels the movie into Act Three.

SELF-REALIZATION

Insight might be of a deeper type. Heroes can sometimes experience a profound **self-realization** after tricking death. They see who they are and how they fit into the scheme of things. They see the ways they've been foolish or stubborn. The scales fall from their eyes and the illusion of their lives is replaced with clarity and truth. Maybe it doesn't last long, but for a moment heroes see themselves clear.

EPIPHANY

Others may see the hero more clearly, too. Others may see in their changed behavior signs that they have been reborn and share in the immortality of gods. This is sometimes called a moment of **epiphany**: an abrupt realization of divinity. The Feast of the Epiphany, observed in the Catholic Church on January 6, celebrates the moment when the Magi, three Wise Old Men, first realized the divinity of the newborn Christ. One of the Rewards of surviving death is that others can see that heroes have changed. Young people coming back from a war or from an ordeal like basic training seem different — more mature, self-confident, and serious, and worthy of a little more respect. There is a chain of divine experience, from enthusiasm, being visited by a god; to apotheosis, becoming a god; to epiphany, being recognized as a god.

Heroes themselves may experience epiphany. A hero may realize suddenly, after a moment of Supreme Ordeal, that he is the son of a god or a king, a chosen one with special powers. Epiphany is a moment of realizing you are a divine and sacred being, connected to all things.

James Joyce expanded the meaning of the word epiphany, using it to mean a sudden perception of the essence of something, seeing to the core of a person, idea, or thing. Heroes sometimes experience a sudden understanding of the nature of things after passing through an Ordeal. Surviving death gives meaning to life and sharpens perceptions.

210

DISTORTIONS

In other stories the conquest of death may lead to some distortions of perception. Heroes may suffer from an inflation of the ego. In other words they get a swelled head. They might turn cocky or arrogant. Perhaps they abuse the power and privilege of being a reborn hero. Their self esteem sometimes grows too large and distorts their perception of their real value.

Heroes may be tainted by the very death or evil they came to fight. Soldiers fighting to preserve civilization may fall into the barbarism of war. Cops or detectives battling criminals often cross the line and use illegal or immoral means, becoming as bad as the criminals themselves. Heroes can enter the mental world of their opponents and get stuck there, like the detective in *Manhunter* who risks his soul to enter the twisted mind of a serial killer.

Bloodshed and murder are powerful forces and may intoxicate or poison a hero. Peter O'Toole as Lawrence of Arabia shows us a man who, after the Ordeal of the battle of Aqaba, is horrified to discover that he loves killing.

Another error heroes may make at this point is simply to underestimate the significance of the Supreme Ordeal. Someone hit by the hammer of change may deny that anything has happened. Denial after an encounter with death is one of the natural stages of grief and recovery described by Dr. Elizabeth Kubler-Ross. Anger is another. Heroes may just let off some steam after the Ordeal, expressing justifiable resentment over having been made to face death.

Heroes may also overestimate their own importance or prowess after a duel with death. But they may soon find out that they were just lucky the first time, and will have other encounters with danger that will teach them their limits.

211

THE WIZARD OF OZ

The immediate aftermath of the Ordeal in The Wizard of Oz
*is an act of Seizing. Instead of a sword, it's the burnt broomstick
of the Wicked Witch that Dorothy takes possession of. Actually
she's much too well mannered to just grab it; she politely asks for
it from the fearsome guards who have now fallen to their knees
to show their loyalty to her. Dorothy had good reason to fear they
would turn on her after the Witch's death. But in fact the guards
are glad the Witch is dead, for now they are free of her awful
slavery. Another Reward of surviving death is that Threshold
Guardians may be completely won over to the hero's side. The
guards give her the broomstick gladly.*

*Dorothy and companions return swiftly to the Wizard's
throneroom where she lays the broom before the ferocious
floating Head. She has fulfilled her bargain with the Wizard,
and completed the seemingly impossible task. Now she and her
friends claim their heroes' Reward.*

*But to their surprise, the Wizard balks at paying up. He gets
furious and argumentative. He is like an old personality
structure or a parent that knows it must yield to a maturing
offspring but is reluctant to let go, putting up one last fight.*

*It's then that the little dog Toto fulfills his purpose in the story.
His animal intuition and curiosity got Dorothy in trouble in the
first place, when he dug in Miss Gulch's flower bed. Now they
are the instrument of salvation. As Toto noses around behind
the throne, he discovers a meek little old man behind a curtain,
controlling the monstrous illusion of Oz, the great and
powerful. This man, not the bellowing head, is the real Wizard
of Oz.*

*This is a typical post-ordeal realization or moment of insight.
The heroes see, through the eyes of the intuitive, curious Toto,
that behind the illusion of the mightiest organization is a*

*human being with emotions that can be reached. (This scene
has always seemed to me a metaphor for Hollywood, which tries
very hard to be scary and awesome, but which is made up of
ordinary people with fears and flaws.)*

*At first the Wizard professes to be unable to help them, but with
encouragement he provides Elixirs for Dorothy's helpers: a
diploma for the Scarecrow, a medal of valor for the lion, and a
windup heart for the Tin Woodman. There is a tone of satire
about this scene. It seems to be saying: These Elixirs are
placebos, meaningless symbols that men give each other. Many
people with degrees, medals, or testimonials have done nothing
to earn them. Those who have not survived death can take the
Elixir all day long but it still won't help them.*

*The true all-healing Elixir is the achievement of inner change,
but the scene acknowledges that it's important to get outward
recognition as well. As a surrogate parent for the lot of them, the
Wizard is granting them the ultimate boon of a father's
approval, a Reward that few people get. Heart, brains, and
courage are inside them and always were, but the physical
objects serve as a reminder.*

*Now the Wizard turns to Dorothy and says sadly there is
nothing he can do for her. He was blown to Oz in a balloon
from the Nebraska state fair, and has no idea how to get back
home himself. He's right – only Dorothy can grant herself the self
acceptance to "get home", that is, be happy inside herself
wherever she is. But he agrees to try and orders a big hot air
balloon to be built by the citizens of Oz. The heroes have seized
everything except the elusive prize of home, which must be
sought in Act Three.*

Facing death has life-changing consequences which heroes experience by Seizing the Sword, but after experiencing their Reward fully, heroes must turn back to the quest. There are more ordeals ahead, and it's time to pack up and face them, on the next stage of the Hero's Journey, the Road Back.

QUESTIONING THE JOURNEY

1. What is the modern equivalent of a campfire scene in *Thelma and Louise? Sister Act? Ghost?*

2. What do the heroes of your stories learn by observing death? By causing death? By experiencing death?

3. What do the heroes of your story take possession of after facing death or their greatest fears? What is the aftermath, the consequence, of the major event of Act Two? Have your heroes absorbed any negative qualities from the Shadow or villain?

4. Does the story change direction? Is a new goal or agenda revealed in the Reward phase?

5. Is the aftermath of the Ordeal in your story an opportunity for a love scene?

6. Do your heroes realize they have changed? Is there self-examination or realization of wider consciousness? Have they learned to deal with their inner flaws?

THE ROAD BACK

STAGE TEN: THE ROAD BACK

"Easy is the descent to the Lower World; but, to retrace your steps and to escape to the upper air – this is the task, this the toil."

The Sibyl to Aeneas in *The Aeneid*

Once the lessons and Rewards of the great Ordeal have been celebrated and absorbed, heroes face a choice: whether to remain in the Special World or begin the journey home to the Ordinary World. Although the Special World may have its charms, few heroes elect to stay. Most take **The Road Back**, returning to the starting point or continuing on the journey to a totally new locale or ultimate destination.

This is a time when the story's energy, which may have ebbed a little in the quiet moments of Seizing the Sword, is now revved up again. If we look at the Hero's Journey as a circle with the beginning at the top, we are still down in the basement and it will take some push to get us back up into the light.

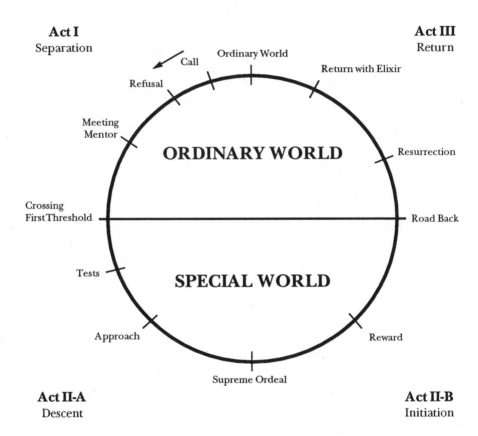

Act I
Separation

Act III
Return

Ordinary World

Call

Refusal

Return with Elixir

Meeting
Mentor

ORDINARY WORLD

Resurrection

Crossing
First Threshold

Road Back

Tests

SPECIAL WORLD

Approach

Reward

Supreme Ordeal

Act II-A
Descent

Act II-B
Initiation

Wake up, Seekers! Shake off the effects of our feast and celebration and remember why we came out here in the first place! People back home are starving and it's urgent, now that we've recovered from the ordeal, to load up our backpacks with food and treasure and head for home. Besides, there's no telling what dangers still lurk on the edge of the hunting grounds. You pause at the edge of camp to look back. They'll never believe this back home. How to tell them? Something bright on the ground catches your eye. You bend to pick it up — a beautiful smooth stone with an inner glow. Suddenly a dark shape darts out at you, all fangs. Run! Run for your life!

In psychological terms this stage represents the resolve of the hero to return to the Ordinary World and implement the lessons learned in the Special World. This can be far from easy. The hero has reason to fear that the wisdom and magic of the Ordeal may evaporate in the harsh light of common day. No one may believe the hero's miraculous escape from death. The adventures may be rationalized away by skeptics. But most heroes determine to try. Like the Boddhisattvas of Buddhist belief, they have seen the eternal plan but return to the world of the living to tell others about it, and share the elixir they have won.

MOTIVATION

The Road Back marks a time when heroes rededicate themselves to the adventure. A plateau of comfort has been reached and heroes must be pried off that plateau, either by their own inner resolve or by an external force.

Inner resolve might be represented by a scene of a tired commander rallying dispirited troops after a battle, or a parent pulling a family together after a death or tragedy. An external force might be an alarm going off, a clock ticking, or a renewed threat by a villain. The heroes may be reminded of the ultimate goal of the adventure.

The Road Back is a turning point, another threshold crossing which marks the passage from Act Two to Act Three. Like crossing the First Threshold, it may cause a change in the aim of the story. A story about achieving some goal becomes a story of escape; a focus on physical danger shifts to emotional risks. The propellant that boosts the story out of the depths of the Special World may be a new development or piece of information that drastically redirects the story. In effect, The Road Back *causes* the third act. It can be another moment of crisis that sets the hero on a new and final road of trials.

The rocket fuel may be fear of retaliation or pursuit. Often heroes are motivated to hit The Road Back when the forces they have defied in the Ordeal now rally and strike back at them. If the elixir was stolen from the central forces rather than given freely, there may be dangerous repercussions.

219

RETALIATION

An important lesson of martial arts is **Finish your opponent.** Heroes often learn that villains or Shadows who are not completely defeated in the crisis can rise up, stronger than before. The ogre or villain that the hero confronted in the Ordeal may pull himself together and strike a counter-blow. A parent who has been challenged for dominance in the family may get over the initial shock and unleash a devastating retaliation. A martial arts opponent knocked off balance may recover his center and deliver a surprise attack. In the Tiananmen Square incident, the Chinese government rallied after several days of confusion to launch a crushing response that drove the students and their Goddess of Liberty from the Square.

One of the most vivid examples of this retaliatory movement in films is in *Red River*, when Tom Dunston has been toppled from his throne by his foster-son Matthew Garth in a central Supreme Ordeal. In the Reward stage, while Matt and his men are celebrating in the town where they've sold the cattle, Dunston is busy recruiting a small army of gunmen. In The Road Back phase, he comes riding after Matt with the force of a railroad train and the stated intention of killing his adopted son. What had been a story of overcoming obstacles on a cattle drive, now becomes a story of a parent stalking his child to get revenge. The peculiar force of this passage is carried in John Wayne's physical acting. He lurches toward the showdown with Clift like a zombie, with the unstoppable energy of a machine, flicking cattle out of his path and shrugging off a bullet from a secondary character who tries to deflect him from his intent. He is the living image of the angry parental energy that can be roused by challenging a Shadow.

The psychological meaning of such counterattacks is that neuroses, flaws, habits, desires, or addictions we have challenged may retreat for a time, but can rebound in a last-ditch defense or a desperate attack before being vanquished forever. Neuroses have a powerful life force of their own and will strike back when threatened. Addicts who have made a first effort at recovery may fall off the wagon with a vengeance as their addiction fights back for its life.

Retaliation can take other forms. If you're hunting bear or killing dragons, you may find that the monster you killed in the Ordeal has a mate who comes chasing after you. A villain's lieutenant may survive him to pursue you, or you may find you have only killed an underling in the Ordeal. There may be a bigger Mr. Big who wants revenge for the loss of his servant.

An avenging force may strike a costly blow to the hero's fortunes, wounding him or killing one of his cohorts. This is when Expendable Friends come in handy. The villain might also steal back the elixir or kidnap one of the hero's friends in retaliation. This could lead to a rescue or chase, or both.

CHASE SCENES

In many cases heroes leave the Special World only because they are running for their lives. Chases may occur in any part of the story, but the end of Act Two is one of the most popular places. Chases are useful for torquing up a story's energy. Audiences may get sleepy at this point, and you have to wake them up with some action or conflict. In the theatre, this stage is called "racing for the curtain", a time when you want to pick up the pace and build momentum for the finish.

Chases are a favorite element of movies, and they figure prominently in literature, art, and mythology as well. The most famous chase in classical mythology is Apollo's pursuit of the shy nymph Daphne, who begged her father, a river god, to transform her into a laurel tree. Transformation is often an important aspect of chases and escapes. Modern heroes may simply assume a disguise in order to escape a tight situation. In a psychological drama, a hero may have to escape a pursuing inner demon by changing behavior or undergoing inner transformation.

MAGIC FLIGHT

Fairy tales often include a chase that involves a whimsical transformation of objects, known as the **magic flight** motif. In a typical story a little girl escapes from the clutches of a witch with the help of gifts from animals she's been kind to. The girl throws down the gifts one by one in the witch's path and they magically transform into barriers that delay the witch. A comb becomes a thick forest that slows the witch while she gobbles it up. A scarf becomes a wide river which she has to drink.

Joseph Campbell gives several illustrations of magical flights, and suggests the motif stands for a hero's attempts to stall the avenging forces in any way possible, by throwing down "protective interpretations, principles, symbols, rationalizations, anything... (to)...delay and absorb" their power.

What the hero throws down in a chase may also represent a sacrifice, the leaving behind of something of value. The little girl of the fairy tales may find it hard to part with the lovely scarf or comb given by the animals. Heroes of movie adventures sometimes have to decide what's really important, and toss money out the window to slow their pursuers and save their lives. Campbell cites the extreme example of Medea. Escaping with Jason from her father, she had Jason cut up her own brother and toss his pieces into the sea to delay the pursuit.

CHASE VARIATIONS: PURSUIT BY ADMIRERS

It's most common for heroes to be chased by villains, but there are other possibilities. An unusual variant of the chase is pursuit by admirers, for example in *Shane*, at the beginning of Act Three. Shane has been out on the farm trying to stay away from gunfighting, but now the brutality of the villains in the town draws him back. He tells the little farm boy (Brandon De Wilde) to stay behind, but the boy follows him at a distance. Behind the boy follows the boy's dog, who has also been told to stay home. The point is made that this kid is as faithful to Shane as a dog. It's a chase scene with a twist: Rather than hero fleeing villain, hero is being pursued by his admirer.

VILLAIN ESCAPE

Another chase scene variant is the pursuit of a escaped villain. A Shadow captured and controlled in the Ordeal escapes at this stage and becomes more dangerous than before. Hannibal "The Cannibal" Lecter in *Silence of the Lambs*, feeling betrayed by FBI agent Clarice, escapes and begins to kill again. King Kong, taken to New York to be displayed in chains, escapes and goes on a rampage. Countless movie and TV Westerns depict a villain trying to make a getaway, then being ridden down and tackled by the hero prior to a final fistfight or gun duel. Such scenes were a staple of the Roy Rogers and Lone Ranger serials and TV shows.

As mentioned above, villains may steal back the treasure from the hero or make off with one of his team members. This could lead to pursuit by the hero and rescue or recovery.

SETBACKS

Another twist of The Road Back may be a sudden catastrophic reversal of the hero's good fortune. Things were going well after surviving the Ordeal, but now reality sets in again. Heroes may encounter setbacks that seem to doom the adventure. Within sight of shore the ship may spring a leak. For a moment, after great risk, effort, and sacrifice, it may look like all is lost.

This moment in the story, the climax of Act Two, may be the Delayed Crisis spoken of earlier. It could be the moment of greatest tension in Act Two and should set the story on the final path to resolution in Act Three.

The Road Back at the end of Act Two may be a brief moment or an elaborate sequence of events. Almost every story needs a moment to acknowledge the hero's resolve to finish, and provide her with necessary motivation to return home with the elixir despite the temptations of the Special World and the trials that remain ahead.

THE WIZARD OF OZ

> *The Wizard has prepared a hot-air balloon with which he hopes to take Dorothy on The Road Back to Kansas. The people of Oz gather to see them off with a brass band. However, it's seldom that easy. Toto, seeing a cat in the arms of a woman in the crowd, runs after it, and Dorothy runs after Toto. In the confusion, the balloon wobbles off with the Wizard aboard and Dorothy is left behind, apparently stuck in the Special World. Many heroes have tried to return using familiar means — old crutches and dependencies. But they find the old ways as artificial and difficult to control as the Wizard's hot-air balloon. Dorothy, guided by her instincts (the dog) knows deep down that this is not the way for her. Yet she is ready to take The Road Back, and keeps looking for the proper branching of the path.*

⊷⊐ ⊏⊷

Heroes gather up what they have learned, gained, stolen, or been granted in the Special World. They set themselves a new goal, to escape, find further adventure, or return home. But before any of those goals are achieved, there is another test to pass, the final exam of the journey, Resurrection.

QUESTIONING THE JOURNEY

1. What is The Road Back in *A League of Their Own? Awakenings? Unforgiven? Terminator II*? From the writer's point of view, what are the advantages and disadvantages of heroes being ejected or chased from the Special World? Of leaving voluntarily?

2. What have you learned or gained from confronting death, defeat, or danger? Did you feel heroic? How can you apply your feelings to your writing, to the reactions of your characters?

3. How do your heroes rededicate themselves to the quest?

4. What is The Road Back in your story? Is it returning to your starting place? Setting a new destination? Adjusting to a new life in the Special World?

5. Find the Act Two/Act Three turning points in three current feature films. Are these single moments or extended sequences?

6. Is there an element of pursuit or acceleration in these sections? In The Road Back section of your own story?

RESURRECTION

STAGE ELEVEN: THE RESURRECTION

"What can I do, old man? I'm dead, aren't I?"
from *The Third Man* by Graham Greene

Now comes one of the trickiest and most challenging passages for the hero and the writer. For a story to feel complete, the audience needs to experience an additional moment of death and rebirth; similar to the Supreme Ordeal, but subtly different. This is the **climax**, not the crisis; the last and most dangerous meeting with death. Heroes have to undergo a final purging and purification before reentering the Ordinary World. Once more they must change. The trick for writers is to <u>show</u> the change in their characters, in behavior or appearance, rather than by just talking about it. Writers must find ways to demonstrate that their heroes have been through a **Resurrection**.

> *We weary Seekers shuffle back towards the village. Look! The smoke of the Home Tribe fires! Pick up the pace! But wait – the shaman appears to stop us from charging back in. You have been to the land of Death, he says, and you look like death itself, covered in blood, carrying the torn flesh and hide of your game. If you march back into the village without purifying and cleansing yourselves, you may bring death back with you. You must undergo one final sacrifice before rejoining the tribe. Your warrior self must die so you can be reborn as an innocent into the group. The trick is to keep the wisdom of the Ordeal, while getting rid of its bad effects. After all we've been through, fellow Seekers, we must face one more trial, maybe the hardest one yet.*

A NEW PERSONALITY

A new self must be created for a new world. Just as heroes had to shed their old selves to enter the Special World, they now must shed the

227

personality of the journey and build a new one that is suitable for return to the Ordinary World. It should reflect the best parts of the old selves and the lessons learned along the way. In the Western *Barbarossa*, Gary Busey's farmboy character goes through a final ordeal from which he is reborn as the new Barbarossa, having incorporated the lessons of his Mentor, Willie Nelson, along the way. John Wayne emerges from the ordeal of death in *Fort Apache* and incorporates some of the dress and attitudes of his antagonist, Henry Fonda.

CLEANSING

One function of Resurrection is to cleanse heroes of the smell of death, yet help them retain the lessons of the ordeal. The lack of public ceremonies and counseling for returning Vietnam War veterans may have contributed to the terrible problems these soldiers have had in reintegrating with society. So-called primitive societies seem better prepared to handle the return of heroes. They provide rituals to purge the blood and death from hunters and warriors so they can become peaceful members of society again.

Returning hunters may be quarantined safely away from the tribe for a period of time. To reintegrate hunters and warriors into the tribe, shamans use rituals that mimic the effects of death or even take the participants to death's door. The hunters or warriors may be buried alive for a period of time or confined in a cave or sweat lodge, symbolically growing in the womb of the earth. Then they are raised up (Resurrected) and welcomed as newborn members of the tribe.

Sacred architecture aims to create this feeling of Resurrection, by confining worshippers in a narrow, dark hall or tunnel, like a birth canal, before bringing them out into an open, well-lit area, with a corresponding lift of relief. Baptism by immersion in a stream is a ritual designed to give the Resurrection feeling, both cleansing the sinner and reviving him from symbolic death by drowning.

TWO GREAT ORDEALS

Why do so many stories seem to have two climaxes or death-and-rebirth ordeals, one near the middle and another just before the end of the story? The college semester metaphor suggests the reason. The central crisis or Supreme Ordeal is like a midterm exam; the Resurrection is the final exam. Heroes must be tested one last time to see if they retained the learning from the Supreme Ordeal of Act Two.

To learn something in a Special World is one thing; to bring the knowledge home as applied wisdom is quite another. Students can cram for a test but the Resurrection stage represents a field trial of a hero's new skills, in the real world. It's both a reminder of death and a test of the hero's learning. Was the hero sincere about change? Will she backslide or fail, be defeated by neuroses or a Shadow at the eleventh hour? Will the dire predictions made about hero Joan Wilder in Act One of *Romancing the Stone* ("You're not up to this, Joan, and you know it,") turn out to be true?

PHYSICAL ORDEAL

At the simplest level, the Resurrection may just be a hero facing death one last time in an ordeal, battle, or showdown. It's often the final, decisive confrontation with the villain or Shadow.

But the difference between this and previous meetings with death is that the danger is usually on the broadest scale of the entire story. The threat is not just to the hero, but to the whole world. In other words, the stakes are at their highest.

The James Bond movies often climax with 007 battling the villains and then racing against time and impossible odds to disarm some Doomsday device, such as the atomic bomb at the climax of *Goldfinger*. Millions of lives are at stake. Hero, audience, and world are taken right to the brink of death one more time before Bond manages to yank the right wire and save us all from destruction.

THE ACTIVE HERO

It seems obvious that the hero should be the one to act in this climactic moment. But many writers make the mistake of having the hero rescued from death by a timely intervention from an Ally — the equivalent of the cavalry coming to save the day. Heroes can get surprise assistance, but it's best for the hero to be the one to perform the decisive action; to deliver the death blow to fear or the Shadow; to be active rather than passive, at this of all times.

SHOWDOWNS

In Westerns, crime fiction, and many action films, the Resurrection is expressed as the biggest confrontation and battle of the story, the **showdown** or shootout. A showdown pits hero and villains in an ultimate contest with the highest possible stakes, life and death. It's the classic gunfight of the Western, the swordfight of the swashbuckler, or the last acrobatic battle of a martial arts movie. It may even be a courtroom showdown or an emotional "shootout" in a domestic drama.

The showdown is a distinct dramatic form with is own rules and conventions. The operatic climaxes of the Sergio Leone "spaghetti Westerns" exaggerate the elements of the conventional showdown: the dramatic music; the opposing forces marching towards each other in some kind of arena (the town street, a corral, a cemetery, the villain's hideout); the closeups of guns, hands, and eyes poised for the decisive moment; the sense that time stands still. Gun duels are almost mandatory in Westerns from *Stagecoach* to *High Noon* to *My Darling Clementine*. The so-called Gunfight at the O.K. Corral in 1881 was a brutal shootout that has become part of the myth of the American West and has spurred more film versions than any other.

Duels to the death form the climaxes of swashbucklers such as *Robin Hood, Prince of Thieves, The Seahawk, Scaramouche* and *The Flame and the Arrow*; knights battle to the death in *Ivanhoe, Excalibur* and *Knights of the Round Table*. Duels or shootouts are not fully satisfying unless the

230

hero is taken right to the edge of death. The hero must clearly be fighting for his life. The playful quality of earlier skirmishes is probably gone now. He may be wounded or he may slip and lose his balance. He may actually seem to die, just as in the Supreme Ordeal.

DEATH AND REBIRTH OF TRAGIC HEROES

Conventionally heroes survive this brush with death and are Resurrected. Often it is the villains who die or are defeated, but some tragic heroes actually die at this point, like the doomed heroes of *They Died With Their Boots On, The Sand Pebbles, Charge of the Light Brigade,* or *Glory*. Robert Shaw's character Quint is killed at this point in *Jaws*. However all these doomed or tragic heroes are resurrected in the sense that they usually live on in the memory of the survivors, those for whom they gave their lives. The audience survives, and remembers the lessons a tragic hero can teach us.

In *Butch Cassidy and the Sundance Kid* the heroes are cornered in an adobe building, surrounded and outnumbered. They run out to face death in a climax that is delayed to the final seconds of the film. The chances are good they're going to die in a hail of bullets, but they'll go down fighting and are granted immortality by a final freeze-frame, which makes them live on in our memories. In *The Wild Bunch* the heroes are elaborately killed, but their energy lives on in a gun which is picked up by another adventurer who we know will carry on in their wild style.

CHOICE

Another possibility for a Resurrection moment may be a climactic choice among options that indicates whether or not the hero has truly learned the lesson of change. A difficult choice tests a hero's values: Will he choose in accordance with his old, flawed ways, or will the choice reflect the new person he's become? In *Witness*, policeman John Book comes to a final showdown with his ultimate enemy, a crooked police official. The Amish people watch to see if Book will follow the violent code of his Ordinary World or the peaceful way he

231

has learned in their Special World. He makes a clear choice not to engage in the expected shootout. Instead he puts down his gun, leaving the villain armed, and stands with the silent Amish. Like them, he is a witness. The villain can't shoot when there are so many witnesses. The old John Book would have shot it out with his opponent, but the new man chooses not to. Here is the test that proves he's learned his lesson and is a new man, resurrected.

ROMANTIC CHOICE

The Resurrection choice may be in the arena of love. Stories like *The Graduate* or *It Happened One Night* take heroes to the altar at the climax, where a choice of spouses must be made. *Sophie's Choice* is about the impossible choice of a mother who is told by the Nazis to pick which of her two children will die.

CLIMAX

The Resurrection usually marks the climax of the drama. **Climax** is a Greek word meaning "a ladder". For us storytellers it has come to mean an explosive moment, the highest peak in energy, or the last big event in a work. It may be the physical showdown or final battle, but it can also be expressed as a difficult choice, sexual climax, musical crescendo, or highly emotional but decisive confrontation.

THE QUIET CLIMAX

The climax need not be the most explosive, dramatic, loud, or dangerous moment of the story. There is such a thing as a **quiet climax**; a gentle cresting of a wave of emotion. A quiet climax can give a sense that all the conflicts have been harmoniously resolved, and all the tensions converted into feelings of pleasure and peace. After a hero has experienced the death of a loved one, there may be a quiet climax of acceptance or understanding. The knots of tension created in the body of the story come untied, perhaps after a gentle tug from a final realization.

ROLLING CLIMAXES

Stories may meed more than one climax, or a series of **rolling climaxes**. Individual subplots may require separate climaxes. The Resurrection stage is another nerve ganglion of the story, a checkpoint through which all the threads of the story have to pass. Rebirth and cleansing may have to be experienced on more than one level.

The hero may experience a climax on different levels of awareness in succession, such as mind, body, and emotion. A hero might go through a climax of mental change or decision which triggers a physical climax or showdown in the material world. This could be followed by an emotional or spiritual climax as the hero's behavior and feelings change.

Gunga Din combines effective physical and emotional climaxes in succession. Cary Grant and his two English sergeant pals have been badly wounded, leaving the water carrier Gunga Din, once a clown, to act as the hero and warn the British army of an ambush. Although wounded himself, Gunga Din climbs to the top of a golden tower to blow a bugle call. The army is warned and many lives are saved in an action scene which is the story's physical climax, but Din himself is shot from the tower and falls to his death. However, his death is not in vain. He is recognized as a hero by his comrades and is Resurrected. In a final emotional climax the Colonel reads a poem which Rudyard Kipling has written in Din's honor. Superimposed on the scene is Din's spirit, dressed in full army uniform and grinning as he salutes, Resurrected and transformed.

Of course, a well-made story can bring all levels — mind, body, and spirit — to climax in the same moment. When a hero takes a decisive action, her whole world can be changed at once.

CATHARSIS

A climax should provide the feeling of **catharsis**. This Greek word actually means "vomiting up" or "purging", but in English has come to mean a purifying emotional release, or an emotional breakthrough. Greek drama was constructed with the intent of triggering a vomiting up of emotions by the audience, a purging of the poisons of daily life. Just as they took purgatives to empty and cleanse their digestive systems from time to time, the Greeks at regular times of the year would go to the theatre to get rid of ill feeling. Laughter, tears, and shudders of terror are the triggers that bring about this healthy cleansing, this catharsis.

In psychoanalysis, catharsis is a technique of relieving anxiety or depression by bringing unconscious material to the surface. The same is true, in a way, of storytelling. The climax you are trying to trigger in your hero and audience is the moment when they are the most conscious, when they have reached the highest point on a ladder of awareness. You are trying to raise the consciousness of both the hero and the participating audience. A catharsis can bring about a sudden expansion of awareness, a peak experience of higher consciousness.

A catharsis can be combined with a simple physical showdown, for a satisfying emotional effect. In *Red River*, Tom Dunston and Matthew Garth come together for an explosive fight to the death. At first Garth won't fight. He is determined not to be provoked into abandoning his principles. Dunston hammers at him until Garth is forced to fight back to save his own life. They commence a titanic battle and it looks for all the world as if one or both of them must be killed. They crash into a wagon loaded with domestic goods — calico, pots and pans — and destroy it, suggesting the death of hope for building home, family, or society on the frontier.

But a new energy enters the scene: Tess, an independent woman who has come to love Matthew Garth. She stops the fight with a gunshot to get their attention. In an emotional climax — a genuine catharsis —

she spews up all her feelings about the two men, and convinces them that their fight is foolish, because they really love each other. She has changed a deadly physical showdown into an emotional catharsis, a moment of highest awareness.

Catharsis works best through physical expression of emotions such as laughter and crying. Sentimental stories can bring an audience to a catharsis of tears by pushing their emotions to a climax. The death of a beloved character, like Mr. Chips or the doomed young woman in *Love Story*, may be the climactic moment. Such characters are inevitably "resurrected" in the hearts and memories of those who loved them.

Laughter is one of the strongest channels of catharsis. A comedy should crest with a gag or a series of gags that create a virtual explosion of laughter, jokes that relieve tension, purge sour emotions, and allow us a shared experience. The classic Warner Bros. and Disney short cartoons are constructed to reach a climax of laughter, a crescendo of absurdity, in only six minutes. Full-length comedies have to be carefully structured to build to a climax of laughter that releases all the boxed-in emotions of the audience.

CHARACTER ARC

A catharsis is the logical climax of a hero's **character arc**. This is a term used to describe the gradual stages of change in a character; the phases and turning points of growth. A common flaw in stories is that writers make heroes grow or change, but do so abruptly, in a single leap because of a single incident. Someone criticizes them or they realize a flaw, and they immediately correct it; or they have an overnight conversion because of some shock and are totally changed at one stroke. This does happen once in awhile in life, but more commonly people change by degrees, growing in gradual stages from bigotry to tolerance, from cowardice to courage, from hate to love. Here is a typical character arc compared with the Hero's Journey model.

CHARACTER ARC	HERO'S JOURNEY
1) limited awareness of a problem	Ordinary World
2) increased awareness	Call to Adventure
3) reluctance to change	Refusal
4) overcoming reluctance	Meeting with the Mentor
5) committing to change	Crossing the Threshold
6) experimenting with first change	Tests, Allies, Enemies
7) preparing for big change	Approach to Inmost Cave
8) attempting big change	Supreme Ordeal
9) consequences of the attempt (improvements and setbacks)	Reward (Seizing the Sword)
10) rededication to change	The Road Back
11) a final attempt at big change	Resurrection
12) final mastery of the problem	Return with the Elixir

The stages of the Hero's Journey are a good guide to the steps needed to create a realistic character arc.

The Character Arc

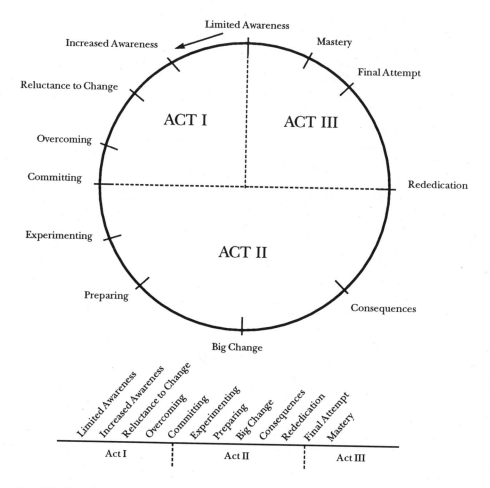

LAST CHANCE

The Resurrection is the hero's final attempt to make major change in attitude or behavior. A hero may backslide at this point, making those around think he's let them down. Hope for that character is temporarily dead, but can be resurrected if he changes his mind. The selfish loner Han Solo in *Star Wars* turns his back on the final attempt to crack the Deathstar, but shows up at the last minute, showing that he has finally changed and is now willing to risk his life for a good cause.

WATCH YOUR STEP

The Resurrection can be a potential misstep for a returning hero who may be walking a narrow sword-bridge from one world to the next. Hitchcock often uses heights at this point in a story to stand for the potential failure to return from the Special World alive. In *North by Northwest* Cary Grant's and Eva Marie Saint's characters end up hanging from the stone portraits on Mount Rushmore, keeping the audience in suspense about their ultimate fates until the last possible moment. The climaxes of Hitchcock's *Vertigo, Saboteur,* and *To Catch a Thief* all take heroes to high places for a final struggle between life and death.

Sometimes great drama comes from heroes dropping the ball at the last moment just before reaching their goal. The heroes of *Quest for Fire* come back to their people with the elixir of flame, but at the threshold of their world, the fire goes out, dropped into the water by accident. This apparent death of all hope is the final test for the hero, the leader of the quest. He reassures the people, for he knows the secret of fire; he has seen the more advanced tribe using a special stick to make fire at his Supreme Ordeal. However when he tries to copy their technique, he finds he has forgotten the trick. Again hope seems dead.

But just then his "wife", a woman he met on the adventure and a member of the more advanced tribe, steps in and gives it a try. The men are not too happy about this, being shown up by a woman and a foreigner at that. However only she knows the secret (spitting on your hands before using the fire-stick). She succeeds, fire blooms, and the possibility of life returns to the tribe. In fact the tribe itself has passed a final test by learning that the combined knowledge of men and women is needed to survive. A stumble at the final threshold has led to resurrection and enlightenment.

The misstep for a hero might not be a physical event, but a moral or emotional stumble at the threshold of return. In *Notorious* there are both physical and emotional tests in the closing moments. Alicia Hueberman (Ingrid Bergman) is in grave physical danger from being poisoned by the Nazis, while Devlin (Cary Grant) is in danger of losing his soul if he doesn't rescue her from the clutches of the enemy where his own devotion to duty has placed her.

THE FALSE CLAIMANT

A common Resurrection moment in fairy tales involves a last-minute threat to a hero who has gone on a quest to achieve impossible tasks. As he stakes his claim on the princess or the kingdom, a pretender or **false claimant** suddenly steps forward questioning the hero's credentials or claiming that he, not the hero, achieved the impossible. For a moment it looks like the hero's hopes are dead. To be reborn, the hero must provide proof that he is the true claimant, perhaps by showing the ears and tail of the dragon he slew, perhaps by besting the pretender (the Shadow) in a contest.

PROOF

Providing proof is a major function of the Resurrection stage. Kids like to bring back souvenirs from summer vacations, partly to remind them of the trips, but also to prove to the other kids that they really visited these exotic locales. Not being believed is a perennial problem of travelers to other worlds.

A common fairy tale motif is that proof brought back from the magic world tends to evaporate. A sack full of gold coins won from the fairies will be opened in the Ordinary World and be found to contain nothing but wet leaves, leading other people to believe the traveler was just sleeping off a drunk in the woods. Yet the traveler knows the experience was real. This motif signifies that spiritual and emotional experiences in a special world are hard to explain to others. They have to go there for themselves. Special World experiences may evaporate if we have not truly made them part of our daily lives. The real treasure from traveling is not the souvenirs, but lasting inner change and learning.

SACRIFICE

Resurrection often calls for a **sacrifice** by the hero. Something must be surrendered, such as an old habit or belief. Something must be given back, like the libation the Greeks used to pour to the gods before drinking. Something must be shared for the good of the group.

In *Terminator II* the shapeshifting villain is destroyed in a physical climax but the story brings the audience to a higher emotional climax in which the robot hero, the Terminator (Arnold Schwarzenegger) must sacrifice himself to keep from causing future violence. In another sense, the boy John Connor is the hero at this point and must sacrifice part of himself, his Mentor/father figure, by allowing the Terminator to leap to his death. A similar self-sacrificial climax is found in *Alien 3*, when Ripley (Sigourney Weaver), knowing she has a monster growing inside her, gives herself up to destruction for the good of the group. The classic sacrifice in literature is found in Charles Dickens' *A Tale of Two Cities*, where a man gives his life on the guillotine to save another man's life.

Sacrifice comes from Latin words meaning "making holy". Heroes are often required to sanctify a story by making a sacrifice, perhaps by giving up or giving back something of themselves. Sometimes the sacrifice is the death of members of the group. Luke Skywalker, at the climax of *Star Wars*, sees many of his comrades killed in the effort to destroy the Deathstar. Luke also gives up part of his personality; his dependence on machines. With Obi Wan's voice in his head, he decides to "Trust the Force", and learns to trust human instinct rather than machinery.

Luke undergoes another personal sacrifice at the climax of the second film in the series, *The Empire Strikes Back*. Here he is escaping from the Emperor and loses a hand in the getaway. In repayment, he gains new control over the Force in the third film of the trilogy, *Return of the Jedi*.

INCORPORATION

Resurrection is an opportunity for a hero to show he has absorbed, or incorporated, every lesson from every character. Incorporation literally means he has made the lessons of the road part of his body. An ideal climax would test everything he's learned, and allow him to show that he has absorbed the Mentor, Shapeshifter, Shadow, Guardians, and Allies along the way. By the time the heroes of *City Slickers* endure their climax, they can apply everything they've learned from a variety of Mentors and antagonists.

CHANGE

The higher dramatic purpose of Resurrection is to give an outward sign that the hero has really changed. The old Self must be proven to be completely dead, and the new Self immune to temptations and addictions that trapped the old form.

The trick for writers is to make the change visible in appearance or action. It's not enough to have people around a hero notice that she's changed; it's not enough to have her talk about change. The audience must be able to see it in her dress, behavior, attitude, and actions.

Romancing the Stone has a well-developed sense of Resurrection that is realized in visual terms. At the action climax of the film, Joan Wilder and Jack Colton unite to defeat the villains, rescue her sister, and reclaim the treasure. But Jack immediately pulls away, putting Joan's romantic plotline in jeopardy. Perfection through a man was within her grasp, but it's snatched away at the last minute. Jack gives her a farewell kiss and tells her she always had what it takes to be a hero, but ultimately he follows money rather than his heart. Colton goes after

241

the emerald which has been swallowed by an alligator. He dives off a high wall, leaving Joan romantically bereaved and unsatisfied. The action plot has ended in triumph, but the emotional plot appears to be a tragedy. In effect, Joan's hope of emotional completion is dead.

From the shot of Joan looking out over the parapet there is a slow dissolve to a matching shot of her Resurrected self in a New York office a few months later. Her agent is reading Joan's latest manuscript, based on her real life adventures. It's apparent from every choice on the screen that Joan Wilder has changed; that in some way she has hit bottom, died, and been emotionally reborn. The manuscript has brought the hard-hearted agent to tears. She pronounces it by far Joan's best book, and notes that it was completed very quickly. The Ordeals of the Special World have made Joan a better writer, and she looks better as well, more "together" than we've ever seen her.

At the end of the scene, Joan is put through a final emotional test. The agent refers to the conclusion of the book, which unlike Joan's real life, ends with the hero and heroine united. She leans in close and, in her forceful way, calls Joan "a world-class hopeless romantic".

Joan could have caved in here, perhaps crying about the sad reality that she didn't get her man. Or she could have agreed with the agent's assessment of her as hopeless. The old Joan might have cracked. But she doesn't. Joan passes this emotional test with her answer. She gently but firmly disagrees, saying "No, a hopeful romantic." Her look tells us she is still in some pain, but that she really is all right. She has learned to love herself regardless of whether or not some man loves her, and she has the self-confidence she lacked before. Later, on the street, she is able to brush off men who would have intimidated her before. She has been through a Resurrection. She has changed, in appearance and action, in ways you can see on the screen and feel in your heart.

THE WIZARD OF OZ

The Wizard of Oz *is not as visual as* Romancing the Stone *in its depiction of how the hero has changed, and yet there is rebirth and learning, expressed in words. The Resurrection for Dorothy is recovering from the apparent death of her hopes when the Wizard accidentally floated off in the balloon. Just when it looks as though Dorothy will never achieve her goal of returning home, there is another appearance by the Good Witch, representing the positive anima that connects us to home and family. She tells Dorothy she had the power to return home all along. She didn't tell Dorothy because "She wouldn't have believed me. She had to learn it for herself."*

The Tin Woodman asks bluntly "What have you learned, Dorothy?" She replies that she's learned to look for her "heart's desire" in her "own back yard". Like Joan Wilder, Dorothy has learned that happiness and completion are within her, but this verbal expression of change is not as effective as the visual and behavioral changes you can see on the screen in the Resurrection scene of Romancing the Stone. *Nevertheless, Dorothy has learned something and can now step up to the last threshold of all.*

⇢▩ ▩⇠

Resurrection is the hero's final exam, her chance to show what she has learned. Heroes are totally purged by final sacrifice or deeper experience of the mysteries of life and death. Some don't make it past this dangerous point, but those who survive go on to close the circle of the Hero's Journey when they Return with the Elixir.

QUESTIONING THE JOURNEY

1. What is the Resurrection in *King Kong? Gone With the Wind? Silence of the Lambs? Death Becomes Her?*

2. What negative characteristics has your hero picked up along the way? What flaws were there from the beginning that still need to be corrected? What flaws do you want to preserve, uncorrected? Which are necessary parts of your hero's nature?

3. What final ordeal of death and rebirth does your hero go through? What aspect of your hero is Resurrected?

4. Is there a need for a physical showdown in your story? Is your hero active at the critical moment?

5. Examine the character arc of your hero. Is it a realistic growth of gradual changes? Is the final change in your character visible in her actions or appearance?

6. Who learns anything in a tragedy where the hero dies, where the hero didn't learn his lessons?

RETURN
WITH THE ELIXIR

STAGE TWELVE : RETURN WITH THE ELIXIR

"No, Aunt Em, this was a real truly live place. And I remember some of it wasn't very nice. But most of it was beautiful. But just the same all I kept saying to everybody was 'I want to go home'".

from *The Wizard of Oz*

Having survived all the ordeals, having lived through death, heroes return to their starting place, go home, or continue the journey. But they always proceed with a sense that they are commencing a new life, one that will be forever different because of the road just traveled. If they are true heroes, they **Return with the Elixir** from the Special World; bringing something to share with others, or something with the power to heal a wounded land.

> *We Seekers come home at last, purged, purified, and bearing the fruits of our journey. We share out the nourishment and treasure among the Home Tribe, with many a good story about how they were won. A circle has been closed, you can feel it. You can see that our struggles on the Road of Heroes have brought new life to our land. There will be other adventures, but this one is complete, and as it ends it brings deep healing, wellness, and wholeness to our world. The Seekers have come Home.*

RETURN

Quest For Fire has a wonderful Return sequence that shows how story-telling probably began, with hunter/gatherers struggling to relate their adventures in the outer world. The film's heroes enjoy the fruits of their quest at a barbecue around a campfire. The Trickster clown of the hunting party now becomes the storyteller, acting out an adventure from the Tests phase, complete with sound effects and a funny mimed impression of a mammoth Threshold Guardian they met on the quest. A wounded hunter laughs as his injuries are tended; in film language, a declaration of the healing power of stories. Returning with the Elixir means implementing change in your daily life and using the lessons of adventure to heal your wounds.

DENOUEMENT

Another name for the Return is *denouement,* a French word meaning "untying" or "unknotting". (noue means knot.) A story is like a weaving in which the lives of the characters are interwoven into a coherent design. The plot lines are knotted together to create conflict and tension, and usually it's desirable to release the tension and resolve the conflicts by untying these knots. We also speak of "tying up the loose ends" of a story in a denouement. Whether tying up or untying, these phrases point to the idea that a story is a weaving and that it must be finished properly or it will seem tangled or ragged. That's why it's important in the Return to deal with subplots and all the issues and questions you've raised in the story. It's all right for a Return to raise new questions — in fact that may be highly desirable — but all the old questions should be addressed or at least restated. Usually writers strive to create a feeling of closing the circle on all these storylines and themes.

TWO STORY FORMS

There are two branches to the end of the Hero's Journey. The more conventional way of ending a story, greatly preferred in Western culture and American movies in particular, is the circular form in which there is a sense of closure and completion. The other way, more popular in Asia and in Australian and European movies, is the open-ended approach in which there is a sense of unanswered questions, ambiguities, and unresolved conflicts. Heroes may have grown in awareness in both forms, but in the open-ended form their problems may not be tied up so neatly.

THE CIRCULAR STORY FORM

The most popular story design seems to be the **circular** or **closed form**, in which the narrative returns to its starting point. In this structure you might bring the hero literally full circle back to the location or world where she started. Perhaps the Return is circular in a visual or metaphoric way, with a replay of an initial image, or the repetition of a line of dialogue or situation from Act One. This is one way of tying up loose ends and making a story feel complete. The image or phrases may have acquired a new meaning now that the hero has completed the journey. The original statement of the theme may be re-evaluated at the Return. Many musical compositions return to an initial theme to rephrase it at the ending.

Having your hero Return to her starting point or remember how she started allows you to draw a comparison for the audience. It gives a measure of how far your hero has come, how she's changed, and how her old world looks different now. To give this circular feeling of completion and comparison, writers will sometimes put their heroes through an experience at the Return that was difficult or impossible for them at the beginning, so the audience can see how they have changed. In *Ghost*, the hero was unable to say "I love you" in his Ordinary World. But at the Return, having died and passed many tests in the land of death, he is able to say these all-important words so that his still-living wife can hear them.

In *Ordinary People*, the young hero Conrad is so depressed in his Ordinary World that he can't eat the French toast his mother makes for him. It's an outward sign of his inner problem, his inability to accept love because he hates himself for surviving his brother. In the Return, having passed through several death-and-rebirth ordeals, he goes to apologize to his girlfriend for acting like a jerk. When she asks him to come inside for some breakfast, this time he finds he has an appetite. His ability to eat is an outward sign of his inner change. This actual change in behavior is more dramatically effective than Conrad just saying he feels different, or someone else noticing that he's grown and remarking on it. It communicates change on the

249

symbolic level, and affects the audience indirectly but more powerfully than a blatant statement. In a subtle way it gives a sense that a phase of his life is over, that a circle has been closed, and a new one is about to begin.

ACHIEVEMENT OF PERFECTION

The "happy endings" of Hollywood films link them with the world of fairy tales, which are often about the achievement of perfection. Fairy tales frequently end with a statement of perfection, like "and they lived happily ever after". Fairy tales bring the shattered family back into balance, back to completion.

Weddings are a popular way to end stories. Marriage is a new beginning, the end of an old life of being single and the beginning of a new life as part of a new unit. New beginnings are perfect and unspoiled in their ideal form.

Striking up a new relationship is another way to show a new beginning at the end of a story. In *Casablanca*, Humphrey Bogart makes a difficult Resurrection sacrifice, giving up the chance to be with the woman he loves. His reward, the Elixir he brings away from the experience, is his new alliance with Claude Rains. As he says, in one of the most famous tag lines in the history of the movies, "Louie, I think this is the beginning of a beautiful friendship."

THE OPEN-ENDED STORY FORM

Storytellers have thought of many ways to create a circular feeling of completion or closure, basically by addressing the dramatic questions raised in Act One. However once in awhile a few loose ends are desirable. Some storytellers prefer an **open-ended** Return. In the open-ended point of view, the story-telling goes on after the story is over; it continues in the minds and hearts of the audience, in the conversations and even arguments people have in coffee shops after seeing a movie or reading a book.

Writers of the open-ended persuasion prefer to leave moral conclusions for the reader or viewer. Some questions have no answers, some have many. Some stories end, not by answering questions or solving riddles, but by posing new questions that resonate in the audience long after the story is over.

Hollywood films are often criticized for pat, fairy tale endings in which all problems are solved and the cultural assumptions of the audience are left undisturbed. By contrast the open-ended approach views the world as an ambiguous, imperfect place. For more sophisticated stories with a hard or realistic edge, the open-ended form may be more appropriate.

FUNCTIONS OF THE RETURN

Like the journey's other stages, Return with the Elixir can perform many functions but there is something special about being the last element in the journey. Return is similar to Reward in some ways. Both follow a moment of death and rebirth and both may depict consequences of surviving death. Some functions of Seizing the Sword may also appear in the Return, such as taking possession, celebrating, sacred marriage, campfire scenes, self-realization, vengeance, or retaliation. But Return is your last chance to touch the emotions of the audience. It must finish your story so that it satisfies or provokes your audience as you intended. It bears special weight because of its unique position at the end of the work, and it's also a place of pitfalls for writers and their heroes.

SURPRISE

A Return can fall flat if everything is resolved too neatly or just as expected. A good Return should untie the plot threads but with a certain amount of surprise. It should be done a little taste of the unexpected, a sudden revelation. The Greeks and Romans often built a "recognition" scene into the endings of their plays and novels. A young man and woman, raised as shepherds, discover to everyone's surprise they are prince and princess, promised to each other in

251

marriage long ago. In the tragic mode, Oedipus discovers the man he killed in the Ordeal was his father and the woman he joined with in sacred marriage was his own mother. Here the recognition is cause for horror rather than joy.

The Return may have a twist to it. This is another case of misdirection: You lead the audience to believe one thing, and then reveal at the last moment a quite different reality. *No Way Out* flips you a totally different perception of the hero in the last ten seconds of the film. *Basic Instinct* makes you suspect Sharon Stone's character of murder for the first two acts, convinces you she is innocent in the climax, then leaps back to doubt again in an unexpected final shot.

There is usually an ironic or cynical tone to such Returns, as if they mean to say "Ha, fooled ya!" You are caught foolishly thinking that human beings are decent or that good does triumph over evil. A less sardonic version of a twist Return can be found in the work of writers like O. Henry, who sometimes used the twist to show the positive side of human nature, as in his short story "The Gift of the Magi". A poor young husband and wife make sacrifices to surprise each other with Christmas presents. They discover that the husband has sold his valuable watch to buy his wife a clip for her beautiful long hair, and the wife has cut off and sold her lovely locks to buy him a fob for his beloved watch. The gifts and sacrifices cancel each other out but the couple is left with a treasure of love.

REWARD AND PUNISHMENT

A specialized job of Return is to hand out final rewards and punishments. It's part of restoring balance to the world of the story, giving a sense of completion. It's like getting your grades after final exams. Villains should earn their ultimate fate by their evil deeds and they should not get off too easily. Audiences hate that. Punishment should fit the crime and have the quality of **poetic justice**. In other words the way the villain dies or gets his just comeuppance should directly relate to his sins.

Heroes should get what's coming to them as well. Too many movie heroes get rewards they haven't really earned. The reward should be proportionate to the sacrifice they have offered. You don't get immortality for being nice. Also if heroes have failed to learn a lesson, they may be penalized for it in the Return.

Of course, if your dramatic point of view is that life isn't fair and you feel justice is a rare thing in this world, then by all means reflect this in the way rewards and punishments are dealt out in the Return.

THE ELIXIR

The real key to the final stage of the Hero's Journey is the **Elixir**. What does the hero bring back with her from the Special World to share upon her Return? Whether it's shared within the community or with the audience, bringing back the Elixir is the hero's final test. It proves she's been there, it serves as an example for others, and it shows above all that death can be overcome. The Elixir may even have the power to restore life in the Ordinary World.

Like everything else in the Hero's Journey, returning with the Elixir can be literal or metaphoric. The Elixir may be an actual substance or medicine brought back to save an endangered community (a feature of several "Star Trek" TV plots and the object of the quest in *Medicine Man*). It may be literal treasure wrested from the Special World and shared within a group of adventurers. More figuratively, it may be any of the things that drive people to undertake adventure: money, fame, power, love, peace, happiness, success, health, knowledge, or having a good story to tell. The best Elixirs are those that bring hero and audience greater awareness. In *The Treasure of the Sierra Madre* , the physical treasure of gold is revealed to be worthless dust, and the real Elixir is the wisdom to live a long and peaceful life.

In the tales of King Arthur, the Grail is the Elixir that, once shared, heals the wounded land. The Fisher King can rest easy again. If Percival and the knights had kept the Grail for themselves, there would have been no healing.

253

If a traveler doesn't bring back something to share, he's not a hero, he's a heel, selfish and unenlightened. He hasn't learned his lesson. He hasn't grown. Returning with the Elixir is the last test of the hero, in which shows if he's mature enough to share the fruits of his quest.

THE ELIXIR OF LOVE

Love is, of course, one of the most powerful and popular Elixirs. It can be a reward the hero doesn't win until after a final sacrifice. In *Romancing the Stone* Joan Wilder has surrendered her old fantasies about men and said goodbye to her old, uncertain personality. The payoff for her is that unexpectedly, Jack Colton comes for her after all, miraculously transporting a romantic sailboat to her New York neighborhood to sweep her away. He has transmuted the Elixir he was after — the precious emerald — into another form, love. Joan gets her reward of romance, but she has earned it by learning that she could live without it.

THE WORLD IS CHANGED

Another aspect of the Elixir is that the wisdom which heroes bring back with them may be so powerful that it forces change not only in them, but also those around them. The whole world is altered and the consequences spread far. There is a beautiful image for this in *Excalibur.* When Percival brings the Grail back to the ailing Arthur, the King revives and rides out with his knights again. They are so filled with new life that flowers burst into bloom at their passing. They are a living Elixir, whose mere presence renews nature.

THE ELIXIR OF RESPONSIBILITY

A common and powerful Elixir is for heroes to take wider responsibility at the Return, giving up their loner status for a place of leadership or service within a group. Families and relationships get started, cities are founded. The hero's center has moved from the ego to the Self, and sometimes expands to include the group. Mad Max, the loner hero of George Miller's *Road Warrior* and *Mad Max: Beyond the Thunderdome,* forsakes his solitude to become Mentor and fosterfather to a race of orphaned children. The Elixir is his skill at survival and his recollection of the old world before the apocalypse, which he passes on to the orphans.

THE ELIXIR OF TRAGEDY

In the tragic mode, heroes die or are defeated, brought down by their tragic flaws. Yet there is learning and an Elixir brought back from the experience. Who learns? The audience, for they see the errors of the tragic hero and the consequences of error. They learn, if they are wise, what mistakes to avoid, and this is the Elixir that they bring away from the experience.

SADDER BUT WISER

Sometimes the Elixir is heroes taking a rueful look back at their wrong turns on the path. A feeling of closure is created by a hero acknowledging that he is **sadder but wiser** for having gone through the experience. The Elixir he bears away is bitter medicine, but it may keep him from making the same error again, and his pain serves as fair warning to the audience not to choose that path. The heroes of *Risky Business* and *White Men Can't Jump* have been down a road of learning that mixed pain and pleasure. They ultimately lose the prize of love, must Return without the woman of their dreams, and have to console themselves with the Elixir of experience. These stories create a feeling that the account is closed and the heroes are being presented with the final balance.

SADDER BUT NO WISER

A "sadder but wiser" hero is acknowledging that he's been a fool, which is the first step to recovery. The worse kind of fool is the one who doesn't get it. Either he never sees the error or he goes through the motions but has not really learned his lesson. Even after enduring terrible ordeals, he slides back to the same behavior that got him in trouble in the first place. He is **sadder but no wiser**. This is another kind of circular closure.

In this style of Return, a roguish or foolish character seems to have grown and changed. Perhaps he is a clown or Trickster, like Bob Hope in the Crosby-Hope pictures or Eddie Murphy in *48 Hours* or *Trading Places*, who swears he has learned his lesson. However, in the end he fumbles the Elixir and returns to an original error. He may fall back to his original, irrepressible attitude, closing the circle and dooming himself to repeat the adventure.

For this is the penalty of failing to return with the Elixir: **The hero, or someone else, is doomed to repeat the Ordeals until the lesson is learned or the Elixir is brought home to share.**

EPILOGUE

Just as some stories may have a prologue that precedes the main action, there may also be a need for an **epilogue** that follows the bulk of the story. An epilogue or postscript on rare occasions can serve to complete the story, by projecting ahead to some future time to show how the characters turned out. *Terms of Endearment* has an epilogue that shows the characters a year after the main story has ended. The feeling communicated is that even though there is sadness and death, life goes on. *Look Who's Talking* has an epilogue that shows the birth of the baby hero's little sister nine months after the main plot has been resolved. Stories that show a group of characters at a formative or critical period, like *American Graffiti* or war movies such as *Glory* or *The Dirty Dozen*, may end with a short segment that tells how the characters died, progressed in life, or were remembered. *A League of Their Own* has an extensive epilogue in which an aging woman ballplayer, having remembered her career in flashback for the main body of the film, visits the Baseball Hall of Fame and sees many of her teammates. The fates of the players are revealed and the surviving women, now in their sixties, stage a game to show that they still know how to play ball. Their spirit is the Elixir that revives the hero and the audience.

These have been a few of the purposes and functions of Return. There are also pitfalls to avoid in Returning with the Elixir.

PITFALLS OF THE RETURN

It's easy to blow it in the Return. Many stories fall apart in the final moments. The Return is too abrupt, prolonged, unfocussed, unsurprising, or unsatisfying. The mood or chain of thought the author has created just evaporates and the whole effort is wasted. The Return may also be too ambiguous. Many people faulted the twist ending of *Basic Instinct* for failing to resolve uncertainty about a woman's guilt.

UNRESOLVED SUBPLOTS

Another pitfall is that writers fail to bring all the elements together at the Return. It's common for writers today to leave subplot threads dangling. Perhaps in the hurry to finish and deal with the main characters, the fate of secondary characters and ideas are forgotten about, even though they may be extremely interesting to the audience. Older films tend to be more complete and satisfying because the creators took time to work out every subplot. Character actors could be counted on to do their bit somewhere at beginning, middle, and end. A rule of thumb: **Subplots should have at least three "beats" or scenes distributed throughout the story, one in each act.** All the subplots should be acknowledged or resolved in the Return. Each character should come away with some variety of Elixir or learning.

TOO MANY ENDINGS

On the other hand, the Return should not seem labored or repetitive. Another good rule of thumb for the Return phase is to operate on the KISS system, that is: **Keep It Simple, Stupid.** Many stories fail because they have too many endings. The audience senses the story is over but the writer, perhaps unable to choose the right ending, tries several. This tends to frustrate an audience, dissipating the energy the writer has created. People want to know the story's definitively over so they can quickly get up and leave the theater or finish the book with a powerful charge of emotion. An overly

257

ambitious film like *Lord Jim*, trying to take on a dense novel, can exhaust an audience with climaxes and endings that seem to go on forever.

An extreme example of keeping it simple might be the karate match that forms the climax of *The Karate Kid*. When the last kick is delivered and the hero wins, the credits roll immediately in a burst of final theme music. There is almost no denouement. We know the kid is bearing the Elixir of lessons learned well in his training.

ABRUPT ENDINGS

A Return can seem too abrupt, giving the sense the writer has quit too soon after the climax. A story tends to feel incomplete unless a certain emotional space is devoted to bidding farewell to the characters and drawing some conclusions. An abrupt Return is like someone hanging up the phone without saying goodbye, or a pilot bailing out without bringing the plane in for a landing.

FOCUS

A Return may feel out of focus if the dramatic questions, raised in Act One and tested in Act Two, are not answered now. Writers may have failed to pose the right questions in the first place. Without realizing it, a writer may have shifted the theme. A tale that started out as a love story may have turned into an expose' of government corruption. The writer has lost the thread. The story will not seem focussed unless the circle is closed by Returning to the original themes.

PUNCTUATION

The final function of Return is to conclude the story decisively. The story should end with the emotional equivalent of a punctuation mark. A story, like a sentence, can end in only four ways: with a period, an exclamation point, a questionmark, or an ellipsis (the three or four little dots that indicate your thoughts have just trailed off vaguely. Example: Do you want to go now, or....).

The needs of your story and your attitude may dictate ending with the feeling of a period, an image or line of dialogue flatly making a declarative statement such as "Life goes on." "Love conquers all." "Good triumphs over evil." "That's the way life is." "There's no place like home."

An ending can give the effect of an exclamation point if the intent of the work is to stir action or create alarm. Science fiction and horror films may end on a note of "We are not alone!" or "Repent or perish!" Stories of social awareness may end with a passionate tone of "Never again!", "Rise up and throw off chains of oppression!", or "Something must be done!"

In a more open-ended approach to structure, you may want to end with the effect of a question mark, and the feeling that uncertainies remain. The final image may pose a question such as "Will the hero Return with the Elixir or will it be forgotten?" An open-ended story may also trail off with the feeling of an ellipsis. Unspoken questions may linger in the air or conflicts may remain unresolved with endings that suggest doubt or ambiguity. "The hero can't decide between two women, and therefore...", "Love and art are irreconcilable, so...", "Life goes on... and on... and on....", or "She proved she's not a killer, but..."

One way or another, the very ending of a story should announce that it's all over — like the Warner Bros. cartoon signature line "That's all, folks". Oral storytellers, in addition to using formulas like "...and they lived happily ever after", will sometimes end folk tales with a ritual statement like "I'm done, that's that, and who'll ease my dry throat with a drink?" Sometimes a final image, such as the hero riding off into the sunset, can sum up the story's theme in a visual metaphor and let the audience know it's over. The final image of *Unforgiven*, a shot of Clint Eastwood's character leaving his wife's grave and returning to his house, signals the end of the journey and sums up the story's theme.

These are only a few of the features of Return with the Elixir. As we come full circle, let's leave a little opening for the unknown, the unexpected, the unexplored.

THE WIZARD OF OZ

Dorothy's Return begins with saying goodbye to her Allies and acknowledging the Elixirs of love, courage, and common sense she has gained from them. Then, tapping her heels and chanting "There's no place like home", she wishes herself back to Kansas where she started.

Back home in the Ordinary World, back to black and white, Dorothy wakes up in bed with a compress on her head. The Return is ambiguous: Was the trip to Oz "real", or was it the dream of a girl with a concussion? In story terms, however, it doesn't matter; the journey was real to Dorothy.

She recognizes the people around her as characters from Oz. But her perceptions of them have changed as a result of her experience in the Special World. She remembers that some of it was horrible, some beautiful, but she focusses on what she's learned — there's no place like home.

Dorothy's declaration that she will never leave home again is not meant to be taken literally. It's not this little frame house in Kansas to which she refers, but her own soul. She is a fully integrated person in possession of her best qualities, in control of the worst, and in touch with the positive forms of masculine and feminine energy within her. She has incorporated every lesson she has learned from every being along the road. She is finally happy in her own skin and will feel at home no matter where she is. The Elixir she brings back is this new idea of home, a new concept of her Self.

⊷⊷ ⊷⊷

And so the Hero's Journey ends, or at least rests for awhile, for the journey of life and the adventure of story never really end. The hero and the audience bring back the Elixir from the current adventure, but the quest to integrate the lessons goes on. It's for each of us to say what the Elixir is — wisdom, experience, money, love, fame, or the thrill of a lifetime. But a good story, like a good journey, leaves us with an Elixir that changes us, makes us more aware, more alive, more human, more whole, more a part of everything that is. The circle of the Hero's Journey is complete.

QUESTIONING THE JOURNEY

1. What is the Elixir of *Basic Instinct*? *Big*? *City Slickers*? *Fatal Attraction*? *Dances with Wolves*?

2. What is the Elixir your hero brings back from the experience? Is it kept to herself or is it shared?

3. Does your story go on too long after the main event or climax is over? What would be the effect of simply cutting it off after the climax? How much denouement do you need to satisfy the audience?

4. In what ways has the hero gradually taken more reponsibility in the course of the story? Is the Return a point of taking greatest responsibility?

5. Who is the hero of the story now? Has your story changed heroes, or have characters risen to be heroes? Who turned out to be a disappointment? Are there any surprises in the final outcome?

6. Is your story worth telling? Has enough been learned to make the effort worthwhile?

7. Where are you in your own Hero's Journey? What is the Elixir you hope to bring back?

EPILOGUE:

LOOKING BACK ON THE JOURNEY

EPILOGUE: LOOKING BACK ON THE JOURNEY

"I've had a hell of a lot of fun, and I've enjoyed every minute of it."
Errol Flynn

Now that we have come to the end of the Road of Heroes, I'd like to demonstrate the approach on a couple of recent film stories so you can see it work in practice. As I was finishing this book I saw two recent hit movies, *The Last of the Mohicans* and *Death Becomes Her*, and analyzed them in the language of the Hero's Journey. It was a fascinating exercise revealing flaws and good points in the movies. I strongly recommend you try this for yourself on a movie, novel, or story of your own. However before presenting these analyses, a few warnings, guidelines, and odd bits of information are in order.

CAVEAT, SCRIPTOR

First, Caveat Scriptor! (Let the writer beware!) **The Hero's Journey model is a guideline.** It's not a cookbook recipe or a mathematical formula to be applied rigidly to every story. To be effective, a story doesn't have to concur with this or any other school, paradigm, or method of analysis. The ultimate measure of a story's success or excellence is not its compliance with any established patterns, but its lasting popularity and effect on the audience. To force a story to conform to a structural model is putting the cart before the horse.

It's possible to write good stories that don't exhibit every feature of the Hero's Journey; in fact, it's better if they don't. People love to see familiar conventions and expectations defied creatively. A story can break all the "rules" and yet still touch universal human emotions.

FORM FOLLOWS FUNCTION

Remember: The needs of the story dictate its structure. Form follows function. Your beliefs and priorities, along with the characters, themes, style, tone, and mood you are trying to get across, will determine the shape and design of the plot. Structure will also be influenced by the audience, and the time and place in which the story is being told.

The forms of stories change with the needs of the audience. New story types with different rhythms will continue to be created. For instance, thanks to television and MTV styles of cutting, the attention span of the world audience is shorter these days and its sophistication is greater than ever before. Writers can build faster-moving stories and can assume the audience will be able to handle twists and shortcuts in familiar structures.

New terms are being created every day and new observations about story are being made every time one is written. The Hero's Journey is only a guideline, a starting point for hammering out your own story language and rules of thumb.

CHOOSE YOUR METAPHOR

The pattern of the Hero's Journey is but one metaphor for what goes on in a story or a human life. I have used hunting, college classes, and human sexual response as metaphors to help explain the pattern I see in story, but these are far from the only possibilities. Work out a different metaphor or several of them, if it helps you understand storytelling better. You might find it useful to compare a story to a baseball game, with nine innings instead of twelve stages, and terms like "Seventh-Inning Stretch" instead of Seizing the Sword. You might decide the process of sailing a boat, baking bread, rafting a river, driving a car, or carving a statue makes a more meaningful comparison to telling a story. Sometimes a combination of metaphors is needed to illuminate different facets of the human journey.

The stages, terms, and ideas of the Hero's Journey can be used as a design template for stories, or as a means of troubleshooting a story, so long as you don't follow these guidelines too rigidly. It's probably best to acquaint yourself with the Hero's Journey ideas and then forget about them as you sit down to write. If you get lost, refer to the metaphor as you would check a map on a journey. But don't mistake the map for the journey. You don't drive with a map pasted to your windshield. You consult it before setting out or when you get disoriented. The joy of a journey is not reading or following a map, but exploring unknown places and wandering off the map now and then. It's only by getting creatively lost, beyond the boundaries of tradition, that new discoveries can be made.

DESIGN TEMPLATE

You may want to experiment with the Hero's Journey as an outline for plotting a new story or trouble-shooting one in the works. In Disney Animation we have used the Hero's Journey model to tighten up storylines, pinpoint problems, and lay out structures. Hundreds of writers have told me they plotted their screenplays, romance novels, or TV sitcom episodes using the Hero's Journey and the guidance of mythology.

Some people begin to plot a movie or novel by writing the twelve stages of the journey on twelve index cards. If you already know some of the major scenes and turning points, write these down where you think they match up with the twelve stages. In this way you begin to map out your story by filling in the gaps in your knowledge of the characters and what happens to them. Use the ideas of the Hero's Journey to ask questions about your characters: What are the Ordinary and Special Worlds for these people? What is my hero's Call to Adventure? How is fear expressed in Refusal? Is it overcome by Meeting with a Mentor? What is the First Threshold my hero has to cross? and so on. Before long the gaps fill and you can progress to chart Hero's Journey's for all the characters and subplots until the complete design is worked out.

You may find that a certain scene matches with the function of one of the stages, but it comes at what seems to be the "wrong" point in the Hero's Journey model. In your story a Mentor might be needed to present a Call and Refusal in Act Two or Three instead of Act One, as the Hero's Journey model appears to indicate. Don't worry about this — put in the scene wherever it seems right to you. The model only shows the most likely place for an event to occur.

Any element of the Hero's Journey can appear at any point in a story. *Dances With Wolves* begins with a hero's Supreme Ordeal or Resurrection that you usually expect to see at the midpoint or end of a Hero's Journey, and yet the story works. All stories are composed of elements of the Hero's Journey, but the units can be arranged in almost any order to serve the needs of your particular story.

This is why you use index cards rather than writing the stages on a single sheet of paper. You can move the cards around to situate scenes as needed, and you can add more cards in case a movement like Call and Refusal needs to be repeated a number of times (as was the case with *Death Becomes Her*).

You may find that as you visualize your story, you will think of some scenes that don't seem to match any particular stage of the journey. You may have to invent your own terminology or metaphors to cover this category of scenes, as well as tailoring the Hero's Journey terminology to suit your own picture of the universe.

DEMONSTRATION OF THE IDEA

To demonstrate how these ideas can be used to analyze a story, I have done a story breakdown on two feature films. First is a Hero's Journey analysis of a fairly conventional adventure film, *The Last of the Mohicans*. Following will be an analysis of a more challenging subject, the supernatural comedy *Death Becomes Her*. Major stages, archetypes, or structural elements will be noted, along with a few other building blocks of structure, such as exposition, complications, motivation scenes, revelations, chases, and turning points.

HERO'S JOURNEY ANALYSIS OF
THE LAST OF THE MOHICANS

ORDINARY WORLD

In the Hudson Valley of 1757, NATHANIEL POE (Daniel Day-Lewis), an orphaned English colonist raised by the Indians, chases down and shoots a stag in the forest. He is aided by his Mohican foster-father CHINGACHGOOK (Russell Means), an experienced hunter and warrior, and Chingachgook's son UNCAS, Nathaniel's foster-brother (and ALLY; also a secondary HERO of the story). The hunt is their ENTRANCE and INTRODUCTION to the audience; a strong OPENING IMAGE. Chingachgook says a shaman's prayer over the dead beast, asking its forgiveness. By his example he is a MENTOR to Nathaniel and Uncas.

Nathaniel and the two Mohicans carry their game to the house of English settler JOHN CAMERON and his WIFE (ALLIES). Uncas and Chingachgook are welcomed as friends, showing an idyllic picture of harmony on the frontier. The discussion at the dinner table turns to rivalry between the French and British for trade with the colonists (OUTER PROBLEM). The settler's wife says it's about time for young Uncas to find himself an Indian bride, to carry on the line of the Mohicans. (INNER PROBLEM or DRAMATIC QUESTION: Will Uncas find love and will the Mohican line be carried on? The audience also might wonder if our hero and star, Nathaniel, will find love.) Nathaniel and his friends speak of the rapid development and resulting tension on the frontier (FORESHADOWING the conflict to come).

CALL TO ADVENTURE

A British recruiting officer (A HERALD) tries to get the colonials, including Nathaniel, to enlist as militia to fight the French.

REFUSAL OF THE CALL

Nathaniel refuses to join up, insisting the settlers have a right to stay and defend their homes. He is a loner with loyalty to no government. The colonists agree to go to a nearby town to discuss fighting for the British, but Nathaniel wants no part of it. Instead he joins a game of lacrosse with young Indians and pioneers.

At this point the story switches to the beginning of a SUBPLOT, introducing DUNCAN, a young British officer who will be ANTAGONIST, RIVAL, and sometimes ALLY of Nathaniel. He is also the HERO of his own journey. He has a magnificent ENTRANCE, crossing a graceful bridge in a fancy carriage, to make CONTRAST with Nathaniel's simpler, natural world. He gazes lovingly at a portrait of his beloved, CORA MUNRO.

Meanwhile the colonists have come to town to discuss enlisting with the British. An OFFICER agrees to their terms, promising they will be allowed to defend their homes if attacked by the French and their Indian allies. Duncan enters, overhears this, and disapproves of making concessions to mere colonists. This gives his CHARACTER, indicating that he is rigid and arrogant, but also courageous and patriotic. He has arrived to escort his sweetheart, Miss CORA MUNRO (Madeline Stowe), and her sister ALICE (Jodhi May) to a fort where their father, a Scottish colonel, is stationed (EXPOSITION). The older officer details a company of soldiers to escort them, and entrusts them to an Indian scout, MAGUA (WES STUDI), who seems to be a potential MENTOR for Duncan, but is later revealed to be the villain or SHADOW.

Duncan goes to Cora, finding her in her ORDINARY WORLD, a peaceful farmyard where beautiful apples are being pressed into cider. He urges her to marry him or at least consider his proposal (a romantic CALL TO ADVENTURE for Cora in which Duncan acts as a HERALD). She feels nothing for him and agrees only to think it over (REFUSAL). Duncan has some good qualities but there are also bad flaws and tendencies. He is a SHAPESHIFTER to Cora, sometimes gallant, brave, and kind; sometimes too forceful, hard-nosed, and demanding.

MEETING WITH THE MENTOR

(There is no specific scene at this point, but the influence of Chingachgook as a Mentor is felt throughout the story. Also Nathaniel will soon function as a Mentor to Cora, teaching her the ways of survival in the forest. She is also a Mentor to him, initiating him to the ways of love and compassion.)

CROSSING THE FIRST THRESHOLD

Cora, Alice, Duncan, and their army escort march and ride out of town into the forest (THE FIRST THRESHOLD). When Alice tires, Duncan tells Magua they will stop for a rest. He disagrees, saying they must go on to better water. Magua slips out a tomahawk, kills a soldier at the end of the column, and screams a war cry to signal the start of an Huron attack.

The soldiers are wiped out and it looks like Cora and Alice will be killed or captured when they are suddenly RESCUED by the appearance of Nathaniel and his friends (CLIMAX of ACT ONE). Magua is just about to murder Cora with his rifle when Nathaniel interferes. Magua turns his aim on Nathaniel, fires and misses, and disappears into the forest. In Vladimir Propp's terms, this is a VILLAIN'S RECONNAISSANCE.

Nathaniel chases off the horses and organizes the survivors to leave the area quickly. There is CONFLICT AND RIVALRY between Nathaniel and Duncan, but Nathaniel quickly asserts his authority. He becomes a kind of MENTOR to the women and Duncan, teaching them the way of the new land.

He asks Duncan why Magua would want to kill Cora, but Duncan has no idea (FORESHADOWING of threat to Cora and Alice).

TESTS, ALLIES, ENEMIES

They enter the SPECIAL WORLD of Nathaniel's wilderness. Uncas helps Alice climb a waterfall and begins to fall in love with her (TEST and ALLIANCE; also FORESHADOWING of danger for these two in high places).

They go to John Cameron's house and find it burned. Cameron and his family have been tortured and murdered by Indians. Because nothing of value was taken from the house, Nathaniel knows it was the work of an Indian war party allied with the French, trying to terrorize the English colonists.

Nathaniel hurries them on to the fort to inform his friends, the colonial militia, of the danger to their homes. There is CONFLICT with Cora, who wants to give the bodies Christian burial. Nathaniel overrules her (becoming a SHAPESHIFTER to Cora, shifting from being her rescuer and Mentor to being a cold-hearted savage).

They take cover in the woods at night. A French and Indian WAR PARTY (ENEMIES or THRESHOLD GUARDIANS) approach, looking for them, but back away in superstitious awe from the Indian burial site where Nathaniel has hidden (Nathaniel has passed a hero's TEST by outwitting these THRESHOLD GUARDIANS). When the danger is passed, Cora asks Nathaniel why he did not bury the bodies of the settlers. He explains they were friends of his, and tells her of his background as an orphan raised by Chingachgook (EXPOSITION AND BACKSTORY). He enlightens her about the injustices suffered by the settlers and tells her that his dead friends live on in the stars. She is deeply moved and begins to fall in love with him (A GETTING-TO-KNOW-YOU scene, also a CAMPFIRE scene after an ordeal. This is also a THRESHOLD CROSSING in the primary romantic relationship of the film, that between Nathaniel and Cora.

APPROACH TO THE INMOST CAVE

By night they cautiously approach the fort, which is being besieged by the French army under GENERAL MONTCALM (an ANTAGONIST). They make their way past French lines in canoes (again successfully passing THRESHOLD GUARDIANS) and enter the fort (an INMOST CAVE).

Cora and her sister are reunited with their father, COLONEL MUNRO. His situation looks bad — the French, with heavier guns and more men, will overwhelm him in three days. Based on information from Duncan, he sends a runner to a nearby fort for help. Nathaniel reports the deaths of his settler friends and warns the colonial militia that their homes and families are in danger. Munro discounts Nathaniel's report and refuses to allow them to leave (thus becoming their ANTAGONIST).

General Montcalm meets with his ALLY, Magua. They agree to intercept Munro's messenger. Magua swears he will eat Munro's heart and wipe out "his seed", that is, kill Cora and Alice (FORESHADOWING).

Nathaniel pleads with Col. Munro to let the colonial militia leave to defend their homes. Duncan reveals his true colors by refusing to back up Nathaniel's report of organized terror attacks on the settlers. He chooses military duty over human values and truth. Cora sees this and loses all affection for him. Munro refuses to let the militia leave.

Duncan tries to explain to Cora but she rejects him and his offer of marriage, saying she misjudged him. (Duncan is becoming more of a SHADOW, manifesting unwelcome aspects of masculinity. He is also a TRAGIC HERO in his own story, whose TRAGIC FLAW is excessive devotion to duty and honor.)

Nathaniel advises his friends in the militia to escape to defend their homes, but remains in the fort, in part because Chingachgook has agreed to help the British, but more because he wants to be with Cora. (Bonds with his ALLIES are strengthened as they APPROACH the ordeal).

Nathaniel and Uncas help Munro's MESSENGER get past the French and Indian sentries by shooting the sentries with their long-range rifles (another way of dealing with THRESHOLD GUARDIANS).

THE SUPREME ORDEAL

Nathaniel seeks out Cora who is nursing the wounded. He takes her outside where men and women are dancing to a country tune even as the French pound the fort. In the shadows behind a building, Nathaniel and Cora become lovers (a SUPREME ORDEAL of intimacy and a SACRED MARRIAGE).

The immediate AFTERMATH is that Nathaniel is arrested by Colonel Munro for encouraging the desertion of the colonial militia. He is thrown into a cell (a DEATH of freedom for this wanderer of the forest).

Cora visits Nathaniel's cell. The French are pounding the fort to pieces (DEATH of the whole enterprise is near). Cora wants to stay with Nathaniel, but he advises her to stay with her father and the officers. The French officers will protect them from Huron massacre. (Nathaniel as a MENTOR is teaching Cora about survival.)

The fort is overwhelmed by French guns (ORDEAL, DEATH of the enterprise). Duncan thinks they should die honorably fighting to the last man, woman, and child. Munro is humiliatingly forced to surrender the fort (an ORDEAL and DEATH of honor for him) because General Webb refused to send reinforcements. Montcalm gallantly allows him to retreat with his weapons and banners (a REBIRTH of Munro's honor and proof that Montcalm is an ANTAGONIST rather than a VILLAIN).

The defeated English march out of the fort with Nathaniel in chains.

Magua complains to General Montcalm that the surrender deprived him of revenge against Munro. He explains why he hates Munro — because Munro's men killed his children, gave him as a slave to his enemies, and caused his wife to marry another man (EXPOSITION, BACKSTORY). He swears to kill Munro's children before killing him (FORESHADOWING).

The retreating English column is attacked by Magua's Hurons and Magua cuts out Munro's heart while promising to kill his children (DEATH for Munro, a TRAGIC HERO, doomed like Duncan by his devotion to duty).

Nathaniel escapes from his bonds (REBIRTH of his freedom).

REWARD

Nathaniel, Uncas, and Chingachgook again RESCUE Cora, Alice, and Duncan, and a young BRITISH SOLDIER.

THE ROAD BACK

They get to canoes and ESCAPE by river, pursued by Magua's warriors (CHASE). They plunge over a waterfall and then send the canoes over a second huge waterfall. They hide in a cave behind the waterfall (a return THRESHOLD).

The love between Cora and Nathaniel grows (REWARD). Alice is woozy and almost slips into the thundering waterfall (FORESHADOWING and a minor ORDEAL in her SUBPLOT) but is RESCUED by Uncas, whose REWARD is a slow-motion embrace.

RESURRECTION

Magua finds them and they have no dry gunpowder to fight with. Nathaniel tells Cora to submit to Magua and survive no matter what, promising to find her (as a MENTOR he continues to teach her about survival.) He ESCAPES with Uncas and Chingachgook, leaping into the mist. The bond between Nathaniel and Cora is temporarily broken (apparent DEATH of relationship, end of ACT TWO).

Magua kills the young British soldier, clubs Duncan senseless, and has Cora and Alice tied up and dragged off (apparent DEATH of their hopes).

Nathaniel and his two friends follow Magua to a Huron village where Magua offers the captives as gifts to the SACHEM (a wise elder or shaman, a MENTOR). Nathaniel walks unarmed into the village and is clubbed by a warrior (a humbling, purifying second ORDEAL and NEAR-DEATH experience).

Nathaniel bargains with the Sachem, who delivers up a judgement worthy of Solomon: Duncan will be released to appease the British, Alice will be given to Magua to replace his lost wife, and Cora will be burned alive to avenge the deaths of Magua's children. Nathaniel offers to take Cora's place, but Duncan heroically rushes in instead (a redemptive act for Duncan, a REBIRTH of his humanity, the CLIMAX of his SUBPLOT).

Alice is taken away by Magua. Nathaniel, Cora, Uncas, and Chingachgook leave the village but stop when they see Duncan being burned alive. Nathaniel uses his long rifle to put a bullet in Duncan's heart (a DEATH for Duncan, but a RESURRECTION of his honor).

Nathaniel and friends pursue Magua's band (CHASE) up a steep mountain trail. The Alice-Uncas SUBPLOT reaches its CLIMAX as Uncas attacks alone and tries to RESCUE Alice. He is killed in a fierce battle with Magua, a SACRIFICE on behalf of his loved one. Magua pushes his body over the cliff.

Alice leaps off the cliff rather than submit to Magua, and joins Uncas in DEATH. (She is a TRAGIC HERO whose flaw was that she was too fragile and could not adjust to the SPECIAL WORLD).

Nathaniel and Chingachgook attack. Uncas is avenged (RESURRECTION) when Chingachgook battles and kills Magua (SHOWDOWN, DEATH OF SHADOW/VILLAIN).

RETURN WITH THE ELIXIR

Chingachgook, Nathaniel, and Cora stand on a mountaintop. Chingachgook says a shaman's prayer, speeding Uncas' spirit to the land of their ancestors. Chingachgook is sad because he is now "The Last of the Mohicans", soon to

275

join his tribe in the spirit world; but he is comforted by Nathaniel and Cora, who have learned from the deeds and wisdom of the Mohicans (ELIXIR), and will pass it on to future generations of Americans (RETURN).

THE END

The Last of the Mohicans is a classic Hero's Journey, with well-developed stages and the full gamut of archetypes. Nathaniel Poe is a complex hero, almost a super-hero in some ways, but in others an anti-hero on the edge of society. Cora is also a hero on a journey, exploring love and the frontier with Nathaniel as her Mentor and lover. The subplots of Duncan and Uncas are also Hero's Journeys, showing two possible fates for heroes. Duncan is a tragic hero doomed by his choices: he generally picks a narrow interpretation of duty and honor over broader human values. He doesn't get the girl, but in the end he learns his lesson and is redeemed by his sacrifice. Uncas also gives his life in noble sacrifice, fighting bravely for his love. Alice has very few positive actions to perform and could be interpreted as a victim, who unlike Cora is unable to adapt and survive. She is a tragic hero in the sense that she fails to learn the lesson.

Magua is a true villain, intent on the death of our heroes, and a true Shadow because he represents the hate and resentment caused by clashes between the red men and the Europeans.

The story can be faulted somewhat for not fully developing the Alice-Uncas love story. It is sketched in, MTV-style, with a few slow-motion close-ups backed up by love music. Their attraction is taken for granted and is not dramatized convincingly.

The only stage of the Hero's Journey which is not fully developed is Meeting with the Mentor, but in a sense this energy is built into the entire story with the powerful Mentoring influence of Chingachgook. Interestingly, although he is not the hero of the story, he is the "last of the Mohicans" referred to in the title. Perhaps the title is also meant to suggest that Nathaniel, as Chingachgook's foster-son, is truly the last of the Mohicans, and shares in the legacy of their harmony with nature. The ambiguity of the title invites us to ask "Who is 'The Last of the Mohicans'?" Perhaps the answer is that we all bear some of the weight of that title, as inheritors of the responsibility to live in harmony with nature and each other.

The film is noteworthy for its extensive use of foreshadowing and for weaving together visual and dramatic themes to make a coherent design, a good example of a conventional Hero's Journey. Now let's examine another film that traces a more atypical journey.

HERO'S JOURNEY ANALYSIS OF
DEATH BECOMES HER

ORDINARY WORLD

Bad actress MADELINE ASHTON (Meryl Streep) steals away DR. ERNEST MENVILLE, (Bruce Willis), fiancé of her childhood friend and RIVAL, writer HELEN SHARP (Goldie Hawn). (ORDINARY WORLD, EXPOSITION, CHARACTERIZATION).

CALLS TO ADVENTURE and REFUSALS

Time passes, Helen gets absurdly fat, (REFUSAL/denial), fantasizes killing Madeline, is hauled away to mental institution, gets idea from social worker to kill Madeline for real (CALL).

More time passes, Madeline gets invitation to Helen's book party, is reluctant to go (CALL & REFUSAL); marriage to plastic surgeon Ernest is a disaster and Madeline is aging (complication).

At the book party, Helen is thin, youthful, and out to seduce Ernest (complication for Madeline).

Madeline goes to makeover clinic, desperate to look younger. Gets card of mysterious woman from owner, but tears up the card (CALL & REFUSAL). However she puts the pieces in her purse, so this is also a **MAGIC GIFT from a MENTOR**.

Helen goes to Ernest to enlist his cooperation in murdering Madeline; he is uncommitted (CALL for Ernest, REFUSAL).

Madeline goes to young boyfriend for reassurance, but gets no comfort there — she's old (complication, equivalent to visiting a MENTOR to get motivation).

277

MEETING WITH THE MENTOR

Upset, in rainstorm, Madeline gets out the card (MAGIC GIFT), goes to Isabella's place (APPROACH). Isabella Rosselini is a dark MENTOR luring her into trouble. She offers the potion (a literal ELIXIR or MAGIC GIFT, also a CALL). Madeline thinks the price is too high (REFUSAL) but after a demonstration, accepts and drinks (FIRST THRESHOLD). She notices changes at once and adjusts (TESTING).

CROSSING THE FIRST THRESHOLD

Madeline goes home and is so mean that Ernest kills her (SUPREME ORDEAL for Madeline, THRESHOLD CROSSING for Ernest) While Ernest reports to Helen, Madeline comes back to life although she is clinically dead (DEATH & REBIRTH). (End of ACT ONE and THRESHOLD CROSSING because direction of story has changed — a story of two women feuding has become a story of a man dealing with his undead wife.)

TESTS, ALLIES, ENEMIES

Ernest takes her to hospital where doctor tests her and pronounces her dead (TESTING). Doctor also dies of heart attack (DEATH. COMPLICATION). Ernest rescues Madeline from body bag in morgue (REBIRTH).

APPROACH TO THE INMOST CAVE

Ernest takes Madeline home, patches her up, finds she needs constant attention to keep her corpse from disintegrating (COMPLICATION, TESTING for Ernest). Helen comes to plot with Ernest, Madeline overhears that they planned to kill her (COMPLICATION, REVELATION).

SUPREME ORDEAL

Madeline kills Helen (ORDEAL for Helen) who revives (DEATH & REBIRTH for Helen, COMPLICATION for Ernest and Madeline). Dead women battle with shovels inconclusively (SUPREME ORDEAL).

REWARD

Realizing they need Ernest to patch them up, they make up (REWARD, RECONCILIATION or SACRED MARRIAGE), but find he has decided to leave them both (COMPLICATION).

THE ROAD BACK

The women decide Ernest must drink the potion and be immortal like them; they try to drug his booze, but he refuses to drink, (CALL & REFUSAL). They hit him with vases, knocking him out (COMPLICATION for Ernest; also THE ROAD BACK and end of ACT TWO because the story's direction has changed again — story of man coping with undead women is now story of man trying to avoid becoming undead.)

Ernest wakes up at Isabella's, she urges him to drink, he almost does but ultimately refuses (CALL & REFUSAL; also, spiritual SUPREME ORDEAL for Ernest). Ernest tries to get away and is pursued (CHASE) by undead women and Isabella's servants (THRESHOLD GUARDIANS).

Ernest passes through party of the dead (a THRESHOLD he has to cross to return to the Ordinary World, thus THE ROAD BACK.

Ernest escapes from killer dogs (Chase by Cerberus-like THRESHOLD GUARDIANS of land of the dead) and ends up hanging from pipe (THE ROAD BACK).

RESURRECTION

Helen and Madeline offer Ernest immortality to escape death but he chooses not to drink the potion (CALL & REFUSAL) and falls to certain death, only to land in a swimming pool (RESURRECTION).

RETURN WITH THE ELIXIR

37 years later, Ernest's funeral. He is dead but triumphant. He had a happy productive life, and was loved by all (RETURN WITH ELIXIR). The undead women, now hideously patched together by each other, have learned nothing, are scornful of Ernest, and go off (SADDER BUT NO WISER), literally falling to pieces.

THE END

This Hero's Journey analysis of *Death Becomes Her* reveals a story strong in the areas of Calls and Refusals, Ordeals and Rewards, with a wonderful twist on shadowy Mentors and dangerous Elixirs. This story defies some conventions about the hero archetype. It was initially confusing because the story is somewhat unclear about who is the hero. You begin by identifying with Helen, the victimized writer character, whose fiance', the plastic surgeon Ernest Menville, is stolen away by Madeline. Helen seems to be the hero because she's the one who suffers a loss at the beginning. We feel for her and assume she is to be the hero.

But when Helen miraculously gets thin again and charms Ernest into plotting Madeline's murder, our sympathies and identification shift toward Madeline, as horrible as her character is supposed to be. She carries the movie as hero through the Journey stages of Call & Refusal, Meeting the Mentor, and First Threshold.

However it eventually becomes clear that Ernest is the true hero, by the definition that he learns the most and Returns with the true Elixir. This movie, by the way, offers a delightful reversal of the idea of the Elixir. The apparent Elixir is a literal magic potion that bestows youth and beauty but with a terrible price. The true Elixir, the film finally gets around to saying, is growing old gracefully after a full, productive life.

Although this movie works on many levels, I found it somewhat disorienting in Act Two. I wasn't sure where I was in the journey, or with whom I was supposed to identify. I didn't know if the big events I was seeing — the deaths and resurrections of the two women — were the central crises of the story or just setups for something else. Ernest is such a weak victim, a passive pawn of the other characters in Act One and Act Two, that I didn't suspect him of being the primary hero of the piece until much later, when he went through his ordeals at Isabella's mansion.

Of course, this interpretation is entirely subjective. Someone else could apply the same Hero's Journey metaphor to the film and come up with a totally different reading. It can be read, in hindsight, as a well-balanced story of three heroes, two of whom, Helen and Madeline, are tragic heroes who fail to learn the lesson. Interestingly, the women come across as the positive heroes of the piece only until they take the potion, the dark Elixir. Then they change masks, becoming the undead Shadows of heroes, villains by definition, and Ernest is almost forced to put on the true hero's mask, by default. It becomes a suspense film in which the suspense is watching Ernest come within a millimeter of making the same fatal mistake the women made. It's like the fairy tales in which three siblings set out, and only the youngest or most naive is able to survive or triumph, where the others, more selfish or cynical, fail or die.

Death Becomes Her reveals many of the functions of the archetypes and stages of the Hero's Journey. The masks and structural elements are used in unexpected ways to give an original twist on the old forms. Some stages are repeated and elaborated upon to make a fascinating design.

-→➣ ⬥←-

THE WRITER'S JOURNEY

The beauty of the Hero's Journey model is that it not only describes a pattern in myths and fairytales, but it's also an accurate map of the territory one must travel to become a writer or for that matter, a human being.

The Hero's Journey and the Writer's Journey are one and the same. Anyone setting out to write a story soon encounters all the tests, trials, ordeals, joys, and rewards of the Hero's Journey. We meet all of its Shadows, Shapeshifters, Mentors, Tricksters, and Threshold Guardians in the interior landscape. Writing is an often perilous journey inward to probe the depths of one's soul and bring back the Elixir of experience — a good story. Low self-esteem or confusion about goals may be the Shadows that chill our work, an editor or one's own judgmental side may be the Threshold Guardians that seem to block our way. Accidents, computer problems, and difficulties with time and discipline may torment and taunt us like Tricksters. Unrealistic dreams of success or distractions may be the Shapeshifters who tempt, confuse, and dazzle us. Deadlines, editorial decisions, or the struggle to sell our work may be the Tests and Ordeals from which we seem to die but are Resurrected to write again.

But take hope, for **writing is magic.** Even the simplest act of writing is almost supernatural, on the borderline with telepathy. Just think: We can make a few abstract marks on a piece of paper in a certain order and someone a world way and a thousand years from now can know our deepest thoughts. The boundaries of space and time and even the limitations of death can be transcended.

Many cultures believed the letters of their alphabets were far more than just symbols for communication, recording transactions, or recalling history. They believed letters were powerful magical symbols that could be used to cast spells and predict the future. The Norse runes and the Hebrew alphabet are simple letters for spelling words, but also deep symbols of cosmic significance.

This magical sense is preserved in our word for teaching children how to manipulate letters to make words: spelling. When you "spell" a word correctly, you are in effect casting a spell, charging these abstract, arbitrary symbols with meaning and power. We say "Sticks and stones may break my bones, but words can never hurt me," but this is manifestly untrue. We know that words have power to hurt or heal. The simple words of a letter, telegram, or phone call can strike you like a hammer blow. They're just words — marks on paper or vibrations of air — but mere words such "Guilty", "Ready, aim, fire!", "I do", or "We'd like to buy your screenplay" can bind us, condemn us, or bring us joy. They can hurt or heal us with their magic power.

The healing power of words is their most magical aspect. Writers, like the shamans or medicine men and women of ancient cultures, have the potential to be healers.

WRITERS AND SHAMANS

Shamans have been called "the wounded healers". Like writers, they are special people set apart from the rest by their dreams, visions, or unique experiences. Shamans, like many writers, are prepared for their work by enduring terrible ordeals. They may have a dangerous illness or fall from a cliff and have nearly every bone broken. They are chewed by a lion or mauled by a bear. They are taken apart and put back together again in a new way. In a sense they have died and been reborn, and this experience gives them special powers. Many writers come to their craft only after they have been shattered by life in some way.

Often those chosen to be shamans are identified by special dreams or visions, in which the gods or spirits take them away to other worlds where they undergo terrible ordeals. They are laid out on a table to have all their bones removed and broken. Before their eyes, their bones and organs are split, cooked, and reassembled in a new order. They are tuned to a new frequency like radio receivers. As shamans, they are now able to receive messages from other worlds.

They return to their tribes with new powers. They have the ability to travel to other worlds and bring back stories, metaphors, or myths that guide, heal, and give meaning to life. They listen to the confusing, mysterious dreams of their people and give them back in the form of stories that provide guidelines for right living.

We writers share in the godlike power of the shamans. We not only travel to other worlds but create them out of space and time. When we write, we truly travel to these worlds of our imagination. Anyone who has tried to write seriously knows this is why we need solitude and concentration. We are actually travelling to another time and place.

As writers we travel to other worlds not as mere daydreamers, but as shamans with the magic power to bottle up those worlds and bring them back in the form of stories for others to share. Our stories have the power to heal, to make the world new again, to give people metaphors by which they can better understand their own lives.

When we writers apply the ancient tools of the archetypes and the Hero's Journey to modern stories, we stand on the shoulders of the mythmakers and shamans of old. When we try to heal our people with the wisdom of myth, we are the modern shamans. We ask the same ageless, childlike questions presented by the myths: Who am I? Where did I come from? What happens when I die? What does it mean? Where do I fit in? Where am I bound on my own Hero's Journey?

APPENDICES

FILMOGRAPHY

Adventures of Robin Hood, The
American Graffiti
Annie Hall
Arabesque
Back to the Future
Barbarossa
Basic Instinct
Beauty and the Beast
Beverly Hills Cop
Big
Big Chill, The
Big Sleep, The
Body Heat
Butch Cassidy and
   the Sundance Kid
Casablanca
Chinatown
Citizen Kane
City Slickers
Clash of the Titans
Close Encounters of
   the Third Kind
Count of Monte Cristo, The
Dances with Wolves
Death Becomes Her
Dirty Dozen, The
Dr. Jekyll and Mr. Hyde
E. T., The Extraterrestrial
East of Eden
Empire Strikes Back, The
Excalibur
Fantasia
Fatal Attraction
Fisher King, The
Fort Apache
48 Hours
Fried Green Tomatoes
From Russia With Love
Ghost
Glory
Godfather, The
Goldfinger
Gone With The Wind
Goodbye, Mr. Chips

Goodfellas
Gorillas in the Mist
Graduate, The
Great Escape, The
Guess Who's Coming to Dinner
Gunga Din
Henry V
High Noon
Hurricane
In-Laws, The
It Happened One Night
Ivanhoe
Jaws
King Kong
Lady from Shanghai, The
Last of the Mohicans, The
Lawrence of Arabia
Life and Times of
   Judge Roy Bean, The
Maltese Falcon, The
Manhunter
Midnight Cowboy
Moby Dick
Mr. Smith Goes to Washington
My Darling Clementine
No Way Out
North by Northwest
Notorious
Officer and a Gentleman, An
On Golden Pond
Ordinary People
Peter Pan
Pinocchio
Pretty Woman
Prime of Miss Jean Brodie, The
Prince of Tides
Public Enemy, The
Quest for Fire
Raiders of the Lost Ark
Rain Man
Rebel Without a Cause
Red River
Return of the Jedi
Risky Business

Road Warrior
Robin Hood, Prince of Thieves
Rocky
Romancing the Stone
Sand Pebbles, The
Scarface
Sea Hawk, The
Searchers, The
Shadow of a Doubt
Shane
Silence of the Lambs
Sister Act
Sleeping Beauty, The
Snow White
Sophie's Choice
Stagecoach
Stand and Deliver
Strangers on a Train
Suspicion
Terminator 2: Judgment Day
Terminator, The
The Stranger
Thelma and Louise
They Died With Their Boots On
To Catch a Thief
Trading Places
Treasure of the Sierra Madre, The
Unforgiven
Vertigo
White Men Can't Jump
Who Framed Roger Rabbit
Wild Bunch, The
Wild Ones, The
Willow
Witness
Wizard of Oz, The

BIBLIOGRAPHY

Benet's Reader's Encyclopedia, Harper & Row 1987

Bolen, Jean Shinoda M. D., *Goddesses in Everywoman,* Harper & Row 1985

Bolen, Jean Shinoda M. D., *Gods in Everyman,* Harper & Row 1989

Bulfinch, Thomas, *Myths of Greece and Rome,* Penguin Books 1981

Campbell, Joseph (with Bill Moyers), *The Power of Myth,* Doubleday 1988

Campbell, Joseph, *The Hero With a Thousand Faces,* Bollingen Series/Princeton University Press 1973

Davidson, H. R. Ellis, *Gods and Myths of Northern Europe,* Penguin Books 1984

Graves, Robert, *The Greek Myths,* Penguin Books 1979

Halliwell, Leslie, *Filmgoer's Companion,* 8th Edition, Charles Scribner's Sons 1983

Homer, *The Odyssey,* transl. by E. V. Rieu, Penguin Books 1960

Johnson, Robert A., *He: Understanding Masculine Psychology,* Harper & Row Perennial Library 1977

Johnson, Robert A., *She: Understanding Feminine Psychology,* Harper & Row 1977

Johnson, Robert A., *We: Understanding the Psychology of Romantic Love,* Harper & Row 1983

Knight, Arthur, *The Liveliest Art,* New American Library 1957

Lattimore, Richmond, *The Iliad of Homer,* University of Chicago Press 1967

Leeming, David, *Mythology,* Newsweek Books, New York 1976

Levinson, Daniel J., *The Seasons of a Man's Life,* Ballantine Books, New York 1978

Luthi, Max, *The Fairytale as Art Form and Portrait of Man,* Indiana University Press 1987

Mast, Gerald, *A Short History of the Movies,* Bobbs-Merrill 1979

Murdock, Maureen, *The Heroine's Journey: Woman's Quest for Wholeness,* Shambala 1990

Pearson, Carol S., *Awakening The Heroes Within,* Harper San Francisco 1991

Propp, V., *Morphology of the Folktale,* University of Texas Press 1979

Wheelwright, Philip, *Aristotle,* The Odyssey Press 1955

THE HERO'S JOURNEY

1. ORDINARY WORLD

2. CALL TO ADVENTURE

3. REFUSAL OF THE CALL

4. MENTOR

5. 1ST THRESHOLD

6. TESTS, ALLIES, ENEMIES

7. APPROACH TO THE INMOST CAVE

8. SUPREME ORDEAL

9. REWARD (SEIZING THE SWORD)

10. THE ROAD BACK

11. RESURRECTION

12. RETURN WITH THE ELIXIR

ARCHETYPES

HERO	HERALD
MENTOR	ALLIES
SHAPESHIFTER	SHADOW
TRICKSTER	THRESHOLD GUARDIANS

The
JOSEPH CAMPBELL
FOUNDATION

The JOSEPH CAMPBELL FOUNDATION, founded in 1990, is a
not-for-profit membership organization seeking to
formulate a mythopoetic response to contemporary
literalism and cultural retrenchment. The Foundation
preserves, protects, and perpetuates Campbell's
pioneering work by collecting and cataloging his books,
papers, and recorded lectures: publishing the *Collected
Works of Joseph Campbell;* promoting mythological
education; creating and disseminating educational
materials; training teachers; providing grants for
mythological research and creative endeavors; sponsoring
conferences, workshops and seminars; supporting
community-based, mythologically-informed activities;
and encouraging inter-cultural mythological dialogue
and exploration.

For further information:
John Lobell, Director of Membership
JOSEPH CAMPBELL FOUNDATION
P. O. Box 457, Madison Square Station
New Your, NY 10159-0457
212-679-2326

Christopher Vogler is president of STORYTECH,
a literary consulting firm to help writers, producers, and studio
executives shape their projects.
STORYTECH provides a complete range of services including
evaluation of screenplays, novels, and concepts;
detailed development notes;
and expert story analysis for copyright litigation.
Rates and other services are available upon request from:

STORYTECH
986 Sunset Avenue
Venice, California 90291

Phone: 310-581-1141
Fax: 310-392-1362

SHAKING THE MONEY TREE
HOW TO GET GRANTS AND DONATIONS
FOR FILM & VIDEO

By Morrie Warshawski

This book provides an insider's look at how to find your way through the confusing world of grants and donations. Producers, writers, directors and entreprenuers will discover step-by-step guidelines on fundraising from the nation's leading fundraising consultant for media artists. Contents include: Preparing Your Project for Funding, Doing Research Right, Meeting and Talking to Funders, Writing the Perfect Grant Proposal, Plus an extensive List of Resources!

$24.95, 192 pp., bibliography
ISBN 0-941188-18-3

PRODUCER TO PRODUCER

The Best of Michael Wiese from VIDEOGRAPHY Magazine

by Michael Wiese

Edited by Brian McKernan,
Editor, VIDEOGRAPHY

Current information about producing, financing, marketing and creativity is vital to the videomaker. Michael Wiese's "Producer to Producer" column in *VIDEOGRAPHY* magazine has provided independent producers with cutting-edge insights on the business of video: program development, production, financing, marketing and distribution.

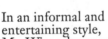

In an informal and entertaining style, Mr. Wiese draws on his own experience and that of other successful video producers to demonstrate forward-thinking industry practices.

Includes: "Shaking the Money Tree," "Zen and the Art of the Steadicam, Jr.," "Where Do you Get the Money?," "Infomercials: Where's the Info?," "Self-Distribution," "You Can Make Desktop Video–But Can You Sell It?" and much more.

176 pp., illustrations
$19.95, ISBN: 0-941188-15-9

Film Directing
SHOT BY SHOT
by Steven D. Katz

The most sought after book in Hollywood by top directors is filled with visual techniques for filmmakers and screenwriters to expand their stylistic knowledge. Includes storyboards from Spielberg, Welles and Hitchcock.

$24.95, 376 pp., 7 x 10
750 illustrations and photos ISBN 0-941188-10-8

Film Directing
CINEMATIC MOTION
A Workshop for Staging Scenes

by Steven D. Katz

The long-awaited sequel to Katz's best-seller —*SHOT BY SHOT*. A staging and blocking guide with 24 basic variations covering many dialogue and dramatic situations.

Includes interviews with John Sayles, Van Ling, Dusty Smith, Ralph Singleton, Allan Daviau, and Harold Michelson.

$24.95, 7 x 10, 320 pp.,
200 illus., ISBN 0-941188-14-0

FILM & VIDEO FINANCING
by Michael Wiese

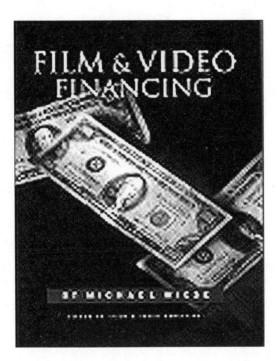

Praised as a book that prepares producers to get the money! A "palette" of creative strategies for producers in financing their feature films and video projects. Interviews with the producers of "sex, lies & videotape," "Trip to Bountiful," and "T2."

$22.95, 300 pp., ISBN 0-941188-11-6

ORDER FORM

To order these products please call 1-800-379-8808 or fax (818) 986-3408 or mail this order form to:

MICHAEL WIESE PRODUCTIONS
11288 Ventura Blvd., Suite 821
Studio City, CA 91604
1-800-379-8808

BOOKS:

_____
_____
_____
_____

Subtotal $_____
Shipping $_____
8.25% Sales Tax (Ca Only) $_____

TOTAL ENCLOSED_____

Please make check or money order payable to
Michael Wiese Productions

(Check one) ___ Master Card ___Visa _____Amex

Company PO#_____

Credit Card Number_____
Expiration Date_____
Cardholder's Name_____
Cardholder's Signature_____

SHIP TO:

Name_____
Address_____
City_____State_____Zip_____
Country_____Telephone_____
CALL 1-800-379-8808 for a Free Book & Software Catalog

VISIT OUR HOME PAGE http://www.earthlink.net/~mwp

Please allow 2-3 weeks for delivery.
All prices subject to change without notice.

CREDIT CARD ORDERS

CALL 1-800-379-8808

OR FAX 818 986-3408

OR E-MAIL WIESE@EARTHLINK.NET

SHIPPING

1ST CLASS MAIL
One Book - $5.00
Two Books - $7.00
For each additional book, add $1.00.

AIRBORNE EXPRESS
2nd Day Delivery
Add an additional $11.00 per order.

OVERSEAS (PREPAID)
Surface - $7.00 ea. book
Airmail - $15.00 ea. book